8th Grade

MARYLAND

MATH TEST PREP

Common Core State Standards

teachers' treasures, inc.

Copyright © 2015 Teachers' Treasures Inc.

Printed in the United States of America. All rights reserved. No part of this publication may be reproduced, stored in a retrieval system, or transmitted in any way or by any means (electronic, mechanical, photocopying, recording, or otherwise) without prior written permission from Teachers' Treasures, Inc., with the following exceptions:

Photocopying of student worksheets by a teacher who purchased this publication for his/her own class is permissible, but not for commercial resale. Reproduction of these materials for an entire school, or for a school system, is strictly prohibited. Reproduction of questions or book format by other state or commercial entities is strictly prohibited. Information taken directly from documents published by the Common Core State Standards Initiative is clearly indicated and not copyrighted.

Send all inquiries to:

sales@teacherstreasures.com
http://www.teacherstreasures.com

INTRODUCTION

Our 8th Grade Math Test Prep for Common Core State Standards is an excellent resource to supplement your classroom's curriculum to assess and manage students' understanding of concepts outlined in the Common Core State Standards Initiative. This resource is divided into three sections: Diagnostic, Practice, and Assessment with multiple choice questions in each section. We recommend you use the Diagnostic section as a tool to determine the students' areas that need to be retaught. We also recommend you encourage your students to show their work to determine *how* and *why* the student arrived at an answer. The Practice section should be used to strengthen the students' knowledge by re-testing the standard to ensure comprehension of each standard. To ensure students' apply taught concepts in the classroom, we advise you use the Assessment section as a final test to verify the students' have mastered the standard.

This resource contains over 600 practice problems aligned to the Common Core State Standards. To view the standards, refer to pages *i* through *vi*.

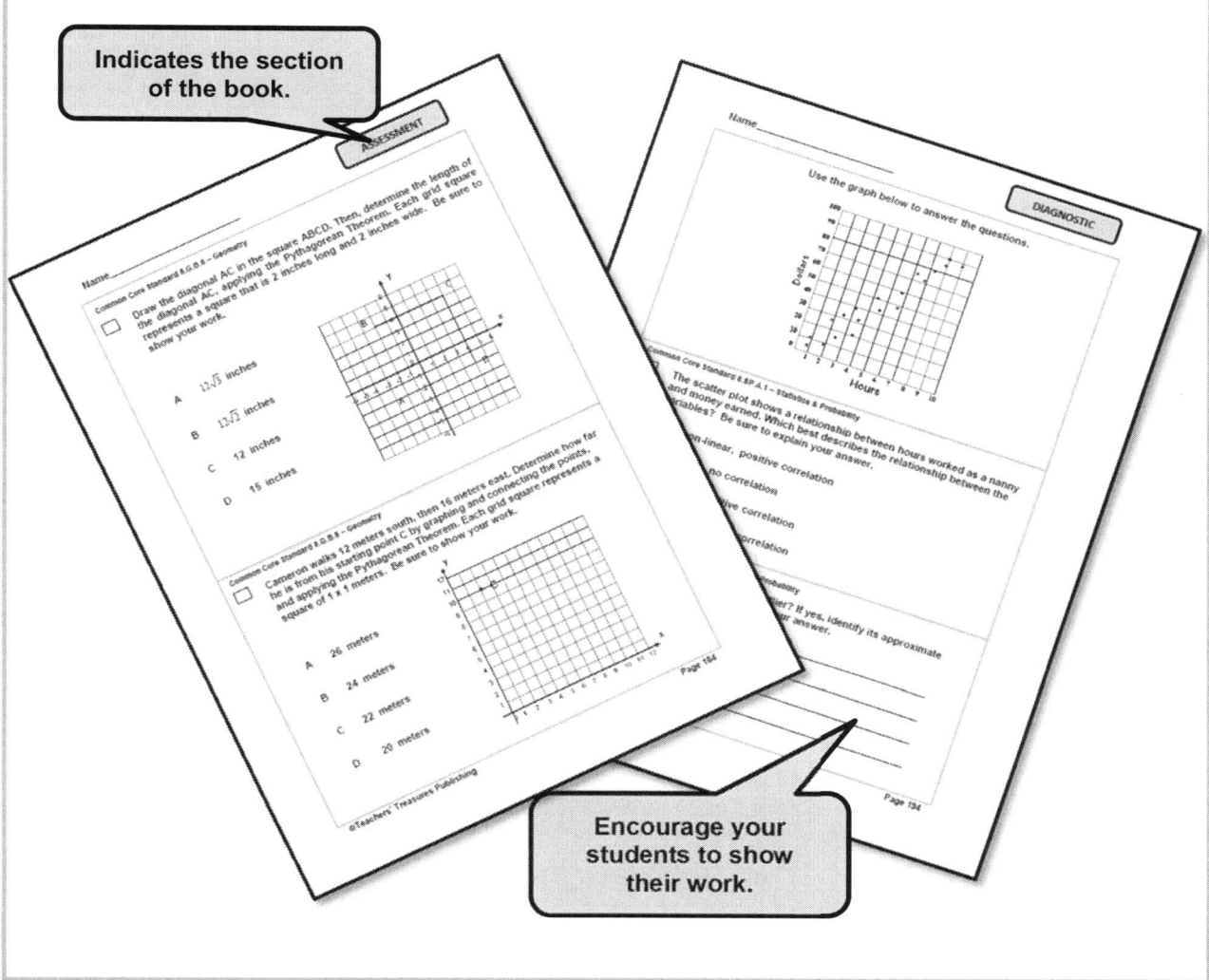

© Teachers' Treasures Publishing

TABLE OF CONTENTS

8th Grade Math Test Prep FOR Common Core Standards

Grade 8 Mathematics Common Core State Standards .... pages i - vi

The Number System Practice Problems
- 8.NS.A.1............ pages 1 – 8
- 8.NS.A.2............ pages 9 – 16

Expressions & Equations Practice Problems
- 8.EE.A.1 .... pages 17 – 24
- 8.EE.A.2 .... pages 25 – 32
- 8.EE.A.3 .... pages 33 – 40
- 8.EE.A.4 .... pages 41 – 48
- 8.EE.B.5 .... pages 49 – 56
- 8.EE.B.6 .... pages 57 – 64
- 8.EE.C.7 .... pages 65 – 72
- 8.EE.C.8 .... pages 73 – 80

Functions Practice Problems
- 8.F.A.1 .... pages 81 – 88
- 8.F.A.2 .... pages 89 – 96
- 8.F.A.3 .... pages 97 – 104
- 8.F.A.4 .... pages 105 – 112
- 8.F.B.5 .... pages 113 – 120

Geometry Practice Problems
- 8.G.A.1 .... pages 121 – 128
- 8.G.A.2 .... pages 129 – 136
- 8.G.A.3 .... pages 137 – 144
- 8.G.A.4 .... pages 145 – 152
- 8.G.A.5 .... pages 153 – 160
- 8.G.B.6 .... pages 161 – 168
- 8.G.B.7 .... pages 169 – 176
- 8.G.B.8 .... pages 177 – 184
- 8.G.B.9 .... pages 185 – 192

Statistics & Probability Practice Problems
- 8.SP.A.1 .... pages 193 – 200
- 8.SP.A.2 .... pages 201 – 208
- 8.SP.A.3 .... pages 209 – 216
- 8.SP.A.4 .... pages 217 – 224

Answer Key .... pages 225 – 229

COMMON CORE STATE STANDARDS

The Number System 8.NS

Know that there are numbers that are not rational, and approximate them by rational numbers.

CCSS.MATH.CONTENT.8.NS.A.1
Know that numbers that are not rational are called irrational. Understand informally that every number has a decimal expansion; for rational numbers show that the decimal expansion repeats eventually, and convert a decimal expansion which repeats eventually into a rational number.

CCSS.MATH.CONTENT.8.NS.A.2
Use rational approximations of irrational numbers to compare the size of irrational numbers, locate them approximately on a number line diagram, and estimate the value of expressions (e.g., π^2). *For example, by truncating the decimal expansion of $\sqrt{2}$, show that $\sqrt{2}$ is between 1 and 2, then between 1.4 and 1.5, and explain how to continue on to get better approximations.*

Expressions & Equations 8.EE

Expressions and Equations Work with radicals and integer exponents.

CCSS.MATH.CONTENT.8.EE.A.1
Know and apply the properties of integer exponents to generate equivalent numerical expressions. For example, $3^2 \times 3^{-5} = 3^{-3} = 1/3^3 = 1/27$.

CCSS.MATH.CONTENT.8.EE.A.1
Use square root and cube root symbols to represent solutions to equations of the form $x^2 = p$ and $x^3 = p$, where p is a positive rational number. Evaluate square roots of small perfect squares and cube roots of small perfect cubes. Know that $\sqrt{2}$ is irrational.

CCSS.MATH.CONTENT.8.EE.A.3
Use numbers expressed in the form of a single digit times an integer power of 10 to estimate very large or very small quantities, and to express how many times as much one is than the other. *For example, estimate the population of the United States as 3 times 10^8 and the population of the world as 7 times 10^9, and determine that the world population is more than 20 times larger.*

CCSS.MATH.CONTENT.8.EE.A.4
Perform operations with numbers expressed in scientific notation, including problems where both decimal and scientific notation are used. Use scientific notation and choose units of appropriate size for measurements of very large or very small quantities (e.g.,

COMMON CORE STATE STANDARDS

use millimeters per year for seafloor spreading). Interpret scientific notation that has been generated by technology.

Understand the connections between proportional relationships, lines, and linear equations.

CCSS.MATH.CONTENT.8.EE.B.5
Graph proportional relationships, interpreting the unit rate as the slope of the graph. Compare two different proportional relationships represented in different ways. For example, compare a distance-time graph to a distance-time equation to determine which of two moving objects has greater speed.

CCSS.MATH.CONTENT.8.EE.B.6
Use similar triangles to explain why the slope m is the same between any two distinct points on a non-vertical line in the coordinate plane; derive the equation $y = mx$ for a line through the origin and the equation $y = mx + b$ for a line intercepting the vertical axis at b.

Analyze and solve linear equations and pairs of simultaneous linear equations.

CCSS.MATH.CONTENT.8.EE.C.7
Solve linear equations in one variable.

   CCSS.MATH.CONTENT.8.EE.C.7.A
   Give examples of linear equations in one variable with one solution, infinitely many solutions, or no solutions. Show which of these possibilities is the case by successively transforming the given equation into simpler forms, until an equivalent equation of the form $x = a$, $a = a$, or $a = b$ results (where a and b are different numbers).

   CCSS.MATH.CONTENT.8.EE.C.7.B
   Solve linear equations with rational number coefficients, including equations whose solutions require expanding expressions using the distributive property and collecting like terms.

CCSS.MATH.CONTENT.8.EE.C.8
Analyze and solve pairs of simultaneous linear equations.

COMMON CORE STATE STANDARDS

CCSS.MATH.CONTENT.8.EE.C.8.A
Understand that solutions to a system of two linear equations in two variables correspond to points of intersection of their graphs, because points of intersection satisfy both equations simultaneously.

CCSS.MATH.CONTENT.8.EE.C.8.B
Solve systems of two linear equations in two variables algebraically, and estimate solutions by graphing the equations. Solve simple cases by inspection. *For example, $3x + 2y = 5$ and $3x + 2y = 6$ have no solution because $3x + 2y$ cannot simultaneously be 5 and 6.*

CCSS.MATH.CONTENT.8.EE.C.8.C
Solve real-world and mathematical problems leading to two linear equations in two variables. *For example, given coordinates for two pairs of points, determine whether the line through the first pair of points intersects the line through the second pair.*

Functions 8.F

Define, evaluate, and compare functions.

CCSS.MATH.CONTENT.8.F.A.1
Understand that a function is a rule that assigns to each input exactly one output. The graph of a function is the set of ordered pairs consisting of an input and the corresponding output.

CCSS.MATH.CONTENT.8.F.A.2
Compare properties of two functions each represented in a different way (algebraically, graphically, numerically in tables, or by verbal descriptions). *For example, given a linear function represented by a table of values and a linear function represented by an algebraic expression, determine which function has the greater rate of change.*

CCSS.MATH.CONTENT.8.F.A.3
Interpret the equation $y = mx + b$ as defining a linear function, whose graph is a straight line; give examples of functions that are not linear. *For example, the function $A = s^2$ giving the area of a square as a function of its side length is not linear because its graph contains the points (1,1), (2,4) and (3,9), which are not on a straight line.*

COMMON CORE STATE STANDARDS

Use functions to model relationships between quantities.

CCSS.MATH.CONTENT.8.F.B.4
Construct a function to model a linear relationship between two quantities. Determine the rate of change and initial value of the function from a description of a relationship or from two (x, y) values, including reading these from a table or from a graph. Interpret the rate of change and initial value of a linear function in terms of the situation it models, and in terms of its graph or a table of values.

CCSS.MATH.CONTENT.8.F.B.5
Describe qualitatively the functional relationship between two quantities by analyzing a graph (e.g., where the function is increasing or decreasing, linear or nonlinear). Sketch a graph that exhibits the qualitative features of a function that has been described verbally.

Geometry   8.G

Understand congruence and similarity using physical models, transparencies, or geometry software.

CCSS.MATH.CONTENT.8.G.A.1
Verify experimentally the properties of rotations, reflections, and translations:

   CCSS.MATH.CONTENT.8.G.A.1.A
   Lines are taken to lines, and line segments to line segments of the same length.

   CCSS.MATH.CONTENT.8.G.A.1.B
   Angles are taken to angles of the same measure.

   CCSS.MATH.CONTENT.8.G.A.1.C
   Parallel lines are taken to parallel lines.

CCSS.MATH.CONTENT.8.G.A.2
Understand that a two-dimensional figure is congruent to another if the second can be obtained from the first by a sequence of rotations, reflections, and translations; given two congruent figures, describe a sequence that exhibits the congruence between them.

COMMON CORE STATE STANDARDS

CCSS.MATH.CONTENT.8.G.A.3
Describe the effect of dilations, translations, rotations, and reflections on two-dimensional figures using coordinates.

CCSS.MATH.CONTENT.8.G.A.4
Understand that a two-dimensional figure is similar to another if the second can be obtained from the first by a sequence of rotations, reflections, translations, and dilations; given two similar two-dimensional figures, describe a sequence that exhibits the similarity between them.

CCSS.MATH.CONTENT.8.G.A.5
Use informal arguments to establish facts about the angle sum and exterior angle of triangles, about the angles created when parallel lines are cut by a transversal, and the angle-angle criterion for similarity of triangles. *For example, arrange three copies of the same triangle so that the sum of the three angles appears to form a line, and give an argument in terms of transversals why this is so.*

Understand and apply the Pythagorean Theorem.

CCSS.MATH.CONTENT.8.G.B.6
Explain a proof of the Pythagorean Theorem and its converse.

CCSS.MATH.CONTENT.8.G.B.7
Apply the Pythagorean Theorem to determine unknown side lengths in right triangles in real-world and mathematical problems in two and three dimensions.

CCSS.MATH.CONTENT.8.G.B.8
Apply the Pythagorean Theorem to find the distance between two points in a coordinate system.

Solve real-world and mathematical problems involving volume of cylinders, cones, and spheres.

CCSS.MATH.CONTENT.8.G.C.9
Know the formulas for the volumes of cones, cylinders, and spheres and use them to solve real-world and mathematical problems.

COMMON CORE STATE STANDARDS

Statistics & Probability 8.SP

Investigate patterns of association in bivariate data.

CCSS.MATH.CONTENT.8.SP.A.1
Construct and interpret scatter plots for bivariate measurement data to investigate patterns of association between two quantities. Describe patterns such as clustering, outliers, positive or negative association, linear association, and nonlinear association.

CCSS.MATH.CONTENT.8.SP.A.2
Know that straight lines are widely used to model relationships between two quantitative variables. For scatter plots that suggest a linear association, informally fit a straight line, and informally assess the model fit by judging the closeness of the data points to the line.

CCSS.MATH.CONTENT.8.SP.A.3
Use the equation of a linear model to solve problems in the context of bivariate measurement data, interpreting the slope and intercept. *For example, in a linear model for a biology experiment, interpret a slope of 1.5 cm/hr as meaning that an additional hour of sunlight each day is associated with an additional 1.5 cm in mature plant height.*

CCSS.MATH.CONTENT.8.SP.A.4
Understand that patterns of association can also be seen in bivariate categorical data by displaying frequencies and relative frequencies in a two-way table. Construct and interpret a two-way table summarizing data on two categorical variables collected from the same subjects. Use relative frequencies calculated for rows or columns to describe possible association between the two variables. *For example, collect data from students in your class on whether or not they have a curfew on school nights and whether or not they have assigned chores at home. Is there evidence that those who have a curfew also tend to have chores?*

MATHEMATICS CHART

LENGTH

Metric

1 kilometer = 1000 meters
1 meter = 100 centimeters
1 centimeter = 10 millimeters

Customary

1 yard = 3 feet
1 foot = 12 inches

CAPACITY & VOLUME

Metric

1 liter = 1000 milliliters

Customary

1 gallon = 4 quarts
1 gallon = 128 ounces
1 quart = 2 pints
1 pint = 2 cups
1 cup = 8 ounces

MASS & WEIGHT

Metric

1 kilogram = 1000 grams
1 gram = 1000 milligrams

Customary

1 ton = 2000 pounds
1 pound = 16 ounces

TIME

1 year = 365 days
1 year = 12 months
1 year = 52 weeks
1 week = 7 days
1 day = 24 hours
1 hour = 60 minutes
1 minute = 60 seconds

MATHEMATICS CHART

Perimeter	square	$P = 4s$
	rectangle	$P = 2l + 2w$ or $P = 2(l + w)$
Circumference	circle	$C = 2\pi r$ or $C = \pi d$
Area	square	$A = s^2$
	rectangle	$A = lw$ or $A = bh$
	triangle	$A = \frac{1}{2}bh$ or $A = \frac{bh}{2}$
	trapezoid	$A = \frac{1}{2}(b_1 + b_2)h$ or $A = \frac{(b_1 + b_2)h}{2}$
	circle	$A = \pi r^2$
Volume	cube	$V = s^3$
	rectangular prism	$V = lwh$
Pi	π	$\pi \approx 3.14$ or $\pi \approx \frac{22}{7}$

Name_____

DIAGNOSTIC

Common Core Standard 8.NS.A.1 – Number System

☐ Write the fraction in decimal form: $\frac{51}{125}$.

A   0.248

B   0.048

C   0.408

D   0.528

Common Core Standard 8.NS.A.1 – Number System

☐ Evaluate the expression below by writing the answer in decimal form. Be sure to show your work.

$$\left(\frac{1}{2} \times \frac{4}{5}\right) \times \left(\frac{1}{2} \times \frac{3}{10}\right) =$$

Common Core Standard 8.NS.A.1 – Number System

☐ Evaluate the expression below by writing the answer in decimal form. Be sure to show your work.

$$(0.045 - 0.0015) \times (0.897 + 1.103) =$$

©Teachers' Treasures Publishing   Page 1

Name_____

DIAGNOSTIC

Common Core Standard 8.NS.A.1 – Number System

☐ Which set of numbers contains at least one irrational number?

A $\quad \sqrt[3]{\dfrac{8}{27}};\ 400;\ \dfrac{14}{25};\ -0.19$

B $\quad 2.\overline{3};\ \dfrac{1}{9};\ \sqrt[3]{64};\ -13.8$

C $\quad 0.5;\ 0.0\overline{9};\ \sqrt{2};\ -1023$

D $\quad 17.\overline{6};\ \dfrac{18}{9};\ \sqrt{144};\ -\dfrac{1}{3}$

Common Core Standard 8.NS.A.1 – Number System

☐ Find the missing number in the expression. Be sure to show your work.

$$\dfrac{4}{5} \div \left(\dfrac{9}{10} \div \dfrac{1}{\boxed{}}\right) = \dfrac{4}{9}$$

Common Core Standard 8.NS.A.1 – Number System

☐ Write the repeating decimal as a fraction: 0.555555555..... Be sure to show your work.

A $\quad \dfrac{55}{100}$ $\qquad\qquad$ C $\quad \dfrac{5}{7}$

B $\quad \dfrac{5}{9}$ $\qquad\qquad$ D $\quad \dfrac{5}{6}$

©Teachers' Treasures Publishing

Name_____

PRACTICE

Common Core Standard 8.NS.A.1 – Number System

☐ Write the fraction in decimal form: $\frac{92}{1000}$.

A   0.092

B   0.0092

C   0.92

D   0.920

Common Core Standard 8.NS.A.1 – Number System

☐ Convert 0.222 to a fraction. Simplify your answer.

A $\frac{222}{100}$

B $\frac{222}{1000}$

C $\frac{111}{1000}$

D $\frac{111}{500}$

Common Core Standard 8.NS.A.1 – Number System

☐ Evaluate the expression. Write the answer in decimal form. Be sure to show your work.

$$\left(\frac{3}{4} \div \frac{2}{5}\right) \times \frac{3}{5} =$$

©Teachers' Treasures Publishing

Name_____

PRACTICE

Common Core Standard 8.NS.A.1 – Number System

☐ Find the missing number in the expression. Be sure to show your work.

$$\frac{5}{33} + \frac{13}{\square} = 1\frac{1}{3}$$

Common Core Standard 8.NS.A.1 – Number System

☐ Evaluate the expression. Write the answer as a fraction. Be sure to show your work.

$$(112.24 \div 0.04) - 2802.5 =$$

Common Core Standard 8.NS.A.1 – Number System

☐ Which of the following statements is true? Be sure to explain your answer.

A   An irrational number is a real number that cannot be written as a simple fraction.

B   Whole numbers cannot be written as fractions.

C   Negative numbers are larger than positive numbers.

D   All rational numbers are integers.

©Teachers' Treasures Publishing

Name_____

PRACTICE

Common Core Standard 8.NS.A.1 – Number System

☐ Which set of numbers contains at least one irrational number? Be sure to explain your answer.

A $\quad \dfrac{14}{35}$; $\sqrt[3]{216}$; 1118; $-\dfrac{23}{70}$

B $\quad -11.\overline{9}$; $\sqrt[4]{\dfrac{16}{81}}$; 543; 10.109

C $\quad \sqrt{3}$; 5; $4.0\overline{9}$; -1023

D $\quad 12.\overline{6}$; $\dfrac{225}{5}$; $\sqrt{169}$; $-\dfrac{1}{9}$

Common Core Standard 8.NS.A.1 – Number System

☐ Convert $\dfrac{1}{9}$ to decimal form. Be sure to show your work.

A $\quad 0.\overline{16}$

B $\quad 0.1\overline{6}$

C $\quad 0.\overline{3}$

D $\quad 0.\overline{1}$

Common Core Standard 8.NS.A.1 – Number System

☐ Express 0.3333333... as a fraction. Be sure to show your work.

A $\quad \dfrac{1}{10}$ $\qquad\qquad$ C $\quad \dfrac{1}{6}$

B $\quad \dfrac{1}{3}$ $\qquad\qquad$ D $\quad \dfrac{2}{7}$

©Teachers' Treasures Publishing

Name_____

PRACTICE

Common Core Standard 8.NS.A.1 – Number System

☐ **Express 0.625 as a fraction. Be sure to show your work.**

A $\dfrac{5}{8}$ C $\dfrac{6}{15}$

B $\dfrac{625}{100}$ D $\dfrac{8}{15}$

Common Core Standard 8.NS.A.1 – Number System

☐ **Express $0.1\overline{6}$ as a fraction. Be sure to show your work.**

A $\dfrac{1}{9}$

B $\dfrac{2}{7}$

C $\dfrac{1}{6}$

D $\dfrac{1}{16}$

Common Core Standard 8.NS.A.1 – Number System

☐ **Evaluate the expression. Write the answer in decimal form. Be sure to show your work.**

$$\dfrac{7}{54} + \left(\dfrac{2}{3} - \dfrac{1}{6}\right) =$$

©Teachers' Treasures Publishing

Name_____

ASSESSMENT

Common Core Standard 8.NS.A.1 – Number System

☐ Which set of numbers contains at least one irrational number? Be sure to explain your answer.

A $\sqrt{144}$; $\sqrt{225}$; $\sqrt{64}$

B $\sqrt{324}$; $\sqrt{196}$; $\sqrt[3]{64}$

C $\sqrt[3]{125}$; $\sqrt{121}$; $\sqrt{576}$

D $\sqrt{\dfrac{169}{625}}$; $\sqrt[3]{729}$; $\sqrt{11}$

Common Core Standard 8.NS.A.1 – Number System

☐ Convert $\dfrac{1}{8}$ to decimal form. Be sure to show your work.

A 0.225

B 0.72

C 0.64

D 0.125

Common Core Standard 8.NS.A.1 – Number System

☐ Find the missing number in the expression. Be sure to show your work.

$$\dfrac{1}{2} \div \left(\dfrac{4}{} \times \dfrac{3}{8}\right) = 1\dfrac{2}{3}$$

©Teachers' Treasures Publishing

Name_____

ASSESSMENT

Common Core Standard 8.NS.A.1 – Number System

☐ **Express $0.1\overline{7}$ as a fraction. Be sure to show your work.**

A $\dfrac{17}{100}$

B $\dfrac{8}{45}$

C $\dfrac{8}{65}$

D $\dfrac{8}{55}$

Common Core Standard 8.NS.A.1 – Number System

☐ **Evaluate the expression. Write the answer in decimal form. Be sure to show your work.**

$$\dfrac{2}{5} \div \left(\dfrac{3}{10} + \dfrac{1}{2} \right) - \dfrac{1}{3} =$$

Common Core Standard 8.NS.A.1 – Number System

☐ **Evaluate the expression. Write the answer as a fraction. Be sure to show your work.**

$$(897.0012 + 0.9988) \times 0.98 =$$

©Teachers' Treasures Publishing

Page 8

Name_____

DIAGNOSTIC

Common Core Standard 8.NS.A.2 – Number System

☐ **Estimate the square root to the nearest tenth: $\sqrt{51}$. Be sure to show your work.**

A   7.1

B   7.4

C   7.6

D   7.8

Common Core Standard 8.NS.A.2 – Number System

☐ **Knowing that the value of $\sqrt{33}$ is between 5.7 and 5.8, estimate the square root to the nearest hundredth. Be sure to show your work.**

A   5.79

B   5.71

C   5.74

D   5.77

Common Core Standard 8.NS.A.2 – Number System

☐ **Estimate the location of $\sqrt{78}$ on the number line. Then, plot and label a point for your estimate. Estimate to the nearest tenth. Be sure to show your work.**

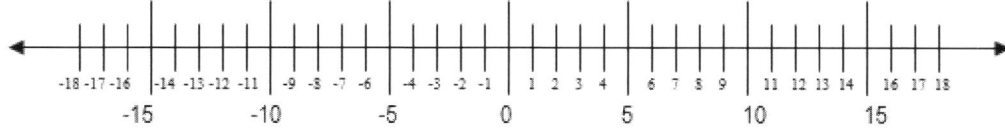

©Teachers' Treasures Publishing

Page 9

Name_____

DIAGNOSTIC

Common Core Standard 8.NS.A.2 – Number System

☐ **Solve to the nearest tenth. Be sure to show your work.**

$$(4\sqrt{22} - \sqrt{22}) - (9\sqrt{10} - 7\sqrt{10}) =$$

Common Core Standard 8.NS.A.2 – Number System

☐ **Simplify the expression. Be sure to show your work.**

$$34\sqrt{5} - 14\sqrt{5} + 5\sqrt{5} \times 2\sqrt{3} =$$

Common Core Standard 8.NS.A.2 – Number System

☐ **Solve to the nearest hundredth. Be sure to show your work.**

$$\frac{2\pi - \sqrt{12}}{\sqrt{4}} =$$

©Teachers' Treasures Publishing

Name_____

PRACTICE

Common Core Standard 8.NS.A.2 – Number System

☐ Compare $\sqrt{5}$ and $\sqrt{7}$. Be sure to explain your answer.

A $\sqrt{5} > \sqrt{7}$

B $\sqrt{5} < \sqrt{7}$

C $\sqrt{5} = \sqrt{7}$

D $\sqrt{5} \geq \sqrt{7}$

Common Core Standard 8.NS.A.2 – Number System

☐ Between which whole numbers on a number line is the value of $\sqrt{22}$. Be sure to explain your answer.

A   4 and 5

B   5 and 6

C   16 and 25

D   20 and 25

Common Core Standard 8.NS.A.2 – Number System

☐ Estimate the value of $\sqrt{14}$ to the nearest tenth. Hint: choose decimals between 3 and 4, and calculate the square of each number to determine which one is the best estimate. Be sure to show your work.

A   3.8

B   3.7

C   3.6

D   3.5

©Teachers' Treasures Publishing

Name_____

PRACTICE

Common Core Standard 8.NS.A.2 – Number System

☐ **Estimate the square root to the nearest tenth: $\sqrt{233}$. Be sure to show your work.**

    A   13.2

    B   14.2

    C   15.2

    D   12.2

Common Core Standard 8.NS.A.2 – Number System

☐ **Estimate the location of $\sqrt{112}$ on the number line. Then, plot and label a point for your estimate. Estimate to the nearest tenth.**

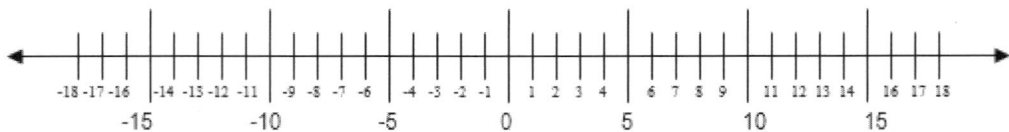

Common Core Standard 8.NS.A.2 – Number System

☐ **Estimate the square root to the nearest hundredth: $\sqrt{70}$. Be sure to show your work.**

    A   8.16

    B   8.36

    C   8.76

    D   8.96

©Teachers' Treasures Publishing

Name_____

PRACTICE

Common Core Standard 8.NS.A.2 – Number System

☐ Estimate the square root to the nearest tenth: $\sqrt{200}$. Be sure to show your work.

A   14.7

B   14.5

C   14.3

D   14.1

Common Core Standard 8.NS.A.2 – Number System

☐ Simplify the expression. Be sure to show your work.

$$30\sqrt{6} + 7\sqrt{6} - 20\sqrt{6} =$$

Common Core Standard 8.NS.A.2 – Number System

☐ Simplify the expression. Be sure to show your work.

$$(18\sqrt{17} \div 3\sqrt{17}) + 15\sqrt{17} - \sqrt{17} =$$

©Teachers' Treasures Publishing

Name_____

PRACTICE

Common Core Standard 8.NS.A.2 – Number System

☐ **Solve to the nearest tenth. Be sure to show your work.**

$$(15\sqrt{8} - 12\sqrt{8}) - (9\sqrt{8} - 7\sqrt{8}) =$$

Common Core Standard 8.NS.A.2 – Number System

☐ **Simplify the expression. Be sure to show your work.**

$$\frac{12\sqrt{6}}{\sqrt{54}} - \frac{7\sqrt{6}}{3\sqrt{6}} - \frac{20\sqrt{6}}{14\sqrt{12}} =$$

Common Core Standard 8.NS.A.2 – Number System

☐ **Solve to the nearest hundredth. Be sure to show your work.**

$$\frac{1}{3} \pi \times \left(\frac{12\sqrt{8}}{\sqrt{32}}\right) =$$

©Teachers' Treasures Publishing   Page 14

Name_____

ASSESSMENT

Common Core Standard 8.NS.A.2 – Number System

☐ Between which whole numbers is $\sqrt{95}$. Be sure to explain your answer.

A 9.1 and 10.3

B 8 and 9

C 9 and 10

D 8.5 and 10

Common Core Standard 8.NS.A.2 – Number System

☐ Knowing that the value of $\sqrt{89}$ is between 9.4 and 9.5, estimate the square root to the nearest hundredth. Be sure to show your work.

A 9.45

B 9.43

C 9.47

D 9.52

Common Core Standard 8.NS.A.2 – Number System

☐ Simplify the expression. Be sure to show your work.

$$\sqrt{44} + \left(5\sqrt{11} - 3\sqrt{11}\right) + 9\sqrt{11} - \sqrt{99} =$$

©Teachers' Treasures Publishing   Page 15

Name_____

ASSESSMENT

Common Core Standard 8.NS.A.2 – Number System

☐ **Estimate the square root to the nearest hundredth: $\sqrt{150}$. Be sure to show your work.**

A   12.16

B   12.26

C   12.24

D   12.34

Common Core Standard 8.NS.A.2 – Number System

☐ **Simplify the expression. Be sure to show your work.**

$$2 \times (2\sqrt{21} + 4\sqrt{21}) + (73\sqrt{5} - 48\sqrt{5}) \div 5 =$$

Common Core Standard 8.NS.A.2 – Number System

☐ **Solve to the nearest tenth. Be sure to show your work.**

$$\frac{14\sqrt{20} - 4\sqrt{20} - 2\sqrt{5}}{2 \times (9\sqrt{10} - 7\sqrt{10})} =$$

©Teachers' Treasures Publishing

Name_____

DIAGNOSTIC

Common Core Standard 8.EE.A.1 – Expressions and Equations

☐ Write the expanded form for the following exponent: $(-12)^4$. Be sure to show your work.

A   1728

B $(-12) \times (-12) \times (-12) \times (-12)$

C $12 \times 12 \times 12 \times 12$

D $(-12) \times (-12) \times (-12) \times (-12) \times (-12)$

Common Core Standard 8.EE.A.1 – Expressions and Equations

☐ Which option below is equivalent to $9^4 \times 5^{-2}$? Be sure to show your work.

A 45^2

B $9 \times 9 \times 9 \times 9 \times 5 \times 5$

C $9 \times 9 \times 9 \times 9 \times \frac{1}{5} \times \frac{1}{5}$

D $9 \times 9 \times 9 \times 9 \times (-5) \times (-5)$

Common Core Standard 8.EE.A.1 – Expressions and Equations

☐ Evaluate the exponential expression. Be sure to show your work.

$$\frac{3^5}{6^2} - \frac{2^{-2}}{13^{-1}} = \boxed{}$$

©Teachers' Treasures Publishing   Page 17

Name_____

DIAGNOSTIC

Common Core Standard 8.EE.A.1 – Expressions and Equations

☐ **Evaluate the exponential expression. Be sure to show your work.**

$$7^4 \times 7^{-6} \times 14 = \boxed{}$$

Common Core Standard 8.EE.A.1 – Expressions and Equations

☐ **Evaluate the exponential expression. Be sure to show your work.**

$$(-0.4)^3 \div 2^2 = \boxed{}$$

Common Core Standard 8.EE.A.1 – Expressions and Equations

☐ **Evaluate the exponent $(-2)^{-8}$. Be sure to show your work.**

A -256

B $\dfrac{1}{256}$

C $\dfrac{1}{128}$

D $-\dfrac{1}{256}$

©Teachers' Treasures Publishing

Name_____

PRACTICE

Common Core Standard 8.EE.A.1 – Expressions and Equations

☐ Write the following in the exponent form: 4 x 4 x 4 x 4 x 4 x 4 x 4. Be sure to show your work.

A 4^6

B 4^5

C 4^7

D 4^8

Common Core Standard 8.EE.A.1 – Expressions and Equations

☐ Write the expanded form for the following exponent: $\left(-\frac{2}{3}\right)^4$. Be sure to show your work.

A $-\frac{2^4}{3}$

B $\left(-\frac{2}{3}\right) \times \left(-\frac{2}{3}\right) \times \left(-\frac{2}{3}\right) \times \left(-\frac{2}{3}\right) \times \left(-\frac{2}{3}\right)$

C $-\left(\frac{2}{3} \times \frac{2}{3} \times \frac{2}{3} \times \frac{2}{3}\right)$

D $\left(-\frac{2}{3}\right) \times \left(-\frac{2}{3}\right) \times \left(-\frac{2}{3}\right) \times \left(-\frac{2}{3}\right)$

Common Core Standard 8.EE.A.1 – Expressions and Equations

☐ Which option below is equivalent to $6^4 \times 7^{-2}$? Be sure to show your work.

A   6 x 6 x 6 x 6 x (−7) x (−7)

B   6 x 6 x 6 x 6 x 7 x 7

C   6 x 6 x 6 x 6 x $\left(-\frac{1}{7}\right)$ x $\left(-\frac{1}{7}\right)$

D   6 x 6 x 6 x 6 x $\frac{1}{7}$ x $\frac{1}{7}$

©Teachers' Treasures Publishing

Name_____

PRACTICE

Common Core Standard 8.EE.A.1 – Expressions and Equations

☐ **Evaluate the exponent $(-10)^1$. Be sure to show your work.**

A -10

B 10

C $\dfrac{1}{10}$

D $-\dfrac{1}{10}$

Common Core Standard 8.EE.A.1 – Expressions and Equations

☐ **Evaluate the exponent $(-0.3)^3$. Be sure to show your work.**

A 0.027

B -0.027

C -0.127

D 0.27

Common Core Standard 8.EE.A.1 – Expressions and Equations

☐ **Evaluate the exponent 0.5^4. Be sure to show your work.**

A 0.625

B 0.0625

C 0.225

D 0.0225

©Teachers' Treasures Publishing

Name_____

PRACTICE

Common Core Standard 8.EE.A.1 – Expressions and Equations

☐ Write the following in the exponent form: $13 \times 13 \times 13 \times 13 \times \frac{1}{11} \times \frac{1}{11} \times \frac{1}{11}$. Be sure to show your work.

A $13^4 \times \left(-\frac{1}{11}\right)$

B $13^4 \times (-11)^3$

C $13^5 - \frac{1}{11}^3$

D $13^4 \times 11^{-3}$

Common Core Standard 8.EE.A.1 – Expressions and Equations

☐ Evaluate the exponential expression $17^6 \times 17^{-4}$. Be sure to show your work.

A   4913

B   289

C   17

D $\frac{1}{49}$

Common Core Standard 8.EE.A.1 – Expressions and Equations

☐ Evaluate the exponential expression $\left(\frac{-5}{2}\right)^{-2}$. Be sure to show your work.

A $\frac{25}{4}$

B $\frac{4}{25}$

C   0.25

D $\frac{4}{25}$

©Teachers' Treasures Publishing

Name_____

PRACTICE

Common Core Standard 8.EE.A.1 – Expressions and Equations

☐ **Evaluate the exponential expression. Be sure to show your work.**

$$52^{-5} \times 52^6 - 4^2 =$$

Common Core Standard 8.EE.A.1 – Expressions and Equations

☐ **Evaluate the exponential expression. Be sure to show your work.**

$$9^2 + 44^8 \times 44^{-7} = \boxed{}$$

Common Core Standard 8.EE.A.1 – Expressions and Equations

☐ **Evaluate the exponential expression. Be sure to show your work.**

$$(-2.1)^2 + 2^2 = \boxed{}$$

Name_____

ASSESSMENT

Common Core Standard 8.EE.A.1 – Expressions and Equations

☐ Evaluate the exponent 10^{-5}. Be sure to show your work.

A $\dfrac{1}{100000}$

B −10000

C $\dfrac{1}{10000}$

D 100000

Common Core Standard 8.EE.A.1 – Expressions and Equations

☐ Evaluate the exponent $(-1.1)^3$. Be sure to show your work.

A − 1.131

B 0.1331

C − 0.1331

D − 1.331

Common Core Standard 8.EE.A.1 – Expressions and Equations

☐ Which is equivalent to $\left(\dfrac{3}{5}\right)^4 \times 36^{-6}$? Be sure to show your work.

A $\dfrac{3}{5} \times \dfrac{3}{5} \times \dfrac{3}{5} \times \dfrac{3}{5} \times 36 \times 36 \times 36 \times 36 \times 36 \times 36$

B $\dfrac{3}{5} \times \dfrac{3}{5} \times \dfrac{3}{5} \times \dfrac{3}{5} \times (-36) \times (-36) \times (-36) \times (-36) \times (-36) \times (-36)$

C $\dfrac{3}{5} \times \dfrac{3}{5} \times \dfrac{3}{5} \times \dfrac{3}{5} \times \dfrac{1}{36} \times \dfrac{1}{36} \times \dfrac{1}{36} \times \dfrac{1}{36} \times \dfrac{1}{36} \times \dfrac{1}{36}$

D $\dfrac{3}{5} \times \dfrac{3}{5} \times \dfrac{3}{5} \times \dfrac{1}{36} \times \dfrac{1}{36} \times \dfrac{1}{36} \times \dfrac{1}{36} \times \dfrac{1}{36} \times \dfrac{1}{36}$

Name_____

ASSESSMENT

Common Core Standard 8.EE.A.1 – Expressions and Equations

☐ **Evaluate the exponential expression. Be sure to show your work.**

$$(-0.2)^2 \times (-1.5)^3 \times 2^0 = \boxed{}$$

Common Core Standard 8.EE.A.1 – Expressions and Equations

☐ **Evaluate the exponential expression. Be sure to show your work.**

$$(-8)^2 + 5^{-2} = \boxed{}$$

Common Core Standard 8.EE.A.1 – Expressions and Equations

☐ **Evaluate the exponential expression. Be sure to show your work.**

$$5^4 - \left(\frac{1}{20}\right)^{-2} = \boxed{}$$

©Teachers' Treasures Publishing

Name_____

DIAGNOSTIC

Common Core Standard 8.EE.A.2 – Expressions and Equations

☐ Find q, if $q^2 = \dfrac{0.64}{1.21}$. Be sure to show your work.

    A $\dfrac{6}{11}$

    B $\dfrac{8}{11}$

    C $\dfrac{0.8}{0.11}$

    D   2

Common Core Standard 8.EE.A.2 – Expressions and Equations

☐ Which row arranges the values from least to greatest? Be sure to explain your answer.

    A $\sqrt[3]{216}$, $\sqrt{121}$, $\sqrt[3]{0.064}$, $\sqrt{6.25}$,

    B $\sqrt[3]{0.064}$, $\sqrt{6.25}$, $\sqrt[3]{216}$, $\sqrt{121}$

    C $\sqrt{6.25}$, $\sqrt[3]{216}$, $\sqrt{121}$, $\sqrt[3]{0.064}$

    D $\sqrt[3]{0.064}$, $\sqrt[3]{216}$, $\sqrt{6.25}$, $\sqrt{121}$

Common Core Standard 8.EE.A.2 – Expressions and Equations

☐ The volume of a cube is 512 cm³. What is the surface area of the cube? Be sure to show your work.

    A   314 cm²

    B   284 cm²

    C   36 cm²

    D   384 cm²

Name_____

DIAGNOSTIC

Common Core Standard 8.EE.A.2 – Expressions and Equations

☐ Connor decided to tile his square-shaped bathroom. He is laying 676 square feet of tile. What is the length of one side of Connor's bathroom? Be sure to show your work.

A   26 feet

B   14 feet

C   24 feet

D   16 feet

Common Core Standard 8.EE.A.2 – Expressions and Equations

☐ The value of which expression is 9? Be sure to show your work.

A $\sqrt[3]{343} - \sqrt{\dfrac{64}{16}}$

B $\sqrt{343} + \sqrt{\dfrac{64}{16}}$

C $\sqrt[3]{343} + \sqrt{\dfrac{64}{16}}$

D $\sqrt[3]{343} \times \sqrt{\dfrac{64}{16}}$

Common Core Standard 8.EE.A.2 – Expressions and Equations

☐ Which of the following equations is true? Be sure to show your work.

A $\sqrt[3]{216} \times \sqrt[3]{8} = \sqrt[3]{1728}$

B $\sqrt[3]{216} \times \sqrt{8} = \sqrt{1728}$

C $\sqrt[3]{216} + \sqrt[3]{8} = \sqrt[3]{1728}$

D $\sqrt[3]{216} - \sqrt[3]{8} = \sqrt[3]{1728}$

©Teachers' Treasures Publishing

Name_____

PRACTICE

Common Core Standard 8.EE.A.2 – Expressions and Equations

☐ Which of the following represents $\sqrt{8100}$? Be sure to show your work.

A   90

B   900

C   9.9

D   0.9

Common Core Standard 8.EE.A.2 – Expressions and Equations

☐ Which of the following represents $\sqrt[3]{512}$? Be sure to show your work.

A   16

B   8

C   14

D   12

Common Core Standard 8.EE.A.2 – Expressions and Equations

☐ Which of the following represents $\sqrt{32}$? Be sure to show your work.

A $4\sqrt{2}$

B $2\sqrt{4}$

C   4

D   8

©Teachers' Treasures Publishing

Name_____

PRACTICE

Common Core Standard 8.EE.A.2 – Expressions and Equations

☐ **Which of the following equations is true? Be sure to explain your answer.**

A $\sqrt{2 \times 2 \times 0.5 \times 5}$ = 1

B $\sqrt{0.2 \times 0.2 \times 0.5 \times 0.5}$ = 1

C $\sqrt{0.2 \times 0.2 \times 5 \times 5}$ = 1

D $\sqrt{2 \times 2 \times 5 \times 5}$ = 1

Common Core Standard 8.EE.A.2 – Expressions and Equations

☐ **Which of the following equations is true? Be sure to explain your answer.**

A $\sqrt{5 \times 5 \times 5 \times 5 \times 7 \times 7}$ = 25 x 7

B $\sqrt{5 \times 5 \times 3 \times 3 \times 3 \times 7 \times 7}$ = 25 x 7

C $\sqrt{4 \times 5 \times 5 \times 4 \times 7 \times 9}$ = 20 x 7

D $\sqrt{5 \times 5 \times 5 \times 5 \times 7 \times 9 \times 7}$ = 25 x 7

Common Core Standard 8.EE.A.2 – Expressions and Equations

☐ **Which of the following equations is true? Be sure to explain your answer.**

A $\sqrt{16}$ x $\sqrt{16}$ = $\sqrt{256}$

B $\sqrt{100}$ + $\sqrt{49}$ = $\sqrt{2.56}$

C $\sqrt{169}$ − $\sqrt{4}$ = $\sqrt{256}$

D $\sqrt{1.96}$ ÷ $\sqrt{16}$ = $\sqrt{256}$

©Teachers' Treasures Publishing

Name_____

PRACTICE

Common Core Standard 8.EE.A.2 – Expressions and Equations

☐ The volume of a cube is 1331 cm³. What is the area of each face of a cube? Be sure to show your work.

A   110

B   15 224

C   121

D   113

Common Core Standard 8.EE.A.2 – Expressions and Equations

☐ Abbie wants to buy a new rug for her bedroom. In a department store she finds a square rug that has an area of 36 ft². How long is each side of the rug? How many of those rugs are needed to cover an area of 144 square foot? Be sure to show your work.

A   8; 4

B   6; 4

C   6; 6

D   8; 2

Common Core Standard 8.EE.A.2 – Expressions and Equations

☐ The value of which expression is 4? Be sure to show your work.

A $\sqrt[3]{\dfrac{64}{0.8}} - \sqrt{\dfrac{144}{0.36}}$

B $\sqrt[3]{\dfrac{0.064}{0.008}} + \sqrt{\dfrac{144}{36}}$

C $\sqrt[3]{\dfrac{0.064}{0.008}} - \sqrt{\dfrac{144}{36}}$

D $\sqrt[3]{\dfrac{0.64}{0.008}} + \sqrt{\dfrac{14.4}{36}}$

©Teachers' Treasures Publishing

Name_____

PRACTICE

Common Core Standard 8.EE.A.2 – Expressions and Equations

☐ **Which row arranges the values from greatest to least? Be sure to explain your answer.**

A $\sqrt{0.81}$, $\sqrt[3]{8}$, $\sqrt{6.25}$, $\sqrt[3]{64}$

B $\sqrt[3]{64}$, $\sqrt[3]{8}$, $\sqrt{6.25}$, $\sqrt{0.81}$

C $\sqrt{0.81}$, $\sqrt{6.25}$, $\sqrt[3]{64}$, $\sqrt[3]{8}$

D $\sqrt{6.25}$, $\sqrt[3]{64}$, $\sqrt{0.81}$, $\sqrt[3]{8}$

Common Core Standard 8.EE.A.2 – Expressions and Equations

☐ **Find the side length of a square with an area of 324 ft^2? Be sure to show your work.**

A 17

B 9

C 18

D 19

Common Core Standard 8.EE.A.2 – Expressions and Equations

☐ **Find q, if $q^2 = \dfrac{81}{169}$. Be sure to show your work.**

A $\dfrac{9}{13}$

B $\dfrac{8}{14}$

C $\dfrac{81}{169}$

D $\dfrac{11}{16}$

©Teachers' Treasures Publishing

Name_____

ASSESSMENT

Common Core Standard 8.EE.A.2 – Expressions and Equations

☐ Find k, if $k^3 = \dfrac{64}{125}$. Be sure to explain your answer.

A $\dfrac{4}{15}$ C $\dfrac{8}{15}$

B $\dfrac{4}{5}$ D $\dfrac{6}{5}$

Common Core Standard 8.EE.A.2 – Expressions and Equations

☐ What is the side length of a square with an area of 144 ft^2 ? Be sure to show your work.

A 8

B 12

C 13

D 14

Common Core Standard 8.EE.A.2 – Expressions and Equations

☐ Which of the following equations is true? Be sure to explain your answer.

A $\sqrt{\dfrac{2 \times 2 \times 3 \times 3 \times 3 \times 3}{5 \times 5 \times 7 \times 7 \times 7 \times 7}} = \dfrac{1}{128}$

B $\sqrt{\dfrac{2 \times 2 \times 3 \times 3 \times 3 \times 3}{5 \times 5 \times 7 \times 7 \times 7 \times 7}} = \dfrac{18}{245}$

C $\sqrt{\dfrac{2 \times 2 \times 3 \times 3 \times 3 \times 3}{5 \times 5 \times 7 \times 7 \times 7 \times 7}} = \dfrac{16}{49}$

D $\sqrt{\dfrac{2 \times 2 \times 3 \times 3 \times 3 \times 3}{5 \times 5 \times 7 \times 7 \times 7 \times 7}} = \dfrac{324}{8575}$

©Teachers' Treasures Publishing

Name_____

ASSESSMENT

Common Core Standard 8.EE.A.2 – Expressions and Equations

☐ The Wilsons want to fence their square garden that has an area of 289 square meters. How long is each side of the garden? Be sure to explain your answer.

A   17 meters

B   18 meters

C   16 meters

D   19 meters

Common Core Standard 8.EE.A.2 – Expressions and Equations

☐ Which row arranges the values from least to greatest? Be sure to show your work.

A $\sqrt[3]{27}$, $\sqrt[3]{125}$, $\sqrt{16}$, $\sqrt{625}$

B $\sqrt{16}$, $\sqrt[3]{27}$, $\sqrt[3]{125}$, $\sqrt{625}$

C $\sqrt[3]{27}$, $\sqrt{16}$, $\sqrt[3]{125}$, $\sqrt{625}$

D $\sqrt{625}$, $\sqrt[3]{27}$, $\sqrt{16}$, $\sqrt[3]{125}$

Common Core Standard 8.EE.A.2 – Expressions and Equations

☐ The value of which expression is 5.8? Be sure to show your work.

A $\sqrt[3]{\dfrac{27}{0.125}} - \sqrt{\dfrac{0.16}{4}}$ C $\sqrt[3]{\dfrac{27}{0.125}} + \sqrt{\dfrac{1.6}{4}}$

B $\sqrt[3]{\dfrac{27}{0.125}} \times \sqrt{\dfrac{0.16}{4}}$ D $\sqrt[3]{\dfrac{27}{1.25}} - \sqrt{\dfrac{0.16}{4}}$

©Teachers' Treasures Publishing

Name_____

DIAGNOSTIC

Common Core Standard 8.EE.A.3 – Expressions and Equations

☐ Which number is larger: 9×10^3 or 6.3×10^5? By how many times? Be sure to explain your answer.

    A 6.3×10^5; 700

    B 6.3×10^5; 70

    C 6.3×10^5; 100

    D 9×10^3; 70

Common Core Standard 8.EE.A.3 – Expressions and Equations

☐ Simplify the expression. Write your answer in scientific notation. Be sure to show your work.

$$6.6 \times 10^6 \div 2 \times 10^7 =$$

Common Core Standard 8.EE.A.3 – Expressions and Equations

☐ Which symbol makes the statement true? 8×10^{17} ? 9.1×10^{14}. Be sure to show your work.

    A   >

    B   <

    C   ≥

    D   ≤

©Teachers' Treasures Publishing

Name_____

DIAGNOSTIC

Common Core Standard 8.EE.A.3 – Expressions and Equations

☐ Simplify the expression. Write your answer in scientific notation. Be sure to show your work.

$$(4.5 \times 10^3) \times (7.8 \times 10^{-8}) =$$

Common Core Standard 8.EE.A.3 – Expressions and Equations

☐ About 54 million Americans participate in fitness activities. The number of people using a stationary bicycle is 9×10^6 in scientific notation. How many times more people perform physical activities other than on a stationary bicycle? Be sure to show your work.

A   60

B   6

C   45

D   5

Common Core Standard 8.EE.A.3 – Expressions and Equations

☐ The Hershey Company produces 1.84 million milk chocolate bars and 9.2×10^5 dark chocolate bars in a month. How many times greater are the milk chocolate bars than the dark chocolate bars? What is the total amount of milk and dark chocolate bars produced by the company in a month? Be sure to show your work.

A $\frac{1}{2}$; 27.6×10^5

B   2; 2.76×10^6

C $\frac{1}{2}$; 2.76×10^5

D   2; 2.76×10^5

©Teachers' Treasures Publishing

Name_____

PRACTICE

Common Core Standard 8.EE.A.3 – Expressions and Equations

☐ Express the number in standard notation: 3.001×10^6. Be sure to show your work.

    A   3.001 000

    B   3, 001, 000

    C   3, 010, 000

    D   3, 100, 000

Common Core Standard 8.EE.A.3 – Expressions and Equations

☐ Express the number in standard notation: 1.23×10^{-10}. Be sure to show your work.

    A   0.000 000 012 300

    B   0.000 000 000 012 300

    C   0.000 000 000 123

    D   0. 000 012 300

Common Core Standard 8.EE.A.3 – Expressions and Equations

☐ Express the number in scientific notation: 1, 000, 000, 000. Be sure to show your work.

    A 1×10^9

    B 1×10^8

    C 10×10^9

    D 1×10^{10}

©Teachers' Treasures Publishing

Name_____

PRACTICE

Common Core Standard 8.EE.A.3 – Expressions and Equations

☐ **Express the number in scientific notation: 0.000 000 007 004. Be sure to show your work.**

A 7.004×10^{-9}

B 7.004×10^{-7}

C 7.400×10^{-9}

D 7.040×10^{-8}

Common Core Standard 8.EE.A.3 – Expressions and Equations

☐ **Simplify the expression. Write your answer in scientific notation. Be sure to show your work.**

$$(2.2 \times 10^6) \div (5 \times 10^{-2}) =$$

Common Core Standard 8.EE.A.3 – Expressions and Equations

☐ **Simplify the expression. Write your answer in scientific notation. Be sure to show your work.**

$$\frac{8 \times 10^7}{5 \times 10^4} \times 10^3 =$$

©Teachers' Treasures Publishing

Name_____

PRACTICE

Common Core Standard 8.EE.A.3 – Expressions and Equations

☐ **Which symbol makes the statement true? 4.56×10^{-7} ? 3.951×10^{-6}. Be sure to show your work.**

A   >

B   <

C   ≥

D   ≤

Common Core Standard 8.EE.A.3 – Expressions and Equations

☐ **Which number is larger: 1.8×10^{-13} or 6.3×10^{-12}? By how many times? Be sure to explain your answer.**

A 1.8×10^{-13} ; 35

B 6.3×10^{-12} ; 35

C 6.3×10^{-12} ; 20

D 1.8×10^{-13} ; 20

Common Core Standard 8.EE.A.3 – Expressions and Equations

☐ **Which number is larger: 8.2×10^8 or 2.46×10^9? By how many times? Be sure to show your work.**

A 2.46×10^9 ; 3

B 2.46×10^9 ; 30

C 8.2×10^8 ; 3

D 8.2×10^8 ; 30

©Teachers' Treasures Publishing

Name_____

PRACTICE

Common Core Standard 8.EE.A.3 – Expressions and Equations

☐ Ann receives $3600 as a scholarship in a year. How much does she receive as scholarship in 3 years? In 6 years? Express your answer in scientific notation. Be sure to show your work.

A 7.2×10^4; 2.16×10^2

B 1.08×10^4; 2.16×10^4

C 7.2×10^4; 2.16×10^3

D 1.08×10^3; 2.16×10^3

Common Core Standard 8.EE.A.3 – Expressions and Equations

☐ Demo-graphologists keep track of how the populations of certain area change. According to their statistics, in 1985 the population of the United State was 2.4×10^8, but in 2005 it increased to 3.0×10^8. How many more people in the US were there in 2005 than in 1985? Be sure to show your work.

A 6×10^8

B 0.6×10^9

C 0.6×10^7

D 6×10^7

Common Core Standard 8.EE.A.3 – Expressions and Equations

☐ The Sun is about 93 million miles away from Earth. Approximately how long would it take for light to reach Earth, if the speed of light is 1.86×10^5 mi/sec? Express your answer in scientific notation. Be sure to show your work.

A 5×10^1 seconds

B 5.0×10^2 seconds

C 0.5×10^2 seconds

D 5.0×10^3 seconds

©Teachers' Treasures Publishing

Name_____

ASSESSMENT

Common Core Standard 8.EE.A.3 – Expressions and Equations

☐ Express the number in standard notation: 4.4391×10^{-8}. Be sure to show your work.

    A   0.000 000 044 391

    B   0.000 044 391

    C   0.000 443 910

    D   0.000 004 439 100

Common Core Standard 8.EE.A.3 – Expressions and Equations

☐ Express the number in scientific notation: 46 320 000 000. Be sure to show your work.

    A 6×10^8

    B 0.6×10^9

    C 0.6×10^7

    D 6×10^7

Common Core Standard 8.EE.A.3 – Expressions and Equations

☐ Simplify the expression. Write your answer in scientific notation. Be sure to show your work.

$$(0.000\ 000\ 635 - 0.000\ 000\ 009) \times 200$$

©Teachers' Treasures Publishing

Name_____

ASSESSMENT

Common Core Standard 8.EE.A.3 – Expressions and Equations

☐ Which symbol makes the statement true? 7.3×10^{27} **?** 5.59×10^{28}. Be sure to explain your answer.

A   >

B   <

C   ≥

D   ≤

Common Core Standard 8.EE.A.3 – Expressions and Equations

☐ The population of India is 1.25×10^9, and the population of Spain is 5×10^7. How many times greater than Spain's population is the population of India? Be sure to show your work.

A   2.5

B   40

C   4

D   25

Common Core Standard 8.EE.A.3 – Expressions and Equations

☐ The Moon is approximately 2.39×10^5 miles away from the Earth. How far would the Moon be from the Earth if the distance between the two increases by 6? Be sure to show your work.

A 1.434×10^5

B 1.434×10^6

C 1.43×10^5

D 1.43×10^4

©Teachers' Treasures Publishing

Name_____

DIAGNOSTIC

Common Core Standard 8.EE.A.4 – Expressions and Equations

☐ One of the most common jobs in the United States is nursing. In scientific notation, there are approximately 2.6×10^6 people working in this field. Each year the number of nurses increases by 3.5%. By how many will the number of nurses increase in one year? Be sure to explain your answer.

    A 9.1×10^4

    B 1.5×10^4

    C 4.5×10^5

    D 8.6×10^3

Common Core Standard 8.EE.A.4 – Expressions and Equations

☐ The half-life of uranium-238 is 4.5×10^9 years. The half-life of uranium-234 is 2.5×10^5 years. How many times greater is the half-life of uranium-238 than that of uranium-234. Be sure to show your work.

    A 4.5×10^3

    B 1.8×10^4

    C 4.5×10^4

    D 1.8×10^5

Common Core Standard 8.EE.A.4 – Expressions and Equations

☐ Write how many particles of dust are present in the house if the total volume of the house is 4,200 cubic meters and there are 3.4×10^9 particles of dust per cubic meter. Be sure to show your work.

    A 6.1×10^{11}

    B 2.6×10^{10}

    C 3.2×10^9

    D 1.4×10^{13}

©Teachers' Treasures Publishing

Name_____

DIAGNOSTIC

Common Core Standard 8.EE.A.4 – Expressions and Equations

☐ The radius of the moon is approximately 1.7×10^3 km. Calculate its approximate volume. Write the answer in scientific notation. Use π = 3. Be sure to show your work.

A 2.7×10^8

B 1.97×10^{10}

C 4.2×10^8

D 2.68×10^{10}

Common Core Standard 8.EE.A.4 – Expressions and Equations

☐ The mass of a dust particle is 7.53×10^{-10} kg. If there were 2.9×10^6 particles on the floor, what would be the total mass of that dust? Be sure to show your work.

A 2.3×10^{-5} kg

B 1.2×10^{-4} kg

C 3.2×10^{-3} kg

D 2.2×10^{-3} kg

Common Core Standard 8.EE.A.4 – Expressions and Equations

☐ Sand particles range in diameter from 2.5×10^{-3} inches to 7.9×10^{-2} inches. Find the difference between the largest and the smallest sand particles. Be sure to show your work.

A 7.7×10^{-2} inches

B 6.6×10^{-2} inches

C 5.7×10^{-1} inches

D 7.5×10^{-3} inches

©Teachers' Treasures Publishing

Name_____

PRACTICE

Common Core Standard 8.EE.A.4 – Expressions and Equations

☐ **Earth is shaped as a sphere with the radius of 6.4 x 10^3 km. The radius of the moon is approximately 1.7 x 10^3 km. How many times is the radius of the Earth larger than the moon's radius? Round to the nearest whole number. Be sure to show your work.**

    A   5

    B   4

    C   3

    D   6

Common Core Standard 8.EE.A.4 – Expressions and Equations

☐ **The wavelength of yellow light is 0.000065. Express the measurement in scientific notation. Be sure to show your work.**

    A   6.5 x 10^{-4}

    B   6.5 x 10^{-5}

    C   0.65 x 10^{-3}

    D   65 x 10^{-5}

Common Core Standard 8.EE.A.4 – Expressions and Equations

☐ **How much is a million days in hours? Write the answer in scientific notation. Be sure to show your work.**

    A   2.4 x 10^8 hours

    B   2.4 x 10^6 hours

    C   24 000 000 hours

    D   2.4 x 10^7 hours

©Teachers' Treasures Publishing

Name_____

PRACTICE

Common Core Standard 8.EE.A.4 – Expressions and Equations

☐ The population of the world in word notation is 7 billion, 274 million, 798 thousand, 604. Write this number in scientific notation. Be sure to explain your answer.

A 7.3×10^6

B 7.2×10^{12}

C 7.3×10^9

D 0.7×10^{11}

Common Core Standard 8.EE.A.4 – Expressions and Equations

☐ The Earth breaks its surface area into water and land segments. The surface area of the Earth is 5.1×10^8 km². How many square kilometers of water are on Earth's surface, if 149 million km² is the land? Write the answer in scientific notation. Be sure to show your work.

A 3.6×10^8 km²

B   361 million km²

C 2.4×10^6 km²

D 4.7×10^8 km²

Common Core Standard 8.EE.A.4 – Expressions and Equations

☐ Tom and Ben calculated the distance between the houses in inches. The number they found was about one million inches. How far is a million inches in miles? Round the answer to the nearest tenth. Be sure to show your work.

A   11.2 miles

B   2.4 miles

C   15.8 miles

D   4.1 miles

©Teachers' Treasures Publishing

Name_____

PRACTICE

Common Core Standard 8.EE.A.4 – Expressions and Equations

☐ About 70% of Earth's surface is water. How many square miles of water are there on Earth's surface, if the Earth total area is 196.9 million sq mi? Express the answer in scientific notation. Be sure to explain your answer.

A 0.4×10^9 sq mi

B 1.3×10^6 sq mi

C 1.4×10^8 sq mi

D 2.2×10^8 sq mi

Common Core Standard 8.EE.A.4 – Expressions and Equations

☐ It has been estimated that there are 2×10^{11} stars in the Milky Way Galaxy. There is also an estimate of 1×10^8 galaxies in the whole universe. Use this to calculate the number of stars in the whole universe. Be sure to show your work.

A 2.0×10^{19}

B 2.1×10^{18}

C 2.0×10^{88}

D 2×10^3

Common Core Standard 8.EE.A.4 – Expressions and Equations

☐ The size of small particles is usually measured in microns. The average size of a bacterium is 30 microns. What is the size of a bacterium in inches, if there are 25400 microns in one inch? Express the answer in scientific notation. Be sure to show your work.

A 7.6×10^5 inches

B 6.9×10^{-4} inches

C 1.2×10^{-3} inches

D 7.6×10^{-5} inches

©Teachers' Treasures Publishing

Name_____

PRACTICE

Common Core Standard 8.EE.A.4 – Expressions and Equations

☐ One micron is one-millionth of a meter. The eye of a needle is approximately 1230 microns. Write the measure of the eye of a needle in meters, using scientific notation. Be sure to explain your answer.

A 2.1×10^{-4} meter

B 9.2×10^{-2} meter

C 3.4×10^{-6} meter

D 1.2×10^{-3} meter

Common Core Standard 8.EE.A.4 – Expressions and Equations

☐ Micron is a metric unit of measure that is used to describe small particles. The average size of a corn starch particle is 0.44 microns. What is the size of a corn starch particle in meters, if one micron is one-millionth of a meter? Express the answer in scientific notation. Be sure to show your work.

A 4.4×10^{5}

B 4.4×10^{-7}

C 4.4×10^{6}

D 4.4×10^{-6}

Common Core Standard 8.EE.A.4 – Expressions and Equations

☐ The number of cells in the human body is about 10^{14} cells. How many cells would 1000 people have in total? Be sure to show your work.

A 1.0×10^{16}

B 1.1×10^{17}

C 0.1×10^{11}

D 1×10^{17}

©Teachers' Treasures Publishing

Name_____

ASSESSMENT

Common Core Standard 8.EE.A.4 – Expressions and Equations

☐ A four-man hot-air balloon is 13.3×10^7 cubic inches in volume. A twelve-man hot-air balloon has the volume of 2.4×10^8 cubic inches. Find the sum of both balloons' volume. Express the answer in scientific notation. Be sure to explain your answer.

    A 1.07×10^8 cubic inches

    B 3.7×10^8 cubic inches

    C 10^8 cubic inches

    D 15.7×10^8 cubic inches

Common Core Standard 8.EE.A.4 – Expressions and Equations

☐ Individual strands of hair range in thickness from 1/1500 to 1/500 of an inch in diameter, depending on the properties of the hair. Find the difference between the diameters of the thickest and thinnest hairs. Express the answer in scientific notation. Be sure to show your work.

    A 1.3×10^{-3} inches

    B 2.3×10^{-2} inches

    C 3.2×10^{-4} inches

    D 2.1×10^{-2} inches

Common Core Standard 8.EE.A.4 – Expressions and Equations

☐ The single gelatin particle measures 45 microns, while a yeast cell is approximately 28 microns. By how much is a particle of gelatin larger than a yeast cell? Write the answer in inches, if there are 25400 microns in one inch. Express the answer in scientific notation. Be sure to show your work.

    A 2.3×10^{-3} inches

    B 5.4×10^{-2} inches

    C 3.8×10^{-5} inches

    D 6.7×10^{-4} inches

©Teachers' Treasures Publishing

Name_____

ASSESSMENT

Common Core Standard 8.EE.A.4 – Expressions and Equations

☐ Scientists found that the body of a 155 lb person consists of 9.3×10^{-3} lbs of iron. In the bodies of 3300 such people, how much iron is present? Be sure to explain your answer.

A   12.4 lbs

B   3.65 lbs

C   23 lbs

D   30.69 lbs

Common Core Standard 8.EE.A.4 – Expressions and Equations

☐ The surface area of the Earth is 510 million km². What is the surface area of Saturn, if its surface area is 84 times larger than Earth? Express the answer in scientific notation. Be sure to show your work.

A 4.3×10^9 km²

B 4.27×10^8 km²

C 4.28×10^{10} km²

D 42.8×10^6 km²

Common Core Standard 8.EE.A.4 – Expressions and Equations

☐ The average raindrop is about 3.0×10^{-3} ounces. How many raindrops are in a gallon of water, if a gallon has 128 ounces? Be sure to show your work.

A   5467 drops in a gallon

B   42667 drops in a gallon

C   17667 drops in a gallon

D   115200 drops in a gallon

©Teachers' Treasures Publishing

Name_____

DIAGNOSTIC

Common Core Standard 8.EE.B.5 – Expressions and Equations

☐ The graph below represents the relationship between the money Jane earned while babysitting and the hours of babysitting. Her brother Jack washed cars to earn some money. The equation below represents the rate at which Jack earned his money. Who earned more money? Be sure to explain your answer.

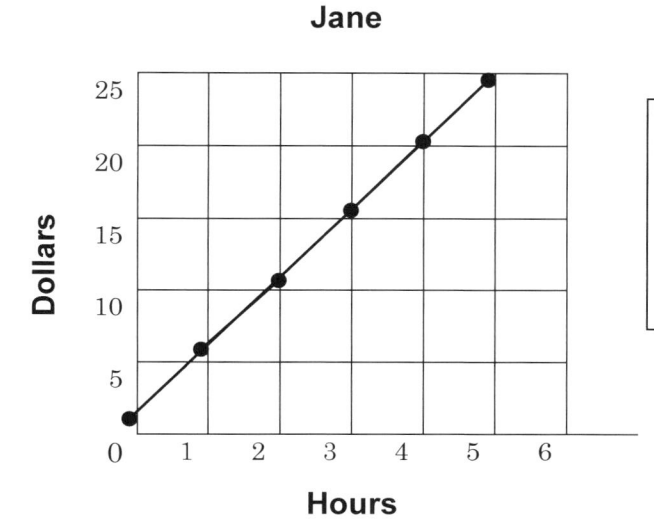

Jane

Jack
$y = 7x$,
where x = hours
y is dollars

Common Core Standard 8.EE.B.5 – Expressions and Equations

☐ Based on the previous problem, how much money will they earn altogether in a week, if each of them worked 3 hours a day? Be sure to show your work.

A   252   C   105

B   36   D   147

Common Core Standard 8.EE.B.5 – Expressions and Equations

☐ Based on the previous problems, how much money did Jack earn at the end of a day, if he worked 5 hours? Be sure to show your work.

A   30   C   25

B   35   D   40

©Teachers' Treasures Publishing

Name_____

DIAGNOSTIC

Common Core Standard 8.EE.B.5 – Expressions and Equations

☐ Tommy and Denny are learning how to type. The graph below represents the number of words typed over time by Tommy. Denny can type at a constant rate represented by the equation below. Who can type at a faster pace? Be sure to explain your answer.

Tommy's Pace

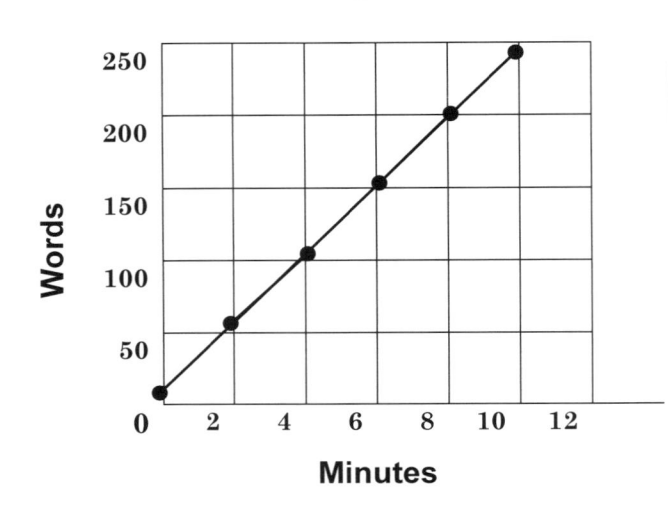

(graph: Words vs Minutes, line passing through approximately (0,10), (2,60), (4,110), (6,160), (8,210), (10,255))

Denny's Pace
$y = 50x$,
where x = minutes
y = words

Common Core Standard 8.EE.B.5 – Expressions and Equations

☐ Based on the previous problem, how many words can Tommy type in 12 minutes? Be sure to show your work.

A   200   C   300

B   350   D   250

Common Core Standard 8.EE.B.5 – Expressions and Equations

☐ Based on the previous problems, in how many minutes will Denny type 450 words? Be sure to show your work.

A   9 minutes   C   11 minutes

B   10 minutes   D   12 minutes

©Teachers' Treasures Publishing

Name_____

PRACTICE

Common Core Standard 8.EE.B.5 – Expressions and Equations

☐ The pet store spent an average of $1.5 a day for each dog they have in stock. Which expression below shows the amount spent in 2 months for the number, *d*, dogs? Be sure to show your work.

- A *d* + 30 x 1.50
- B *d* x 60 + 1.50
- C *d* x 60 x 1.50
- D *d* x 30 x 1.50

Common Core Standard 8.EE.B.5 – Expressions and Equations

☐ A 12-pack of soft drink costs $4.79 at the grocery store. One can of soft drink costs $1.50 in a vending machine. How much money would you save by purchasing a dozen cans at the grocery store instead of a dozen at the vending machine? Be sure to show your work.

- A 11.32
- B 13.21
- C 12.31
- D 12.21

Common Core Standard 8.EE.B.5 – Expressions and Equations

☐ The ratio of boys to girls in a class is 2 to 3. There are 10 boys in the class. How many girls are there? Be sure to show your work.

- A 25
- B 10
- C 30
- D 15

©Teachers' Treasures Publishing

Name_____

PRACTICE

Common Core Standard 8.EE.B.5 – Expressions and Equations

☐ The French club is selling berets to raise money. The supplier charges a one-time fee of $34 for each order and $8 for each beret. Write an equation to calculate the cost C for any number of berets b. Be sure to show your work.

A $C = 8b + 34$

B $C = 34b + 8$

C $b = 8C + 34$

D $b = 34C + 8$

Common Core Standard 8.EE.B.5 – Expressions and Equations

☐ Liz's and Taylor's hiking times and mileages for summer break are shown on the graph. Which equation represents Liz's pace? Be sure to show your work.

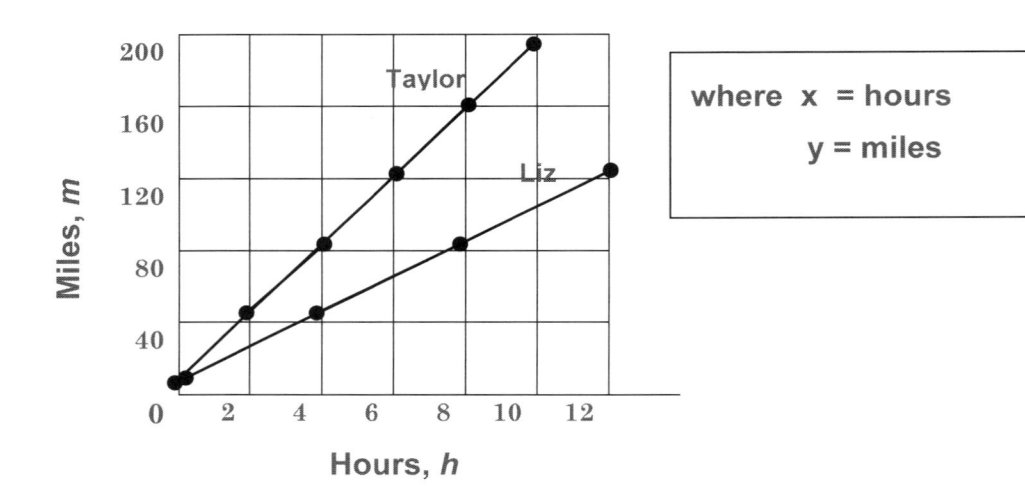

where x = hours
       y = miles

A $y = 40x$

B $x = 10y$

C $y = 10x$

D $x = 40y$

©Teachers' Treasures Publishing

Name_____

PRACTICE

Common Core Standard 8.EE.B.5 – Expressions and Equations

☐ During a fundraiser, the boys made lemonade and the girls made cocoa drinks. The graph below represents the number of cups of lemonade the boys made and the amount of sugar used. The equation represents the number of cups of cocoa drink the girls made and the amount of sugar used. Who spent more sugar making the same amount of cups of beverage? Be sure to explain your answer.

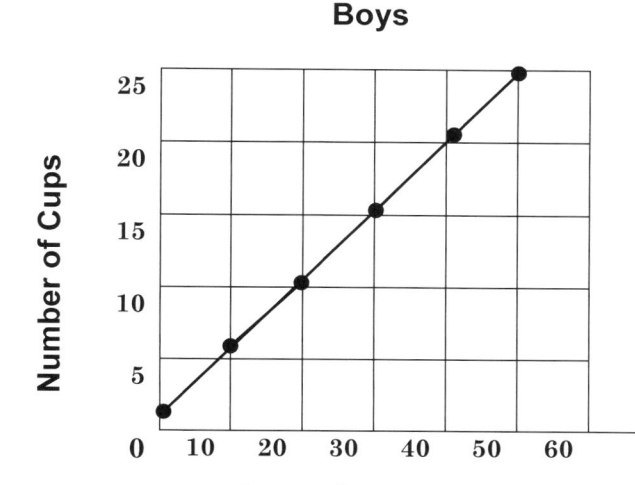

Boys

[Graph: Number of Cups vs Sugar (teaspoons)]

Girls

$y = \frac{1}{3}x$,

where x = sugar (tsp)
        y = cups

Common Core Standard 8.EE.B.5 – Expressions and Equations

☐ Based on the previous problem, how many cups of cocoa drink will the girls make if they use 54 tea-spoons of sugar? Be sure to show your work.

A   16   C   28

B   18   D   26

Common Core Standard 8.EE.B.5 – Expressions and Equations

☐ Based on the previous problems, how much sugar will the boys need if they make 30 cups of lemonade? Be sure to show your work.

A   60   C   15

B   10   D   90

©Teachers' Treasures Publishing

Common Core Standard 8.EE.B.5 – Expressions and Equations

☐ Adam and Leon jog every weekend to warm up before a soccer game. The graph below represents the number of miles Adam runs each hour. The equation represents the rate at which Leon runs. Who jogs at a slower pace? Be sure to explain your answer.

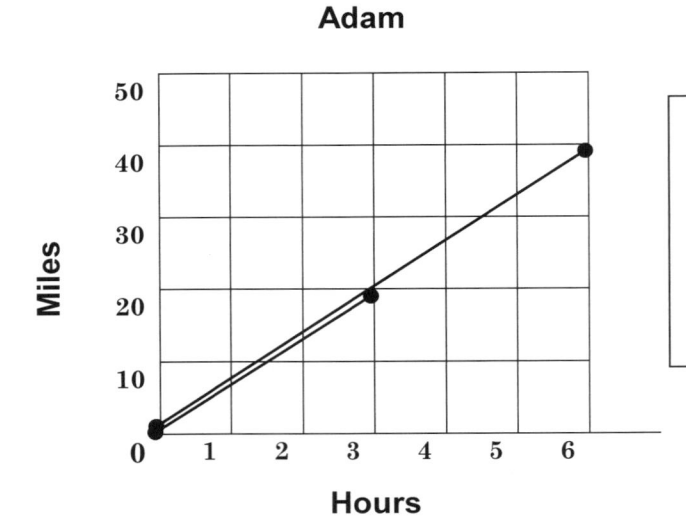

Adam

(Graph: Miles vs. Hours, showing points at approximately (0,0), (3,20), and (6,40))

Leon
$y = 4x$,
where x = hours
y = miles

Common Core Standard 8.EE.B.5 – Expressions and Equations

☐ Based on the previous problem, how many miles will Adam jog if he jogs a total of 9 hours? Be sure to show your work.

A 45 C 35

B 50 D 60

Common Core Standard 8.EE.B.5 – Expressions and Equations

☐ Based on the previous problem, how many miles will Leon jog in 30 minutes? Be sure to show your work.

A 4 C 2

B 6 D 8

Name_____

ASSESSMENT

Common Core Standard 8.EE.B.5 – Expressions and Equations

☐ Two shops, YumCake and the Hobby's want to open their shops in a new shopping center. The graph below represents YumCake's rent payment per month. The equation below represents the Hobby's rent payments. Who will pay more rent? Be sure to explain your answer.

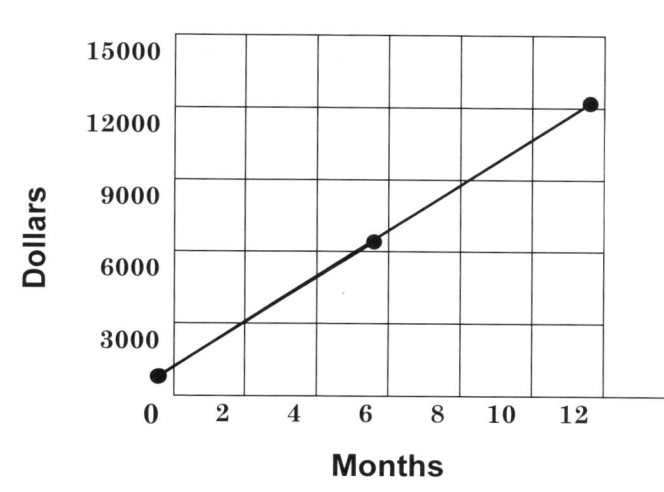

YumCake

(Graph: Dollars vs. Months, with points approximately at (0, 1000), (6, 7000), (12, 13000))

Hobby's
$y = 800x$,
where x = months
y = dollars

Common Core Standard 8.EE.B.5 – Expressions and Equations

☐ Based on the previous problem, determine the monthly rent for each shop. Be sure to show your work.

A   3000; 800

B   2000; 800

C   4000; 800

D   1000; 800

Common Core Standard 8.EE.B.5 – Expressions and Equations

☐ Based on the previous problems, how much is Hobby's rent payment per year? Be sure to show your work.

A   12000

B   9000

C   8000

D   9600

©Teachers' Treasures Publishing

Page 55

Name_____

ASSESSMENT

Common Core Standard 8.EE.B.5 – Expressions and Equations

☐ City High School's basketball and volleyball teams compete by selling school buttons to raise money for an end-of-year party. The graph below represents the costs and the number of buttons sold by the basketball team. The equation below represents how many buttons were sold and the earned money by the volleyball team. Who earns at a faster pace? Be sure to explain your answer.

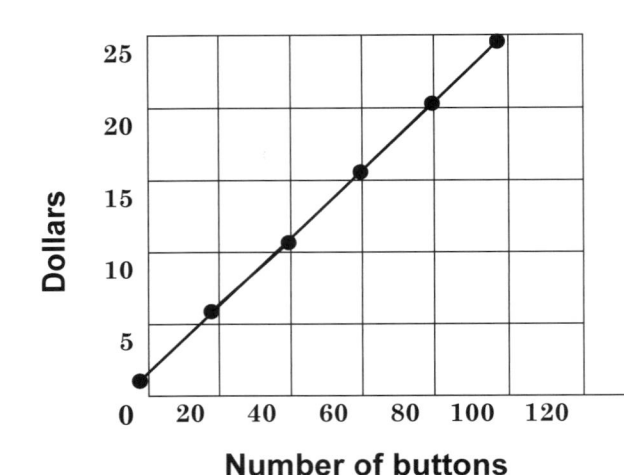

Basketball Team

(graph: Dollars vs Number of buttons)

Volleyball Team
$y = \frac{1}{8} x,$
where
x = number of buttons
y = dollars

Common Core Standard 8.EE.B.5 – Expressions and Equations

☐ Based on the previous problem, how much will the volleyball team have if they sell 240 buttons? Be sure to show your work.

A 60   C 50

B 90   D 30

Common Core Standard 8.EE.B.5 – Expressions and Equations

☐ Based on the previous problem, how much will the basketball team have if they sell 240 buttons? Be sure to show your work.

A 60   C 70

B 40   D 50

©Teachers' Treasures Publishing

Name_____

DIAGNOSTIC

Common Core Standard 8.EE.B.6 – Expressions and Equations

☐ Find the slope of the line using the similar triangles as a guide. Write the equation of the line. Be sure to show your work.

A $\frac{2}{3}$; $y = \frac{2}{3}x - 3$

B   3; $y = 3x - 3$

C   2; $y = 2x - 3$

D $\frac{2}{5}$; $y = \frac{2}{5}x - 3$

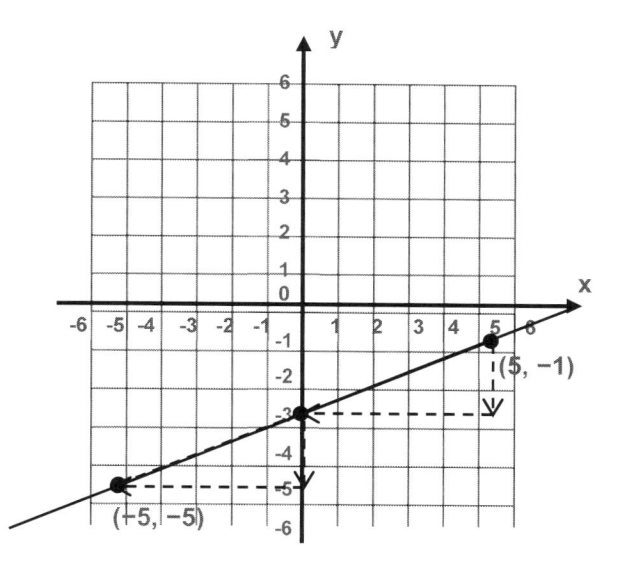

Common Core Standard 8.EE.B.6 – Expressions and Equations

☐ Write the equation of the line G using the similar triangles. Write the equation of the line F that is parallel to the line G and passes through the origin. Be sure to show your work.

A $y = 5x - 11$; $y = -5x$

B $y = 1.5x + 11.5$; $y = -1.5x$

C $y = 5x + 11$; $y = -5x$

D $y = -1.5x + 11.5$; $y = -1.5x$

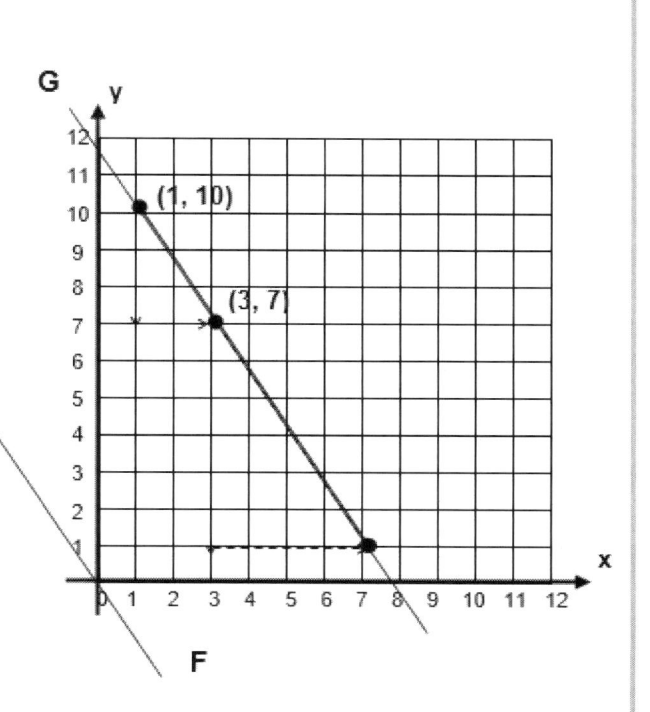

©Teachers' Treasures Publishing

Name_____

DIAGNOSTIC

Common Core Standard 8.EE.B.6 – Expressions and Equations

☐ Find the equation of each line if they are parallel. Be sure to show your work.

A   W: $y = -x$
       V: $y = -x + 6$

B   W: $y = -2x$
       V: $y = 2x + 6$

C   W: $y = x$
       V: $y = 2x - 6$

D   W: $y = 3x + 2$
       V: $y = -3x + 6$

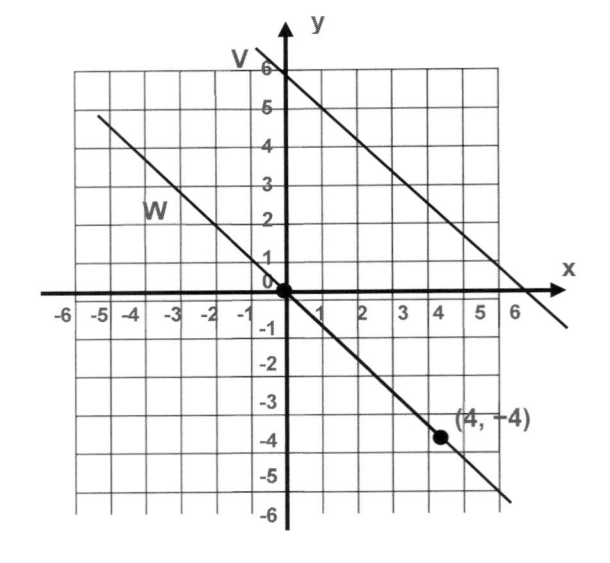

(4, -4)

Common Core Standard 8.EE.B.6 – Expressions and Equations

☐ Write an equation to represent the graph. Be sure to show your work.

A $y = 3.5x + 5$

B $y = 1.75x + 5.5$

C $y = -3.25x + 5.5$

D $y = -1.5x + 6$

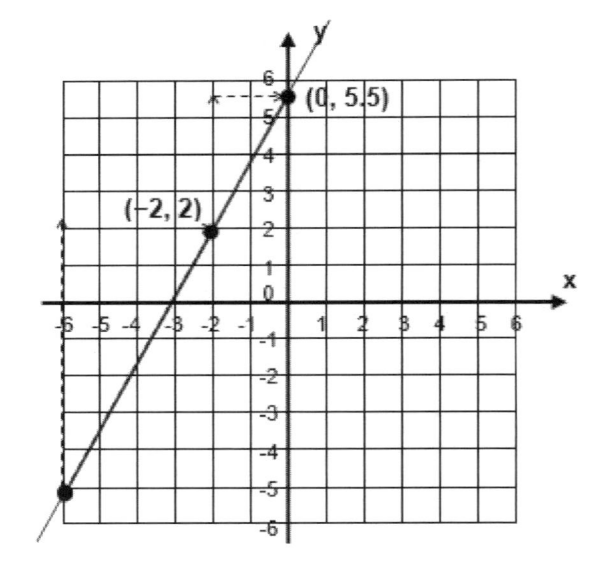

(0, 5.5)
(-2, 2)

©Teachers' Treasures Publishing   Page 58

Name_____

PRACTICE

Common Core Standard 8.EE.B.6 – Expressions and Equations

☐ Find the slope and the y- intercept of the graph of the equation: $y = \frac{x}{9} + 3$.
Be sure to show your work.

A $m = \frac{1}{9}$; b = 3

B   m = 9; b = 3

C $m = \frac{1}{9}$; b = −3

D $m = \frac{x}{9}$; b = 3

Common Core Standard 8.EE.B.6 – Expressions and Equations

☐ Find an equation for the line that passes through (−3, 5) with a slope of 2.
Be sure to show your work.

A   y = −2x + 1

B   y = 2x + 11

C   y = −2x + 11

D   y = 2x + 10

Common Core Standard 8.EE.B.6 – Expressions and Equations

☐ Write an equation of the line with the given characteristics: slope 1, y-intercept −5. Be sure to show your work.

A   y = −x − 5

B   y = −5x + 1

C   y = −x + 5

D   y = x − 5

©Teachers' Treasures Publishing

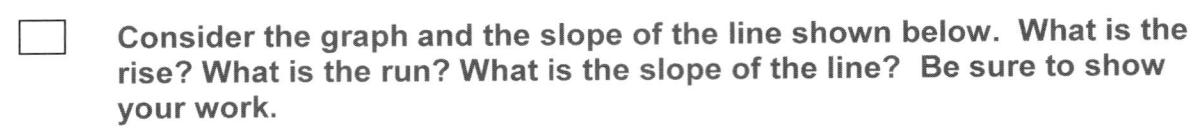

Name_____

PRACTICE

Common Core Standard 8.EE.B.6 – Expressions and Equations

☐ Consider the graph and the slope of the line shown below. What is the rise? What is the run? What is the slope of the line? Be sure to show your work.

A   – 8; 4; $\frac{1}{2}$

B   – 4; 8; $-\frac{1}{2}$

C   8; – 4; $\frac{1}{2}$

D   4; – 4; $-\frac{1}{2}$

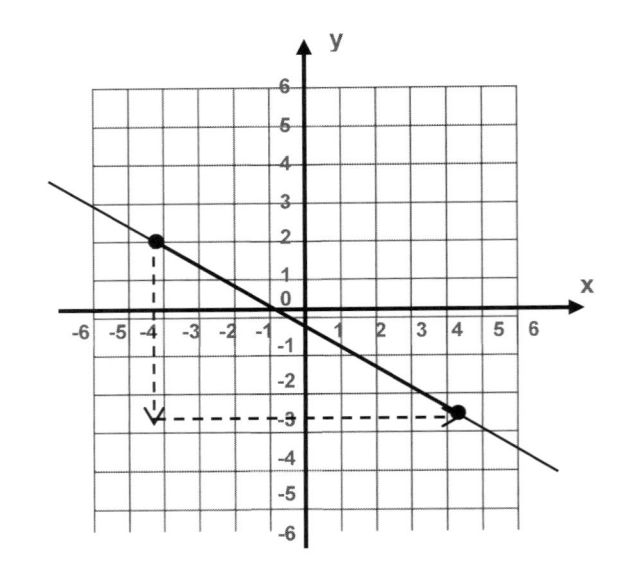

Common Core Standard 8.EE.B.6 – Expressions and Equations

☐ Graph the line that passes through (-4, 3) and (-1, 5). Find the slope m of the line. Be sure to show your work.

A   m = 2

B   m = $\frac{2}{5}$

C   m = $\frac{2}{3}$

D   m = 5

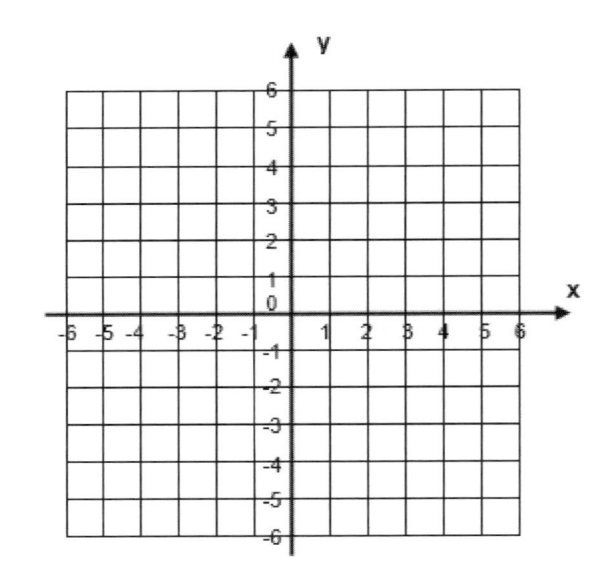

©Teachers' Treasures Publishing

Name_____

PRACTICE

Common Core Standard 8.EE.B.6 – Expressions and Equations

☐ Which of the following equations represents the line that passes through the origin. Be sure to show your work.

A $y = \frac{4}{5}x + 3$

B $y = 5x + 15$

C $y = -5x + 12$

D $y = -\frac{4}{5}x$

Common Core Standard 8.EE.B.6 – Expressions and Equations

☐ Write an equation to represents this graph. Be sure to show your work.

A $y = -x + 13$

B $y = x - 13$

C $y = -x - 13$

D $y = x + 13$

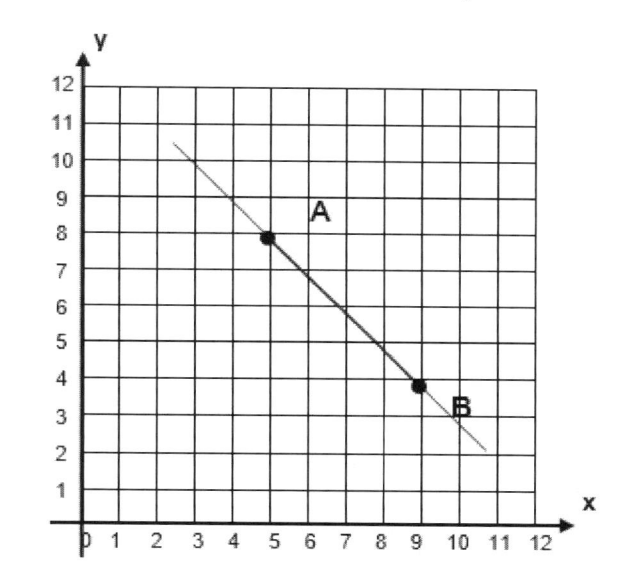

Common Core Standard 8.EE.B.6 – Expressions and Equations

☐ Write the equation of the line with slope $-\frac{1}{4}$ that passes through the point (7, 1). Write the answer in the point-slope form. Be sure to show your work.

A $1 - y = -\frac{1}{4}(x - 7)$

B $y + 1 = -\frac{1}{4}(x + 7)$

C $y - 1 = -\frac{1}{4}(x - 7)$

D $y - 2 = -\frac{1}{4}(7 - x)$

©Teachers' Treasures Publishing

Name_____

PRACTICE

Common Core Standard 8.EE.B.6 – Expressions and Equations

☐ **Find the slope of the line using the similar triangles as a guide. Write the equation of the line. Be sure to show your work.**

A $\frac{2}{5}$; $y = \frac{2}{5}x + 5$

B   0.4; $y = 0.4x + 5$

C   5; $y = 5x + 2$

D $\frac{3}{4}$; $y = \frac{3}{4}x - 5$

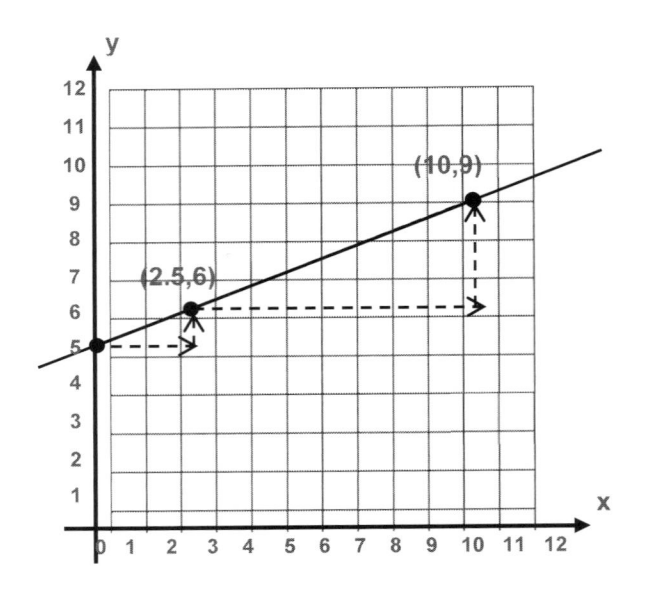

Common Core Standard 8.EE.B.6 – Expressions and Equations

☐ **Find the slope of the line using the similar triangles as a guide. Write the equation of the line. Be sure to show your work.**

A $-\frac{1}{2}$; $y = -\frac{1}{2}x$

B -2; $y = -2x$

C   2; $y = 2x$

D $\frac{1}{2}$; $y = \frac{1}{2}x$

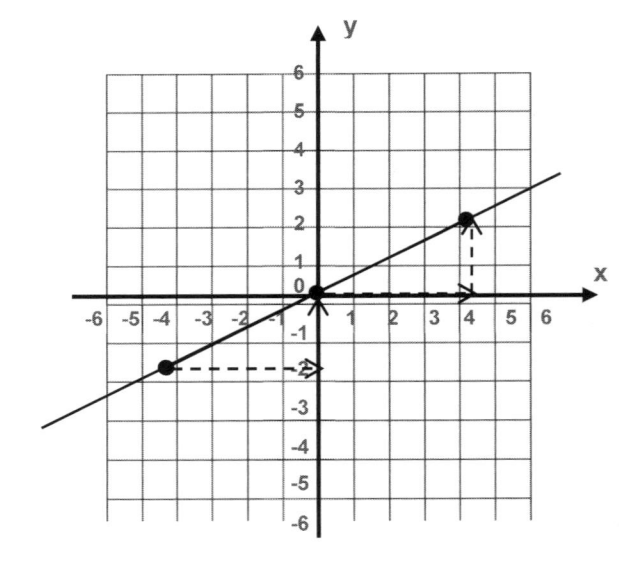

©Teachers' Treasures Publishing   Page 62

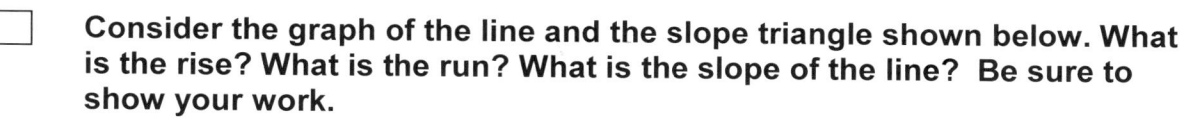

Name_____

ASSESSMENT

Common Core Standard 8.EE.B.6 – Expressions and Equations

☐ Consider the graph of the line and the slope triangle shown below. What is the rise? What is the run? What is the slope of the line? Be sure to show your work.

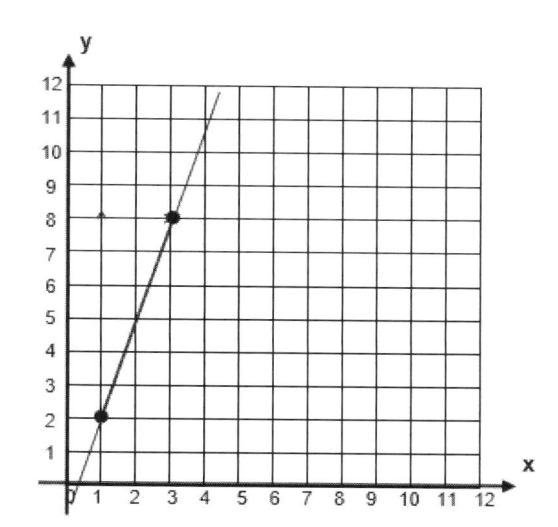

A   6; 3; 2

B   4; 2; 2

C   6; 2; 3

D   5; 2; 2.5

Common Core Standard 8.EE.B.6 – Expressions and Equations

☐ Write the equation of the line with slope −5 that passes through the point (−9, 8). Write the answer in slope-intercept form. Be sure to show your work.

A $y = -5x - 3$

B $y = -5x - 37$

C $y = -5x + 7$

D $y = -5x - 7$

Common Core Standard 8.EE.B.6 – Expressions and Equations

☐ Which of the following pairs of equations represents two parallel lines? Be sure to show your work.

A $y = 2x - 7$; $y = -2x$

B $y = 1.3x - 1$; $y = 13x + 5$

C $y = 5.2x - 7$; $y = 5.2x + 5$

D $y = \frac{7}{8}x$; $y = -\frac{7}{9}x + 1$

©Teachers' Treasures Publishing

Name_____

ASSESSMENT

Common Core Standard 8.EE.B.6 – Expressions and Equations

☐ Find the slope of the line using the similar triangles as a guide. Write the equation of the line. Be sure to show your work.

A   3; $y = 3x - 1.2$

B -3; $y = -3x - \frac{1}{3}$

C $\frac{2}{3}$; $y = \frac{2}{3}x - \frac{1}{3}$

D $-\frac{2}{3}$; $y = -\frac{2}{3}x - \frac{1}{3}$

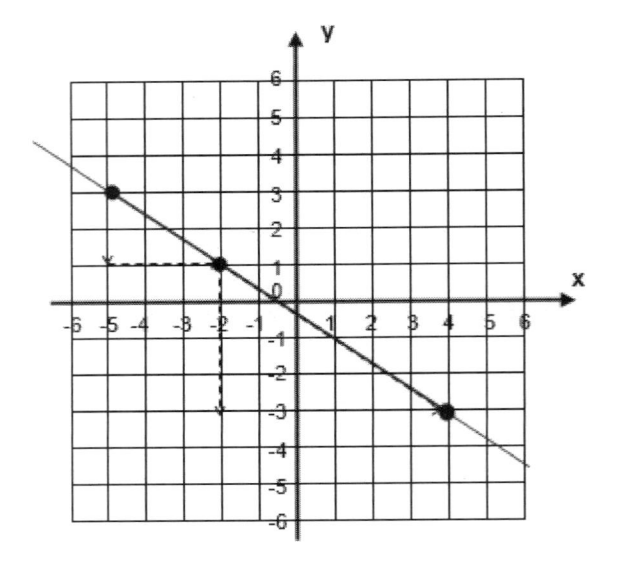

Common Core Standard 8.EE.B.6 – Expressions and Equations

☐ Write an equation to represent this graph. Be sure to show your work.

A $y = x$

B $y = 2x$

C $y = 3x$

D $y = -2x$

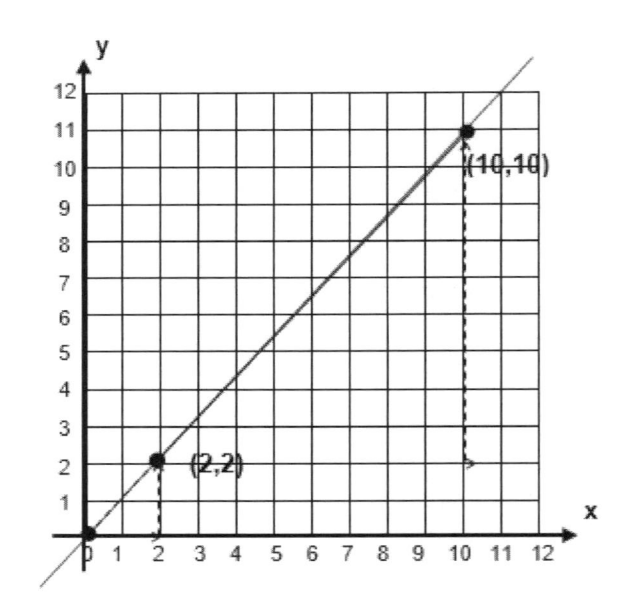

©Teachers' Treasures Publishing   Page 64

Name_____

DIAGNOSTIC

Common Core Standard 8.EE.C.7 – Expressions and Equations

☐ How many solutions does this equation have? $3(n + 4) = 3n + 11$. Be sure to explain your answer.

A   one solution

B   no solution

C   infinitely many solutions

D   two solutions

Common Core Standard 8.EE.C.7 – Expressions and Equations

☐ 13 less than fourteen times a certain number is twenty-nine more than 7 times that number. What is the number? Be sure to show your work.

A   12

B   6

C   7

D   9

Common Core Standard 8.EE.C.7 – Expressions and Equations

☐ Solve for h. $11h - 4h + 1 - 53 = 11$. Be sure to show your work.

A   9

B   7

C   11

D   5

©Teachers' Treasures Publishing

Name_____

DIAGNOSTIC

Common Core Standard 8.EE.C.7 – Expressions and Equations

☐ Solve for *c*. $16.5c - 2(c + 0.6) = 288.8$. Be sure to show your work.

A   12

B   20

C   2

D   21

Common Core Standard 8.EE.C.7 – Expressions and Equations

☐ Solve for *x*. $\dfrac{6-x}{6x-23} = 2$. Be sure to show your work.

A   16

B   12

C   8

D   4

Common Core Standard 8.EE.C.7 – Expressions and Equations

☐ Solve for *f*. $\dfrac{1}{6}(16f - 64) = 32$. Be sure to show your work.

A   16

B   8

C   18

D   26

©Teachers' Treasures Publishing

Name_____

PRACTICE

Common Core Standard 8.EE.C.7 – Expressions and Equations

☐ How many solutions does this equation have? 4x + 6 = 4x + 9. Be sure to explain your answer.

    A   one solution

    B   no solution

    C   infinitely many solutions

    D   two solutions

Common Core Standard 8.EE.C.7 – Expressions and Equations

☐ 20 more than nine of a certain number is eighty more than 3 times of that number. What is the number? Be sure to show your work.

    A   10

    B   6

    C   18

    D   9

Common Core Standard 8.EE.C.7 – Expressions and Equations

☐ How many solutions does this equation have? 9x + 13 = 9x + 13. Be sure to explain your answer.

    A   one solution

    B   no solution

    C   infinitely many solutions

    D   two solutions

©Teachers' Treasures Publishing

Name_____

PRACTICE

Common Core Standard 8.EE.C.7 – Expressions and Equations

☐ 9 less than three of a certain number is fifteen more than 5 times of that number. What is the number? Be sure to show your work.

A −12

B 12

C 2

D − 2

Common Core Standard 8.EE.C.7 – Expressions and Equations

☐ How many solutions does this equation have? $18(\frac{1}{2}x - 3) = 9x + 14$. Be sure to explain your answer.

A one solution

B no solution

C infinitely many solutions

D two solutions

Common Core Standard 8.EE.C.7 – Expressions and Equations

☐ Solve for y. $4y - 23 + 2y - 2 = y + 5$. Be sure to explain your answer.

A 3

B 5

C 8

D 6

©Teachers' Treasures Publishing

Name_____

PRACTICE

Common Core Standard 8.EE.C.7 – Expressions and Equations

☐ **Solve for *x*.   8 (x − 1.5) = 4(x + 5). Be sure to show your work.**

A   1

B   0

C   8

D   6

Common Core Standard 8.EE.C.7 – Expressions and Equations

☐ **Solve for *u*.   1.9u − (− 0.5u) = −72. Be sure to show your work.**

A   − 30

B   30

C   50

D   − 50

Common Core Standard 8.EE.C.7 – Expressions and Equations

☐ **Solve for *a*. $\frac{a}{3} + \frac{2a}{3} - 4 = 10$. Be sure to show your work.**

A   14

B   10

C   8

D   6

©Teachers' Treasures Publishing

Name_____

PRACTICE

Common Core Standard 8.EE.C.7 – Expressions and Equations

☐ Solve for g. $5.1g - 2.7g - 19 = 101$. Be sure to show your work.

A   5

B   50

C   60

D   6

Common Core Standard 8.EE.C.7 – Expressions and Equations

☐ Solve for b. $\frac{1}{6}b - 6b - 5 + 5b = 20$. Be sure to show your work.

A   8

B $\frac{5}{6}$

C   30

D   6

Common Core Standard 8.EE.C.7 – Expressions and Equations

☐ Solve for s. $0.008s + 2.001 - 0.005s = 2.601$. Be sure to show your work.

A   −20

B   20

C   100

D   200

©Teachers' Treasures Publishing

Name_____

ASSESSMENT

Common Core Standard 8.EE.C.7 – Expressions and Equations

☐ 31 less than seventeen times a certain number is twenty-nine more than 2 times that number. What is the number? Be sure to show your work.

A   5

B   4

C   6

D   7

Common Core Standard 8.EE.C.7 – Expressions and Equations

☐ How many solutions does this equation have? $-2(x + 3) = -3x + 16$ Be sure to explain your answer.

A   one solution

B   no solution

C   infinitely many solutions

D   two solutions

Common Core Standard 8.EE.C.7 – Expressions and Equations

☐ How many solutions does this equation have? $-2(x + 3) = -2x - 6$ Be sure to explain your answer.

A   one solution

B   no solution

C   infinitely many solutions

D   two solutions

©Teachers' Treasures Publishing

Name_____

ASSESSMENT

Common Core Standard 8.EE.C.7 – Expressions and Equations

☐ **Solve for w.** $6w - 4(\frac{3}{4}w - 2) + 5 = 43$ Be sure to show your work.

A   8

B   10

C   9

D   11

Common Core Standard 8.EE.C.7 – Expressions and Equations

☐ **Solve for u.** $13u - 16 = -8 + 9u$ Be sure to show your work.

A   1

B   4

C   3

D   2

Common Core Standard 8.EE.C.7 – Expressions and Equations

☐ **Solve for b.** $\frac{6 - 5b}{3b - 12} = 3$ Be sure to show your work.

A   7

B   3

C   9

D   6

©Teachers' Treasures Publishing

Name_____

DIAGNOSTIC

Common Core Standard 8.EE.C.8 – Expressions and Equations

☐ Solve the system of equations by graphing. First graph the equations, and then write the solution: $\begin{cases} y = x \\ y = 2x + 3 \end{cases}$ Be sure to show your work.

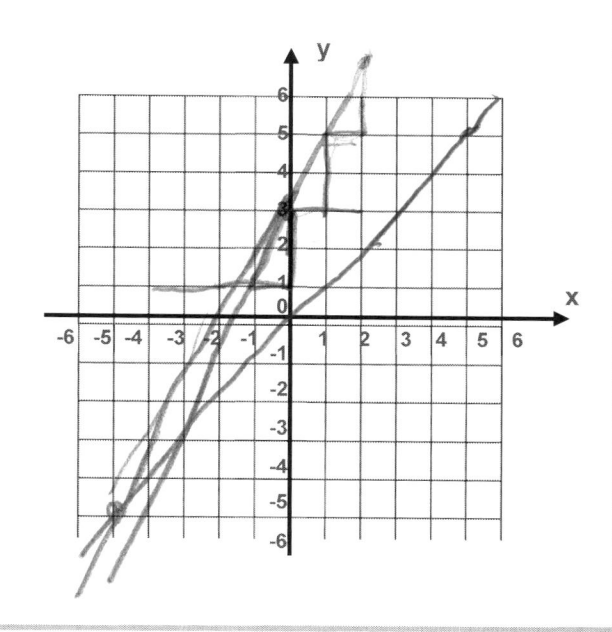

A (−2, 3)

Ⓑ (−3, −3)

C (3, −3)

D (3, −2)

Common Core Standard 8.EE.C.8 – Expressions and Equations

☐ Solve the following system of equations by graphing: $\begin{cases} x = y - 3 \\ y = -2x - 3 \end{cases}$
Be sure to show your work.

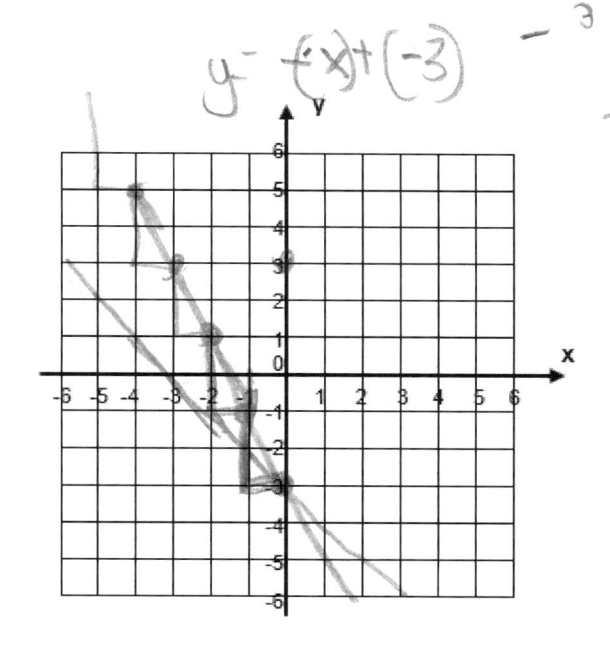

A (3, 4)

B (−2, 1)

C (5, −2)

D (−3, −1)

©Teachers' Treasures Publishing

Name_____

DIAGNOSTIC

Common Core Standard 8.EE.C.8 – Expressions and Equations

☐ The following points are for Line F and G:
Line F: (6, −4) and (−4, −4);
Line G: (1, 4) and (−1, −6).
Find the point where the two lines intersect. Be sure to show your work.

A   (−0.6, −4)

B   (3, −4)

C   (0.6, −4)

D   (0.3, 4)

Common Core Standard 8.EE.C.8 – Expressions and Equations

☐ Mrs. Robinson has two sons, William and Martin. William is half as old as Martin. The sum of their ages is 18. How old are the brothers? Be sure to show your work.

A   4;   14

B   7;   11

C   8;   10

D   6;   12

Common Core Standard 8.EE.C.8 – Expressions and Equations

☐ Three boxes of pears and two pineapples cost $33 altogether. Two boxes of pears cost as much as 6 pineapples. How much does a box of pears cost? How much does one pineapple cost? Solve using systems of equations. Be sure to show your work.

A $8; $2

B $9; $3

C $4; $12

D $3; $6

©Teachers' Treasures Publishing

Name_____

PRACTICE

Common Core Standard 8.EE.C.8 – Expressions and Equations

☐ Solve this system of equations by graphing. First graph the equations, and then write the solution: $\begin{cases} x = 5 - y \\ y = 2x - 4 \end{cases}$ Be sure to show your work.

A (−2, 3)

B (−3, 3)

C (3, −3)

(D) (3, 2)

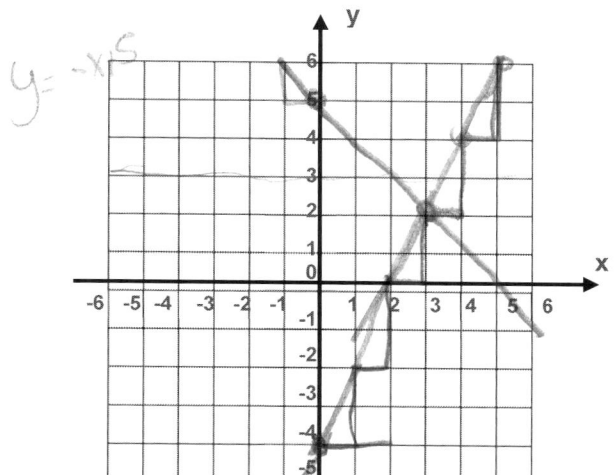

Common Core Standard 8.EE.C.8 – Expressions and Equations

☐ Does the system of equations have a solution? Be sure to explain your answer.

$$\begin{cases} y = 0.9x - 1 \\ y = 0.9x + 3 \end{cases}$$

No it is parallel line

Common Core Standard 8.EE.C.8 – Expressions and Equations

☐ Do the graphs of these equations intersect? Be sure to explain your answer.

$$\begin{cases} y = -x \\ x = 3 \end{cases}$$

Yes the are perpendicular

©Teachers' Treasures Publishing

Name_____

PRACTICE

Common Core Standard 8.EE.C.8 – Expressions and Equations

☐ The sum of two numbers is 12 and their difference is 8. What are the numbers? Be sure to show your work.

    A   8, 4

    (B)   10, 2

    C   6, 6

    D   12, 0

Common Core Standard 8.EE.C.8 – Expressions and Equations

☐ Which of following systems of equations has no solution? Be sure to explain your answer.

A $\begin{cases} y = -0.2x \\ x = 3 \end{cases}$ C $\begin{cases} y = -x + 15 \\ y = -6 \end{cases}$

(B) $\begin{cases} y = 3x - 2 \\ y = 3x + 1 \end{cases}$ D $\begin{cases} y = -12x \\ x + 3 = y - 4 \end{cases}$

Common Core Standard 8.EE.C.8 – Expressions and Equations

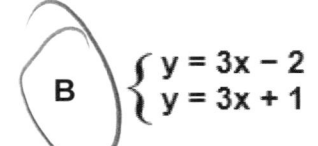

☐ To take 126 eighth graders to the Opera House, the school administration rented 3 vans and 2 buses. Each van and each bus carried the same number of students. One bus can carry twice as many students as a van. How many students can a van carry? How many students can a bus carry? Be sure to show your work.

    A   12, 24

    B   18, 36

    C   20, 40

    D   14; 28

©Teachers' Treasures Publishing

Name_____

PRACTICE

Common Core Standard 8.EE.C.8 – Expressions and Equations

☐ Graph the system. Find the coordinates of the point of intersection:

$y = x + 2$
$y = -3$ Be sure to show your work.

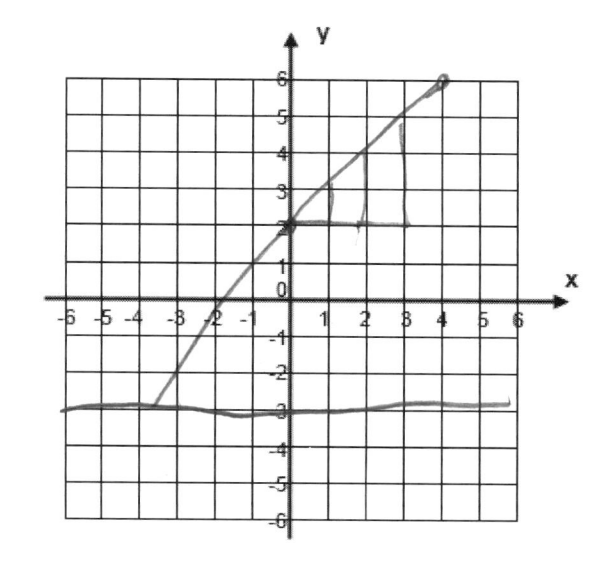

A   (3, −2)

(B) (−4, 3)

C   (−5, −3)

D   (5, −2)

Common Core Standard 8.EE.C.8 – Expressions and Equations

☐ Solve the system of equations by graphing. First graph the equations, and then write the solution: $\begin{cases} y = -2 \\ x = 5 \end{cases}$ Be sure to show your work.

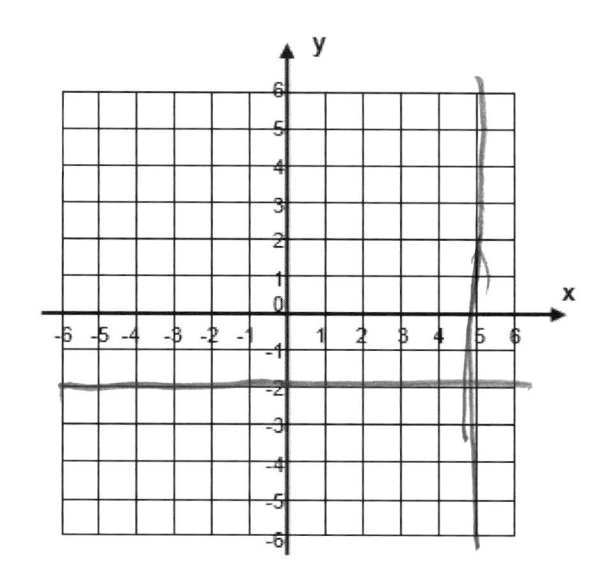

(A) (5, −2)

B   (−5, −2)

C   (5, 2)

D   (−5, 2)

©Teachers' Treasures Publishing

Name_____

PRACTICE

Common Core Standard 8.EE.C.8 – Expressions and Equations

☐ The sum of two numbers is 45. The larger number is three more than twice the smaller. Find the numbers. Be sure to show your work.

A 15, 30

B 8, 37

C 16, 29

D 14, 31

Common Core Standard 8.EE.C.8 – Expressions and Equations

☐ The following points are for Line V and E:
Line V: (4, 0) and (−2, 3);
Line E: (3, 1) and (−6, 7).
Find the point where the two lines intersect. Be sure to explain your answer.

A (6, −4)

B (6, −1)

C (−1.6, −4)

D (0.4, 2)

Common Core Standard 8.EE.C.8 – Expressions and Equations

☐ The following points are for Line J and K:
Line J: (3, −2) and (−6, −5);
Line K: (4, −1) and (−3, −1).
Find the point where the two lines intersect. Be sure to show your work.

A (−5, −3)

B (7, −4)

C (6, −1)

D (2, −5)

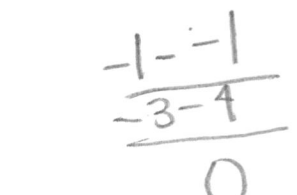

©Teachers' Treasures Publishing

Name_____

ASSESSMENT

Common Core Standard 8.EE.C.8 – Expressions and Equations

☐ Solve the system of equations by graphing. First graph the equations, and then write the solution: $\begin{cases} y = -2x - 3 \\ y = -6x + 1 \end{cases}$ Be sure to show your work.

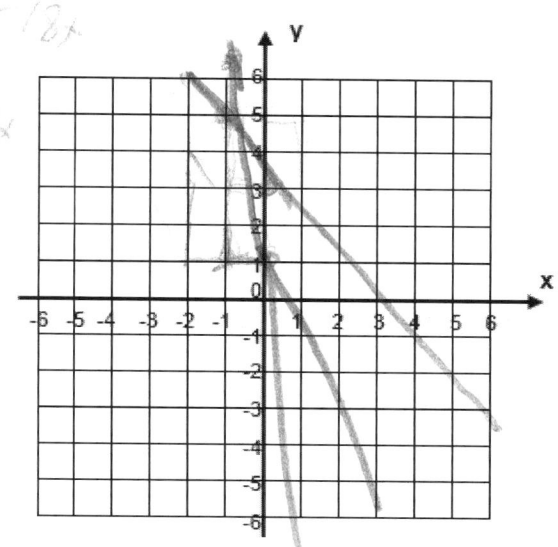

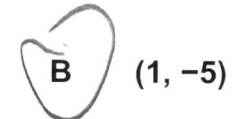

A (−4, 6)

B (1, −5)

C (5, −8)

D (4, −2)

Common Core Standard 8.EE.C.8 – Expressions and Equations

☐ Solve the following system of questions by graphing:

$\begin{cases} y = -3x + 4 \\ y = x - 4 \end{cases}$ Be sure to show your work.

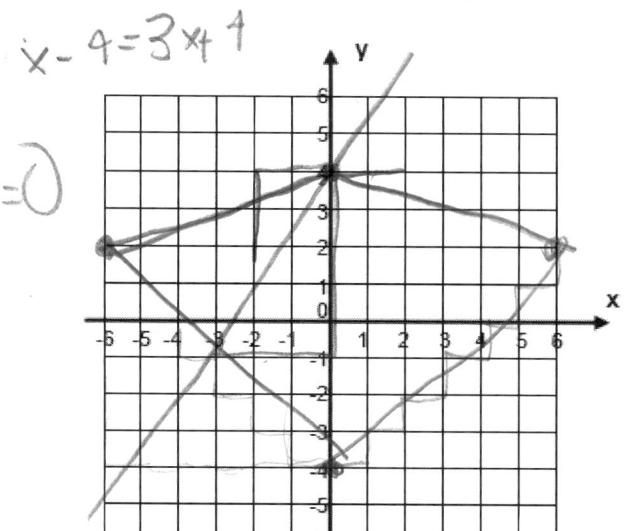

A (−4, 2)

B (2, −3)

C (2, −2)

D (3, −4)

Name_____

ASSESSMENT

Common Core Standard 8.EE.C.8 – Expressions and Equations

☐ The following points are for Line L and M:
Line L: (2, −7) and (0, −4);
Line M: (6, −3) and (8, −4).
Find the point where the two lines intersect. Be sure to show your work.

A   (1, −1)

B   (2.5, −1.5)

C   (6.5, 4)

D   (−4, 2)

Common Core Standard 8.EE.C.8 – Expressions and Equations

☐ The difference between two numbers is 2. If two times the smaller is added to one-half the larger, the result is 18.5. Find the numbers. Be sure to explain your answer.

A   9, 11

B   5, 7

C   6, 8

D   7, 9

Common Core Standard 8.EE.C.8 – Expressions and Equations

☐ Annie's and Lucy's families went to the Art Museum. Annie's father paid $39 for 3 adult tickets and 2 child tickets. Lucy's mom paid $24 for 2 adult tickets and one child ticket. How much do an adult ticket and a child ticket cost? Be sure to show your work.

A   10, 6

B   9, 6

C   12, 6

D   8, 5

©Teachers' Treasures Publishing

Name_____

DIAGNOSTIC

Common Core Standard 8.F.A.1 – Functions

☐ Complete the table. Be sure to show your work.

A   3

B   −5

C   5

D   12

$f(x) = 2x + 5$	
x	f(x)
2	9
4	13
−3	−1
?	−5

Common Core Standard 8.F.A.1 – Functions

☐ Fill in the missing number to complete the linear equation that gives the rule for the table: y = ▓x + 15. Be sure to show your work.

A   −7

B   −11

C   12

D   9

x	y
8	21
1	7
−2	1
−7	−9

Common Core Standard 8.F.A.1 – Functions

☐ Which equation gives the rule for this table? Be sure to show your work.

A   y = 3.4x − 2.5

B   y = 4.2x − 0.5

C   y = −1.8x − 5

D   y = 14.2x − 0.15

x	y
2	7.9
1.5	5.8
−2	−8.9
0.5	1.6

©Teachers' Treasures Publishing

Name_____

DIAGNOSTIC

Common Core Standard 8.F.A.1 – Functions

☐ Use the following function rule to find *f*(2): f(x) = 12x − 7. Be sure to show your work.

A   13

B   17

C   21

D   12

Common Core Standard 8.F.A.1 – Functions

☐ Graph the function, using the table below. Write a function that satisfies the set of points. Be sure to show your work.

A   f(x) = x − 11

B   f(x) = 2x + 3

C   f(x) = −x − 2

D   f(x) = 2x + 5

x	f(x)
2	−4
1	−3
−4	2
−6	4

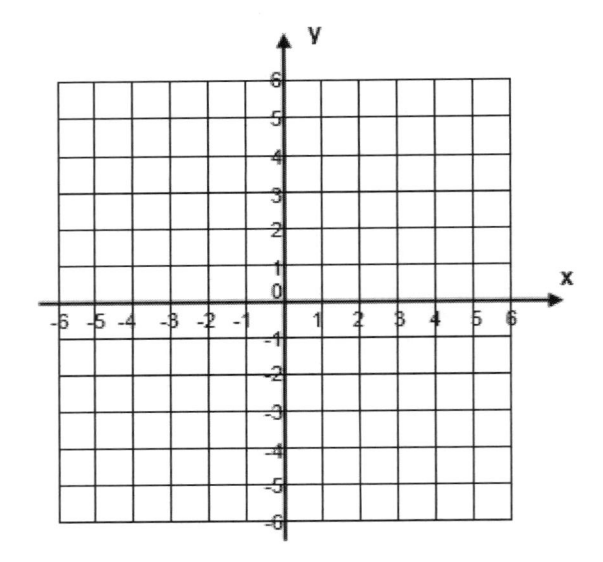

Common Core Standard 8.F.A.1 – Functions

☐ This graph shows how the total number of recipes Cecile recorded in her cookbook depends on the number of months she started recording recipes. After 8 months, how many recipes will Cecile have recorded? Be sure to show your work.

A   50

B   60

C   40

D   70

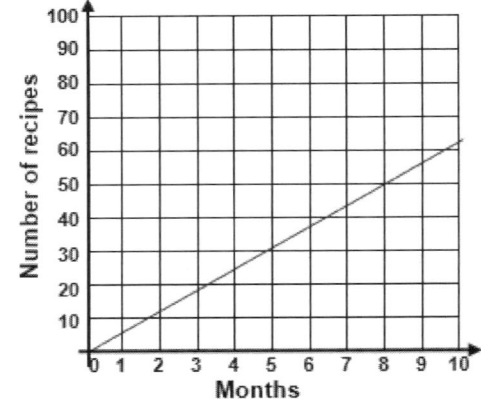

©Teachers' Treasures Publishing

Name_____

PRACTICE

Common Core Standard 8.F.A.1 – Functions

☐ Does the point (5, −0.25) make the equation true? Be sure to explain your answer.

$$y = 0.45x - 2.5$$

_____

_____

_____

Common Core Standard 8.F.A.1 – Functions

☐ Use the following function rule to find $f(-0.4)$: $f(x) = 10x + 71$. Be sure to show your work.

A   24

B   67

C   42

D   59

Common Core Standard 8.F.A.1 – Functions

☐ Complete the table. Be sure to show your work.

A   4; −14

B   −2; 10

C   4; 7.5

D   −5; 5

| $f(x) = 0.1x + 6$ ||
x	f(x)
10	7
5	6.5
?	5.5
−10	?
−20	4

©Teachers' Treasures Publishing

Common Core Standard 8.F.A.1 – Functions

Which equation gives the rule for this table? Be sure to show your work.

A   y = 4.9x − 10

B   y = 4.5x + 5

C   y = 2.5x − 8.5

D   y = 5x + 6.9

x	y
5	14.5
2	−0.2
−4	−29.6
−6	−39.4

Common Core Standard 8.F.A.1 – Functions

Fill in the missing number to complete the linear equation that gives the rule for this table: y = ▒x +11. Be sure to show your work.

A   0.24

B   2.02

C   0.02

D   20.2

x	y
50	12
10	11.2
−5	10.9
−10	10.8

Common Core Standard 8.F.A.1 – Functions

Does the point (6, 36) satisfy the equation? Be sure to explain your answer.

$$y = 7x + 8$$

©Teachers' Treasures Publishing   Page 84

Name_____

PRACTICE

Common Core Standard 8.F.A.1 – Functions

☐ Graph the function, using the table below. Write a function that satisfies the set of points. Be sure to show your work.

A   f(x) = x − 1.7

B   f(x) = 0.7x

C   f(x) = 6x + 1

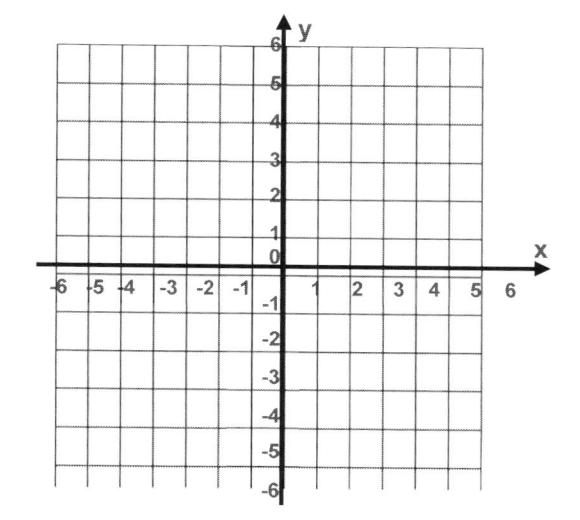

D   f(x) = 0.6x + 1

x	f(x)
6	4.2
4	2.8
3	2.1
−5	−3.5

Common Core Standard 8.F.A.1 – Functions

☐ This graph shows how much money Max spent on books at the school book fair. If Max purchases 4 books, how much money will he spend, given that they all cost the same? Be sure to show your work.

A   40

B   30

C   28

D   35

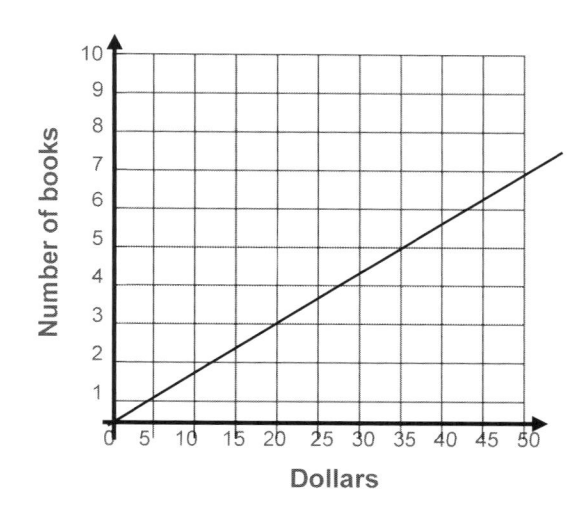

©Teachers' Treasures Publishing   Page 85

Name_____

PRACTICE

Common Core Standard 8.F.A.1 – Functions

☐ Complete the table. Be sure to show your work.

A   −3; −12

B   −2;   7

C   −1; 30

D   0; −27

| $f(x) = 4x - 7$ ||
x	f(x)
4	9
1	−3
?	−7
−5	?

Common Core Standard 8.F.A.1 – Functions

☐ Which equation gives the rule for this table? Be sure to show your work.

A $y = \frac{1}{9}x + 1$

B $y = \frac{2}{3}x + 1$

C $y = x - \frac{1}{25}$

D $y = -x + 1\frac{2}{5}$

x	y
6	5.96
3	2.96
−1	−1.04
−4	−4.04

Common Core Standard 8.F.A.1 – Functions

☐ Fill in the missing number to complete the linear equation that gives the rule for the table: $y = 2.1x + \_\_$. Be sure to show your work.

A   8

B   0.6

C   2.7

D   4.6

x	y
8	17.4
2	4.8
−2	−3.6
−7	−14.1

©Teachers' Treasures Publishing

Name_____

ASSESSMENT

Common Core Standard 8.F.A.1 – Functions

☐ Fill in the missing number to complete the linear equation that gives the rule for the table: y = ▨x − 8.5. Be sure to show your work.

A   y = 7x − 8.5

B   y = 4.2x − 8.5

C   y = −2.5x − 8.5

D   y = 0.5x − 8.5

x	y
0	−8.5
5	−6
−3	−10
−5	−11

Common Core Standard 8.F.A.1 – Functions

☐ Complete the table. Be sure to show your work.

A   10; −10.2

B   −8; 12

C   12; −12.4

D   9; 16.2

f(x) = 2.3x − 1	
x	f(x)
?	22
6	12.8
−4	?
−10	−24

Common Core Standard 8.F.A.1 – Functions

☐ Which equation gives the rule for this table? Be sure to show your work.

A   y = 4x − 2.2

B   y = 4x − 5

C   y = 8x + 5

D   y = 1.2x − 1.5

x	y
9	31
7	23
−2	−13
−5	−25

©Teachers' Treasures Publishing

Name_____

ASSESSMENT

Common Core Standard 8.F.A.1 – Functions

☐ Does the point (8, 5.8) satisfy the equation? Be sure to explain your answer.

$$y = \frac{3}{4}x - \frac{1}{5}$$

_____

_____

Common Core Standard 8.F.A.1 – Functions

☐ Graph this function, using the table below. Write a function rule. Be sure to show your work.

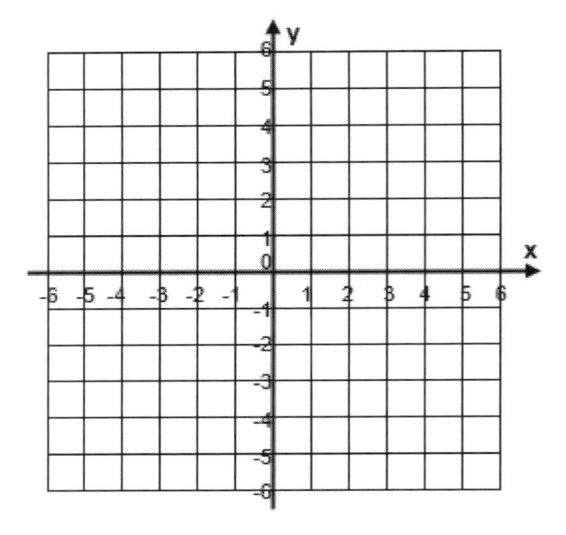

A   f(x) = −6x + 5

B   f(x) = −4x + 6

C   f(x) = 2x + 5

D   f(x) = 6x − 5

x	f(x)
2	−7
1.5	−4
0	5
−0.5	8

Common Core Standard 8.F.A.1 – Functions

☐ This graph shows how much money Arin spent on her school snacks. How much will she spend in total after purchasing her 10th snack? Be sure to show your work.

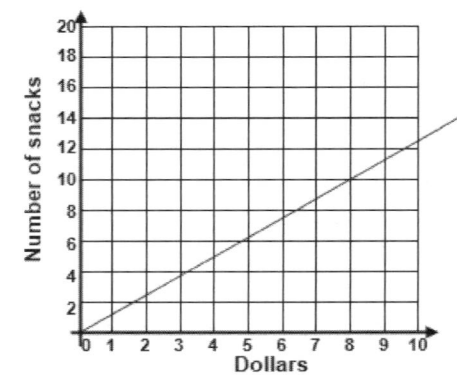

A   12

B   8

C   10

D   11

©Teachers' Treasures Publishing

Name_____

DIAGNOSTIC

Common Core Standard 8.F.A.2 – Functions

☐ Compare the following functions to determine which has a greater rate of change. Be sure to explain your answer.

A   function 1

B   function 2

Function 1

$f(x) = 1.2x + 9$

Function 2

x	f(x)
6	11
4	4
2	−3
−2	−17

Common Core Standard 8.F.A.2 – Functions

☐ Compare the two linear functions listed below and determine which has a negative slope. Be sure to explain your answer.

Function 1:
During the first day, Geraldine knitted 8 cm of her new scarf. Afterwards, she continued knitting 3 cm each day. Write an equation that shows the relationship between the days x and the length of the scarf y.

A   function 1

B   function 2

Function 2

x	y
12	−21
4	−7
8	−14
−6	10.5

Common Core Standard 8.F.A.2 – Functions

☐ Compare the two linear functions listed below and determine which has a greater slope. Be sure to explain your answer.

Function 1

$f(x) = 2x + 3.4$

Function 2:
When Alex planted a sapling in the garden, it was 35 cm in height. For the next few months, it grew 9 cm a month. Write an equation that shows the relationship between the total height in cm and months.

A   function 1

B   function 2

©Teachers' Treasures Publishing

Name_____

DIAGNOSTIC

Common Core Standard 8.F.A.2– Functions

☐ Compare the two linear functions listed below and determine which has a negative slope. Be sure to explain your answer.

Function 1

x	f(x)
2	−13
1	−9
−3	7
−4	11

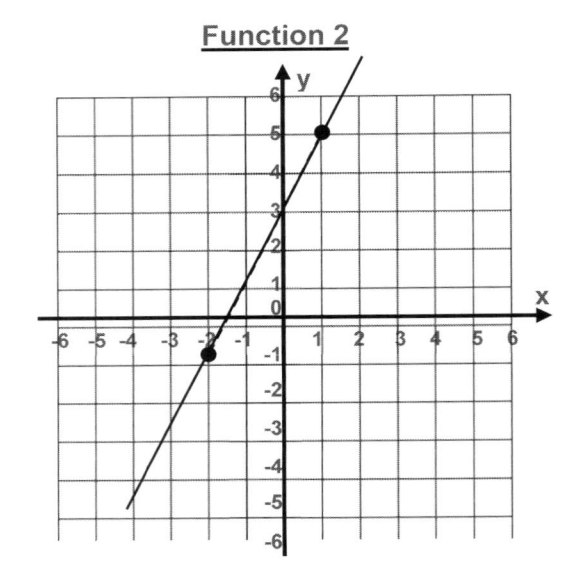

Function 2

A function 1

B function 2

Common Core Standard 8.F.A.2 – Functions

☐ Compare the following functions to determine which has the greater rate of change. Be sure to explain your answer.

Function 1

x	f(x)
6	11
4	6
−8	−24
−2	−9

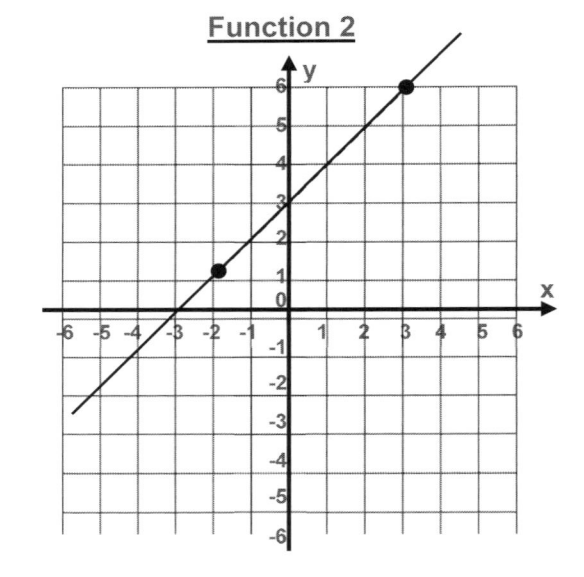

Function 2

A function 1

B function 2

©Teachers' Treasures Publishing

Name_____

PRACTICE

Common Core Standard 8.F.A.2 – Functions

☐ Compare the two linear functions listed below and determine which has a negative slope. Be sure to explain your answer.

Function 1:

When Travis opened his piggy bank, he discovered $52. He decided to use this money to go bowling every Sunday. The admission fee was $5. Write an equation that shows the relationship between the amount of bowling visits *x* and his budget *y*.

Function 2

x	y
7	35
5	21
2.5	3.5
−2	−28

A   function 1

B   function 2

Common Core Standard 8.F.A.2 – Functions

☐ Compare the two linear functions listed below and determine which has a greater slope. Be sure to explain your answer.

Function 1

f(x) = 9x − 70

Function 2:

Mr. Davis graded 10 math papers in an hour. If he continues at the same rate, which equation will show the relationship between the papers he has graded *y* and the time *x*?

A   function 1

B   function 2

Common Core Standard 8.F.A.2 – Functions

☐ Which of these functions is increasing faster? Be sure to show your work.

A   f(x) = −2x + 3

B   f(x) = −9x + 5

C   f(x) = 7x + 12

D   f(x) = 4x − 1

Name_____

PRACTICE

Common Core Standard 8.F.A.2– Functions

☐ Which of these functions is decreasing faster? Be sure to show your work.

A $f(x) = -x + 3.2$

B $f(x) = x - 3$

C $f(x) = -9x + 11$

D $f(x) = 2x - 5$

Common Core Standard 8.F.A.2 – Functions

☐ Which two functions have the same rate of change? Be sure to explain your answer.

A $f(x) = -4x + 8$ and $f(x) = x + 23$

B $f(x) = 0.7x + 0.15$ and $f(x) = 6x + 23$

C $f(x) = -x - 10$ and $f(x) = x + 4$

D $f(x) = 0.5x + 23$ and $f(x) = \frac{1}{2}x - 2.3$

Common Core Standard 8.F.A.2 – Functions

☐ Which function produces 52 at a greater *x*-value? Be sure to show your work.

A $f(x) = 3.4x + 1$

B $f(x) = 4x - 5$

C $f(x) = -7x + 3$

D $f(x) = 1.5x - 6$

©Teachers' Treasures Publishing

Name_____

PRACTICE

Common Core Standard 8.F.A.2 – Functions

☐ Compare the two linear functions listed below and determine which has a negative slope. Be sure to explain your answer.

Function 1

x	f(x)
10	−24
5	−14
3	−10
1	−6

Function 2

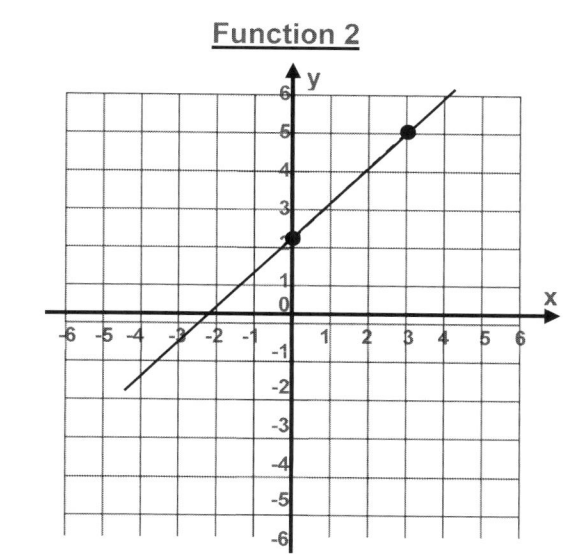

A   function 1

B   function 2

Common Core Standard 8.F.A.2 – Functions

☐ Compare the following functions to determine which has the greater rate of change. Be sure to explain your answer.

Function 1

x	f(x)
7	4.1
3	1.7
2	1.1
−1	−0.7

Function 2

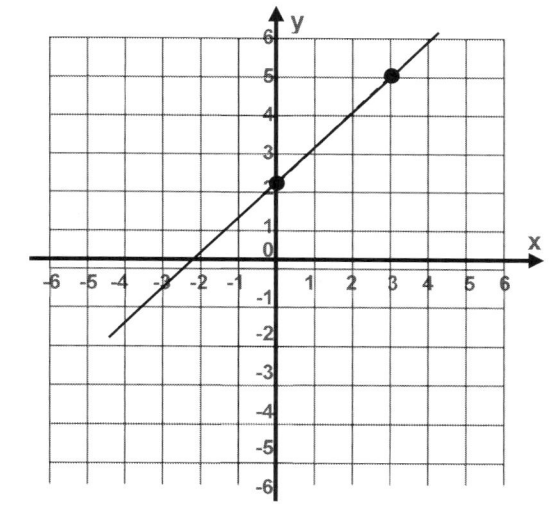

A   function 1

B   function 2

©Teachers' Treasures Publishing

Name_____

PRACTICE

Common Core Standard 8.F.A.2– Functions

☐ Compare the following functions to determine which has the greater rate of change. Be sure to explain your answer.

Function 1

$f(x) = 34x + 5$

A   function 1

B   function 2

Function 2:

x	f(x)
5	84
3	64
-2	14
-3	4

Common Core Standard 8.F.A.2 – Functions

☐ Compare the two linear functions listed below and determine which has a negative slope. Be sure to explain your answer.

Function 1:

Griffin bought a puppy along with a 50 lb bag of dog food. Every day, he fills out the puppy's bowl with 0.5 lb of dog food from that bag. Write an equation that shows the relationship between the number of days *x* and the amount of food left *y*.

A   function 1

B   function 2

Function 2

x	y
3	-62
2	-66
-4	-90
-5	-94

Common Core Standard 8.F.A.2 – Functions

☐ Compare the two linear functions listed below and determine which has a greater slope. Be sure to explain your answer.

Function 1

$f(x) = 7x + 0.5$

Function 2:

To become a member of the Beading Society, Ms. Morris paid a $45 registration fee, and proceeded to pay $25 per month of her membership. Write an equation that shows the relationship between the months *x* and the total amount of money *y*.

A   function 1

B   function 2

©Teachers' Treasures Publishing   Page 94

Name_____

ASSESSMENT

Common Core Standard 8.F.A.2– Functions

☐ Compare the two linear functions listed below and determine which has a negative slope. Be sure to explain your answer.

Function 1

x	f(x)
7	−26
4	−17
1	−8
−4	7

Function 2

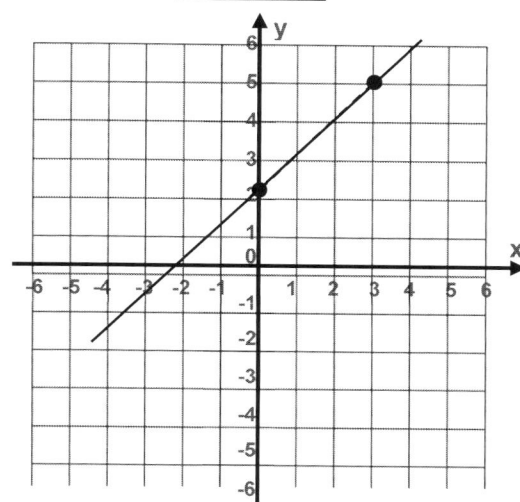

A   function 1

B   function 2

Common Core Standard 8.F.A.2 – Functions

☐ Compare the following functions to determine which has the greater rate of change. Be sure to explain your answer.

Function 1

x	f(x)
6	10
2	8
−2	6
−4	5

Function 2

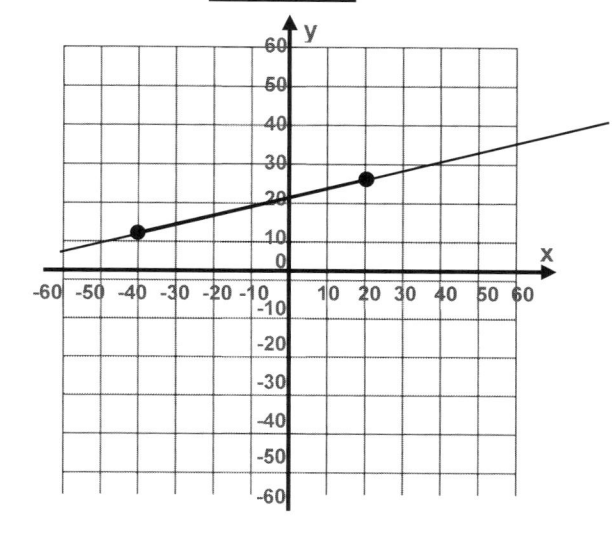

A   function 1

B   function 2

©Teachers' Treasures Publishing

Name_____

ASSESSMENT

Common Core Standard 8.F.A.2– Functions

☐ Which function produces 20 at a greater x-value? Be sure to show your work.

A f(x) = 4x + 3

B f(x) = 2x + 12

C f(x) = x − 6

D f(x) = −x − 1

Common Core Standard 8.F.A.2 – Functions

☐ Compare the two linear functions listed below and determine which has a negative slope. Be sure to explain your answer.

Function 1:
Each roll of tape is 750 inches. Armand uses 4 inches of tape for every present he wraps. Write an equation that shows the relationship between the number of presents x and the tape used y.

A function 1

B function 2

Function 2

x	y
15	−3
10	−2
−5	1
−20	4

Common Core Standard 8.F.A.2 – Functions

☐ Compare the following functions to determine which has the greater rate of change. Be sure to explain your answer.

Function 1

f(x) = x + 2

Function 2:

x	f(x)
1	1
6	1.5
−2	0.7
−8	0.1

A function 1

B function 2

©Teachers' Treasures Publishing

Page 96

Name_____

DIAGNOSTIC

Common Core Standard 8.F.A.3 – Functions

☐ Does the graph represent a linear or non-linear function? Be sure to explain your answer.

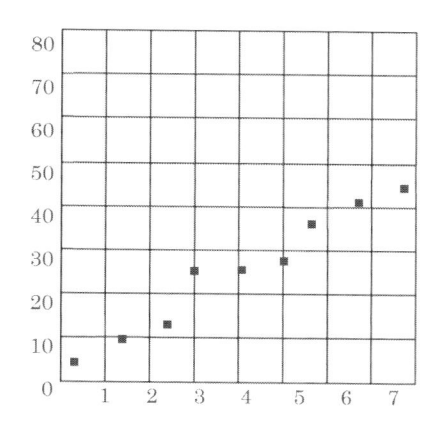

_____

_____

_____

_____

_____

Common Core Standard 8.F.A.3 – Functions

☐ Which of the following graphs is linear? Be sure to explain your answer.

A

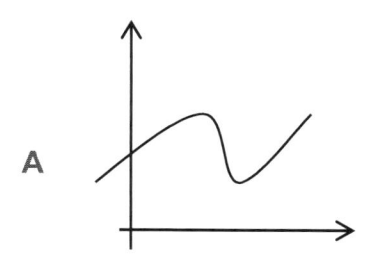

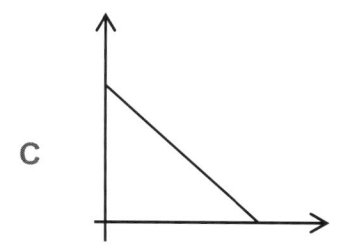

B

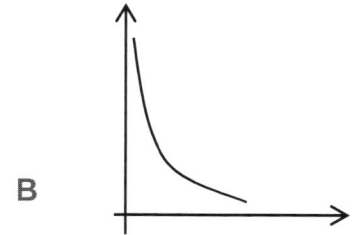

C

D

©Teachers' Treasures Publishing

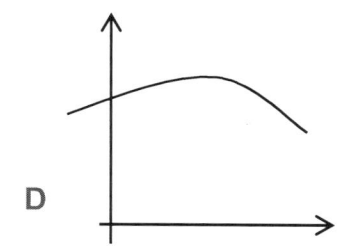

Name _____

DIAGNOSTIC

Common Core Standard 8.F.A.3 – Functions

☐ The table below shows the volume V of a cube with a side length of x feet. Does the table represent a linear or non-linear function? Be sure to explain your answer.

x	V
1	1
3	27
5	125
7	343

_____
_____
_____
_____

Common Core Standard 8.F.A.3 – Functions

☐ Anna walks to her friend Hasmik's house and, together, they ride the bus to the cafe. They spend 1 hour there, then return home by bus. Sketch the graph representing their speed over time. Does the graph display a linear relationship? Be sure to explain your answer.

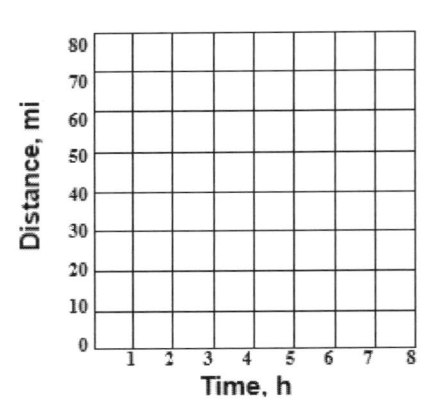

_____
_____
_____
_____

Common Core Standard 8.F.A.3 – Functions

☐ Which equation represents a non-linear function? Be sure to show your work.

A $y = 2.3x^1 + 1$

B $y = -12x + 10$

C $y + 17 = 9 - 3x$

D $2x^2 + 5 = 10 + y$

©Teachers' Treasures Publishing   Page 98

Name_____

PRACTICE

Common Core Standard 8.F.A.3 – Functions

☐ Which of following graphs is non-linear? Be sure to explain your answer.

A

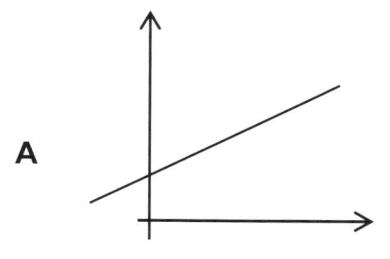

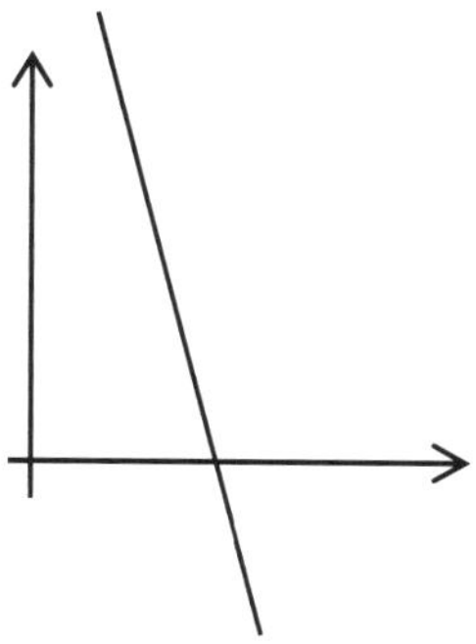

B

C

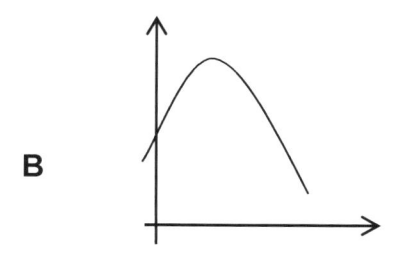

D

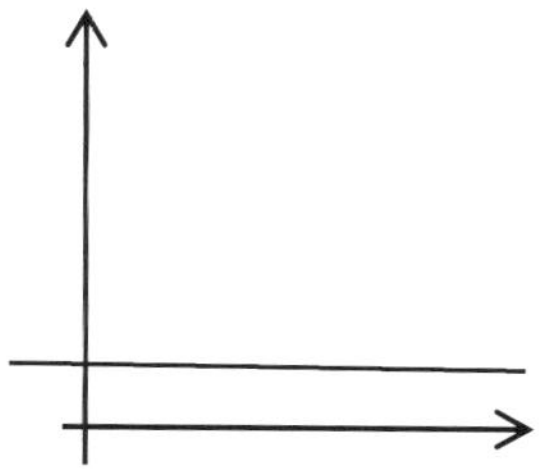

Common Core Standard 8.F.A.3 – Functions

☐ Is this a graph of a linear or non-linear equation? Be sure to explain your answer.

_____

_____

_____

_____

_____

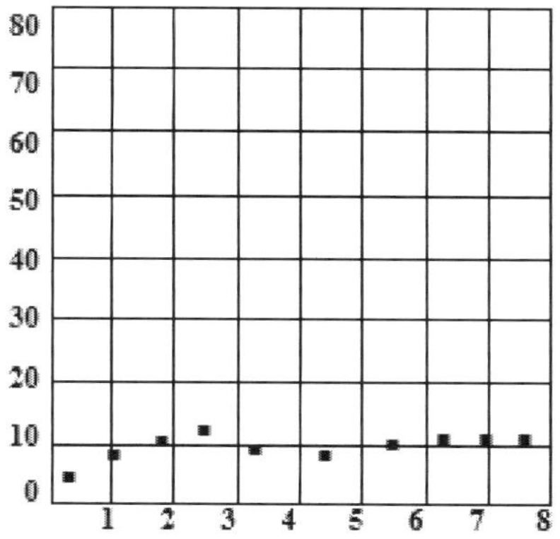

©Teachers' Treasures Publishing   Page 99

Name_____

PRACTICE

Common Core Standard 8.F.A.3 – Functions

☐ Which of the following graphs represents a non-linear function? Be sure to explain your answer.

A   G

B   E

C   F

D   V

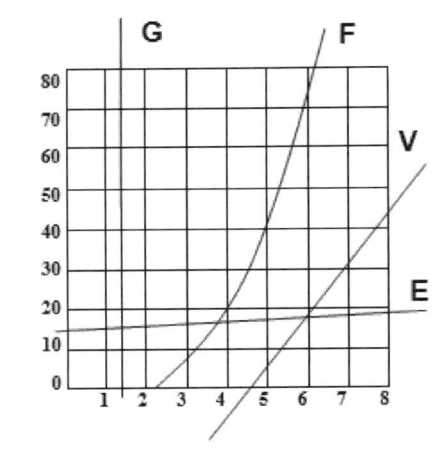

Common Core Standard 8.F.A.3 – Functions

☐ The points below are created by an equation. Is the equation linear or non-linear? Be sure to explain your answer.

_____

_____

_____

_____

x	f(x)
1	24
2	47
4	93
5	116

Common Core Standard 8.F.A.3 – Functions

☐ Which of the following equations is linear? Be sure to show your work.

A $n = -3m + 14$

B $n = -2.3m^3$

C $n = 9 - \dfrac{1}{m}$

D $n = 8x^2 + 5$

©Teachers' Treasures Publishing

Name_____

PRACTICE

Common Core Standard 8.F.A.3 – Functions

☐ **Which of the following tables represents a linear function? Be sure to show your work.**

A

x	y
2	2
1	5
−1	−7
−2	−4

C

x	y
2	12
1	4
−1	4
−2	12

B

x	y
2	3
1	-3
−1	-15
−2	−21

D

x	y
2	−13
1	−9
−1	-8
−2	-7.5

Common Core Standard 8.F.A.3 – Functions

☐ **Sydney borrowed a book for a week. On the first day, she read 38 pages. For the next two days, she read 12 pages a day, and for the remaining four days, she read 8 pages a day. Draw a graph that represents the number of pages read over time. Does the graph display a linear relationship? Be sure to explain your answer.**

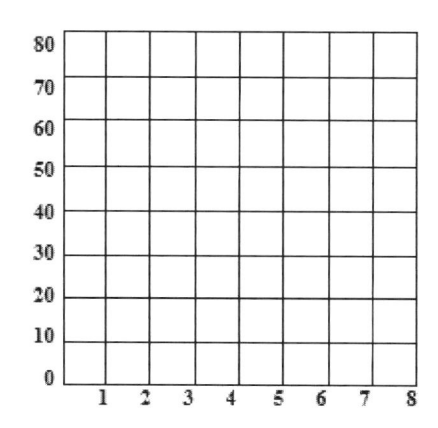

_____
_____
_____
_____
_____

©Teachers' Treasures Publishing

Page 101

Name_____

PRACTICE

Common Core Standard 8.F.A.3 – Functions

☐ The table below shows the volume V of a sphere with a radius of x cm. Does the table represent a linear or non-linear function? Be sure to explain your answer.

x	V
1	4
2	32
3	108
4	256

Common Core Standard 8.F.A.3 – Functions

☐ Do the points (1; −0.5), (3; 2.5), and (2; 1) represent a linear or non-linear function? Be sure to explain your answer.

Common Core Standard 8.F.A.3 – Functions

☐ David was writing his term paper. During the first 30 minutes, he wrote one page, then worked at a constant rate for 4 hours, writing eight pages. Draw a graph that represents the pages written over time. Does the graph display a linear relationship? Be sure to explain your answer.

©Teachers' Treasures Publishing

Name_____

ASSESSMENT

Common Core Standard 8.F.A.3 – Functions

☐ Which equation is non-linear? Be sure to show your work.

A $\quad g = 9 - s$

B $\quad s = 8g^2 + 5$

C $\quad s = -\dfrac{1}{6} g + 14$

D $\quad s = -0.2g$

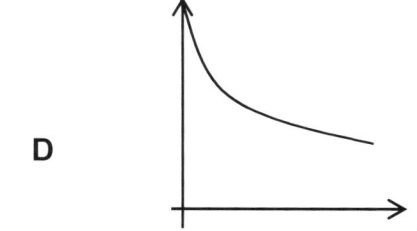

Common Core Standard 8.F.A.3 – Functions

☐ Do the points (2; 7), (6; 8), and (10; 18) represent a linear or non-linear function? Be sure to show your work. Be sure to explain your answer.

_____
_____
_____
_____

Common Core Standard 8.F.A.3 – Functions

☐ Which function is linear? Be sure to explain your answer.

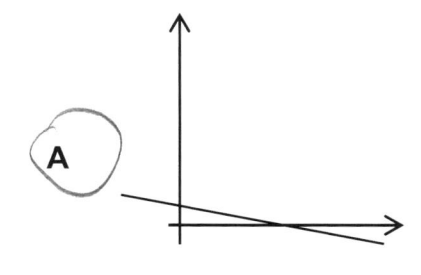

(A) [graph — circled]

B

C

D

©Teachers' Treasures Publishing

Name_____

ASSESSMENT

Common Core Standard 8.F.A.3 – Functions

☐ Does the graph represent a linear or non-linear function? Be sure to explain your answer.

_____

_____

_____

_____

_____

Common Core Standard 8.F.A.3 – Functions

☐ The radius of the base of a cylinder is 3 feet. Is the volume of the cylinder V a linear or a non-linear function of the height of the cylinder x? Be sure to explain your answer.

_____

_____

_____

_____

x	V
1	28.26
2	56.52
3	84.78
4	113.04

Common Core Standard 8.F.A.3 – Functions

☐ Gabrielle registers for a gym. The registration fee was $50, and her monthly fee was $25. Fill out the table that represents Gabrielle's total payments y in relation to the number of months she exercised x. Does the table represent a linear or non-linear function? Be sure to explain your answer.

_____

_____

_____

_____

x	y
1	75
2	100
3	125
4	150

©Teachers' Treasures Publishing

Page 104

Name_____

DIAGNOSTIC

Common Core Standard 8.F.B.4 – Functions

☐ Find the slope and y-intercept of the line that passes through the points (5; −5) and (−4; 5). Be sure to show your work.

    A   −10; −3

    B $-\frac{10}{9}; \frac{5}{9}$

    C $-\frac{1}{9}; -\frac{1}{6}$

    D   −4; 10

Common Core Standard 8.F.B.4 – Functions

☐ Find the slope and y-intercept of the graph below. Be sure to show your work.

    A $\frac{1}{2}$; 4

    B   2; 3

    C $\frac{1}{4}$; −2

    D   4; 4

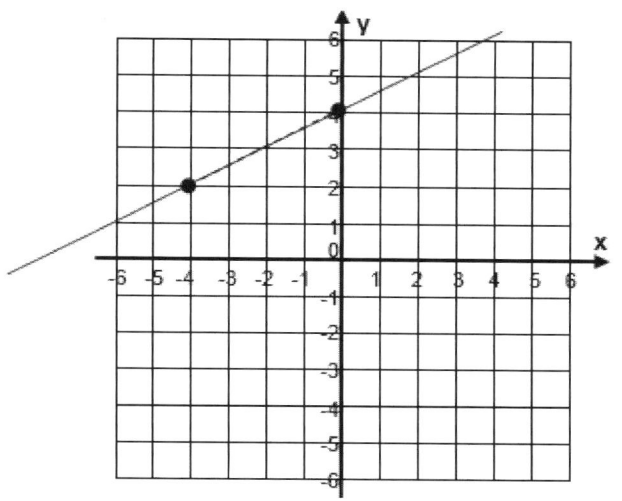

Common Core Standard 8.F.B.4 – Functions

☐ Write an equation that models the linear relationship in the table below. Be sure to show your work.

    A $f(x) = 3x - 2$

    B $f(x) = 0.3x - 1$

    C $f(x) = 0.2x + 3$

    D $f(x) = 0.5x - 4$

x	f(x)
5	0.5
10	2
−10	−4
−20	−7

©Teachers' Treasures Publishing

Name_____

DIAGNOSTIC

Common Core Standard 8.F.B.4 – Functions

☐ Find the slope and y-intercept of the line that models the linear relationship in the table below. Be sure to show your work.

A   4; −8

B   2; −4

C   6; 3

D   2; −6

x	f(x)
7	8
4	2
2	−2
−3	−12

Common Core Standard 8.F.B.4 – Functions

☐ Kerry lends his vacuum cleaner to a friend for $35 for the first day and $15 daily from thereafter. Write an equation that models the linear relationship between the days x and the amount of money y. Be sure to show your work.

A   15x = 35 − y

B   y = 35x + 15

C   35 + y = 15x

D   y = 35 + 15x

Common Core Standard 8.F.B.4 – Functions

☐ Write an equation that models the linear relationship between the two points in the graph below. Be sure to show your work.

A   f(x) = −10x + 30

B   f(x) = x + 40

C   f(x) = 10x + 20

D   f(x) = −x + 40

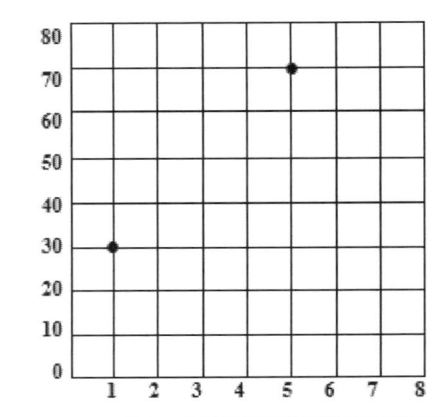

©Teachers' Treasures Publishing   Page 106

Name_____

PRACTICE

Common Core Standard 8.F.B.4 – Functions

☐ Find the slope and y-intercept of the equation $y = \frac{x}{9} + 3$. Be sure to show your work.

A   −9; 3

B   9;   3

C $\frac{1}{9}$; −3

(D) $\frac{1}{9}$; 3

Common Core Standard 8.F.B.4 – Functions

☐ Find the slope and y-intercept of the line that passes through the points (0; 3) and (−4; −1). Be sure to show your work.

A   −1; −3

B   1;   3

C   3;   4

D   −4; 3

Common Core Standard 8.F.B.4 – Functions

☐ Aubrey has 85 push pins to hang pictures. She uses 4 push pins per picture. Which function models the relationship between the push pins left over y after hanging the pictures x? Fill out the missing spaces in the table. Be sure to show your work.

A   y = 4x − 85;   13; 29; 67; 55

B   y = −4x + 85; 32; 66; 81; 43

C   y = 85 + 4x;   65; 23; 16; 64

D   y = 85 − 4x;   57; 69; 77; 41

x	y
7	
4	
2	
11	

©Teachers' Treasures Publishing   Page 107

Name_____

PRACTICE

Common Core Standard 8.F.B.4 – Functions

☐ Find the slope and y-intercept for the graph below. Be sure to show your work.

A $\frac{3}{2}$; –2

B –6; –3

C $\frac{1}{6}$; –3

D 4; 4

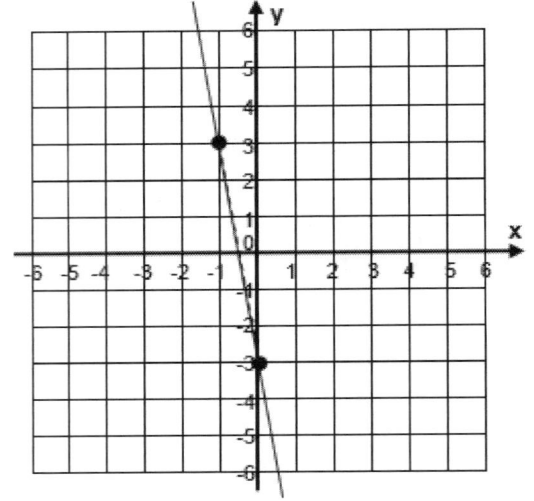

Common Core Standard 8.F.B.4 – Functions

☐ Write an equation that models the linear relationship between points in the graph below. Be sure to show your work.

A f(x) = 4x – 2

B f(x) = 6x + 3

C f(x) = 3x + 1

D f(x) = 5x

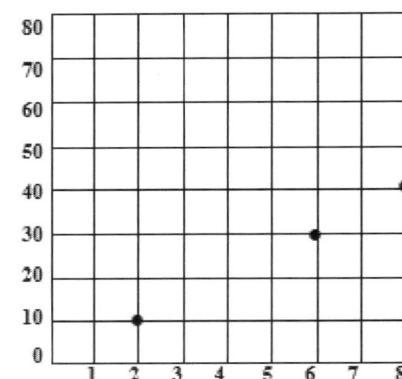

Common Core Standard 8.F.B.4 – Functions

☐ The table represents how many greeting cards Layla makes in a month. Write an equation that models the linear relationship in the table below. Be sure to show your work.

A f(x) = 11x – 4

B f(x) = 12x + 1

C f(x) = 13x

D f(x) = 16x

x	f(x)
5	65
7	91
4	52
9	117

©Teachers' Treasures Publishing

Name_____

PRACTICE

Common Core Standard 8.F.B.4 – Functions

☐ Find the y-intercept of the line that has a zero slope and passes through the point (−2, 6). What is the equation of the line? Be sure to show your work.

A   6; y = 6

B   7; y = 6x + 4

C   8; y = 2x − 3

D   9; y = 9x

Common Core Standard 8.F.B.4 – Functions

☐ Write an equation of the line that has a slope of 0.8 and passes though the point (5, 4.5). Write the y-intercept of that line. Be sure to show your work.

A   y = x + 1.5;   0.5

B   y = 0.8x + 0.5;   0.5

C   y = 0.6x + 4.3;   4.3

D   y = 0.8x + 5;   5

Common Core Standard 8.F.B.4 – Functions

☐ Find the slope and y-intercept of the line that passes through (−3, 5) and (−4, −2). Be sure to show your work.

A   12; 12

B   7; 26

C   5; 8

D   14; 16

©Teachers' Treasures Publishing

Name_____

PRACTICE

Common Core Standard 8.F.B.4 – Functions

☐ $y = -2x + 9$ is an equation that represents a line parallel to the line $8x + 4y = 28$. Is the statement true or false? Be sure to explain your answer.

Common Core Standard 8.F.B.4 – Functions

☐ Does the graph of the straight line with the slope of 0.7 and y-intercept of 5 pass through the point (10, 12)? Be sure to explain your answer.

Common Core Standard 8.F.B.4 – Functions

☐ The graph G represents how much candy Gary eats in a week. The graph S represents how much candy Sammy eats in a week. Who eats candy at a faster rate? Be sure to show your work.

A   Gary

B   Sammy

C   they eat at the same rate

D   None of above

©Teachers' Treasures Publishing

Name_____   ASSESSMENT

Common Core Standard 8.F.B.4 – Functions

☐ Theodore sells electronics. He gets $300 monthly and $12 per item sold. Write an equation that models his income. Be sure to show your work.

A $-x + 300 = 12y$

B $300 - y = 12x$

C $y - 300 = -12x$

D $y = 300 + 12x$

Common Core Standard 8.F.B.4 – Functions

☐ Find the slope and y-intercept of the line that passes through the points (5; 10.5) and (−4; -3). Be sure to show your work.

A   −2; −3

B $\frac{2}{3}$; 3

C $\frac{3}{2}$; 3

D   −3; 5

Common Core Standard 8.F.B.4 – Functions

☐ Find an equation for the line that passes through (−3, −9) with a slope of 4. Be sure to show your work.

A $f(x) = 4x + 3$

B $f(x) = 5x + 2$

C $f(x) = 6x - 9$

D $f(x) = 7x - 5$

©Teachers' Treasures Publishing

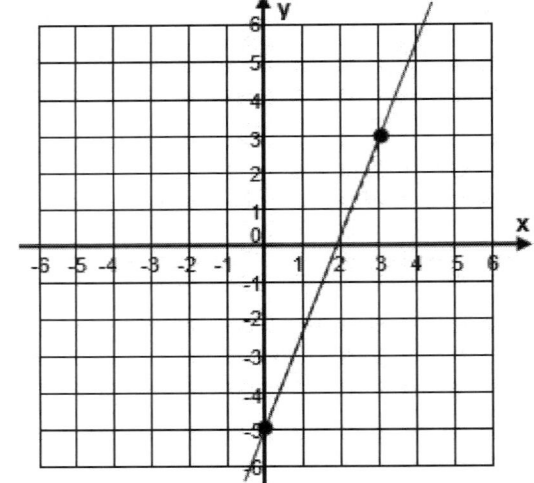

Name _____

ASSESSMENT

Common Core Standard 8.F.B.4 – Functions

☐ Find the slope and y-intercept for the graph below. Be sure to show your work.

A $-\dfrac{2}{3}$;   6

B   6;   −2

C $\dfrac{8}{3}$;   −5

D   −4;   5

Common Core Standard 8.F.B.4 – Functions

☐ Does the graph of the straight line with slope of −1 and y-intercept of −4 pass through the point (9, −12)? Be sure to explain your answer.

_____

_____

_____

_____

Common Core Standard 8.F.B.4 – Functions

☐ The table H represents how many bracelets Rita made in a day. The table K represents how many bracelets Karen made in a day. Who works at a faster rate? Be sure to show your work.

A   both have the same rate

B   Hanna

C   Karen

D   none of them

Table H

x	f(x)
8	56
2	14
5	35
3	21

Table K

x	f(x)
7	42
9	54
6	36
4	24

©Teachers' Treasures Publishing

Name_____

DIAGNOSTIC

Common Core Standard 8.F.B.5 – Functions

☐ Ellis sells wrapping paper for a fundraiser for about 2 weeks. Each day for 5 days he sold 10 rolls. Then, he went out of town for 2 days and sold none. When he returned, he sold 6 rolls each day for the last 5 days. Draw a graph represents Ellis' sales. Does he sell at a constant rate? Be sure to explain your answer.

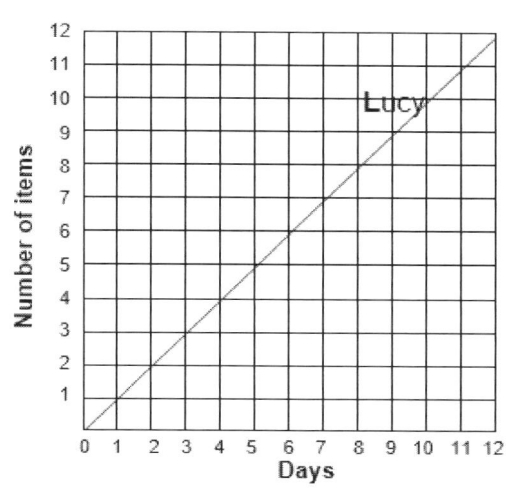

_____

_____

_____

_____

Use the graph above to answer the questions.

☐ Ellis' sister Lucy makes origami flowers to help him raise money. Line L represents her progress over the days. Is the line L increasing? Is this function linear or non-linear? Be sure to explain your answer.

A   yes; non-linear   C   no; non-linear

B   yes; linear   D   no; linear

Use the graph above to answer the questions.

☐ How many origami flowers did Lucy make while her brother was out of town? Be sure to show your work.

A   2

B   9

C   10

D   8

Name_____

DIAGNOSTIC

Common Core Standard 8.F.B.5 – Functions

☐ Julia and Sonya are both coffee lovers, but Emma prefers tea. Graph 1 represents how many cups of tea Emma drinks during the week. Table 2 and table 3 represent how many cups of coffee Julia and Sonya drink during the week. Who drinks coffee at a faster rate? Be sure to explain your answer.

Graph 1

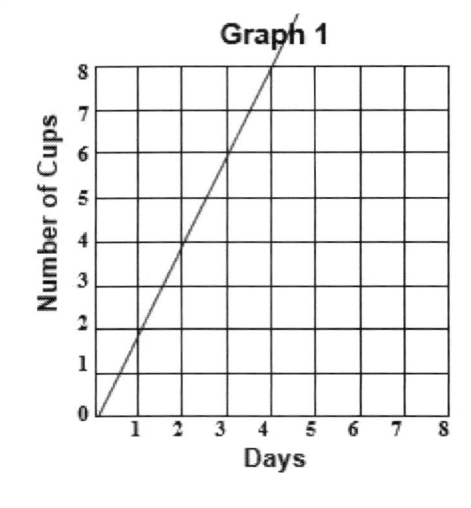

Table 2

d	1	2	5	6
J	3	6	15	21

Table 3

d	2	4	6	7
S	8	16	24	28

A   Emma   C   Sonya

B   Julia   D   none of the above

Use the graph above to answer the questions.

☐ What is the rate of change of Emma's tea drinking habits? Is this function increasing? Be sure to explain your answer.

A   2; yes   C   2; no

B   3; yes   D   3; no

Use the graph above to answer the questions.

☐ Which of the graphic organizers above represents a decreasing function? Be sure to show your work.

A   graph 1   C   table 3

B   table 2   D   none of the above

©Teachers' Treasures Publishing

Name_____

PRACTICE

Common Core Standard 8.F.B.5 – Functions

☐ Which of the following functions is increasing? Be sure to show your work.

A f(x) = 2x − 9

B f(x) = −3x + 5

C f(x) = 9

D f(x) = 12 − x

Common Core Standard 8.F.B.5 – Functions

☐ Which of the following functions is decreasing? Be sure to show your work.

A f(x) = 7x + 9

B f(x) = −x − 1

C f(x) = 3 + 8x

D f(x) = x

Common Core Standard 8.F.B.5 – Functions

☐ Which of the tables below represents a decreasing function? Be sure to show your work.

Table 1

x	y
4	4.4
2	0
−2	−8.8
−8	−22

Table 2

x	y
−6	−9
−4	−7
2	−1
5	2

Table 3

x	y
6	−2
0	4
2	2
1	3

A table 1

B table 2

C table 3

D none of the above

©Teachers' Treasures Publishing

Page 115

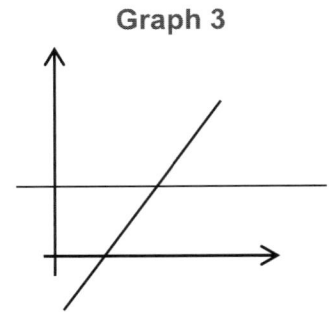

Name_____

PRACTICE

Common Core Standard 8.F.B.5 – Functions

☐ Each graph represents 2 functions. Which of the following graphs shows 2 increasing functions? Be sure to show your work.

A   Graph 1

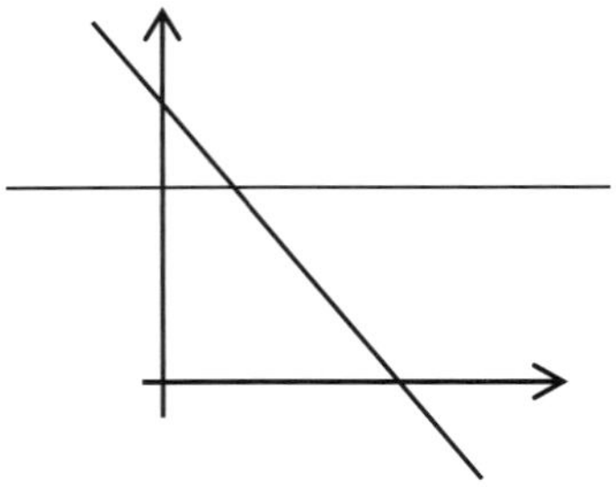

B   Graph 2

C   Graph 3

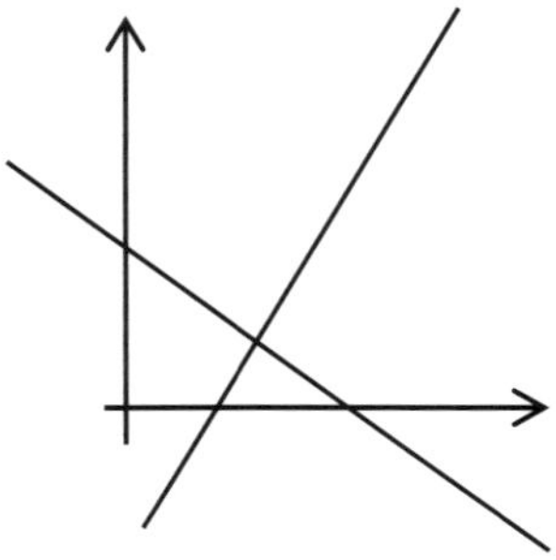

D   Graph 4

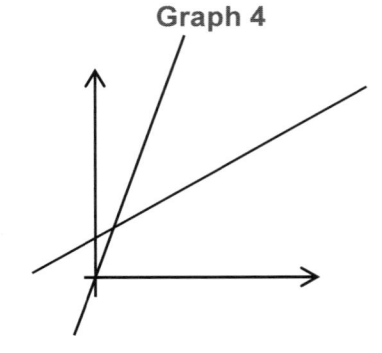

Use the graphs above to answer the questions.

☐ Which of the following graphs shows both increasing and decreasing functions? Be sure to show your work.

A   graph 1

B   graph 2

C   graph 3

D   graph 4

©Teachers' Treasures Publishing

Name_____

PRACTICE

Common Core Standard 8.F.B.5 – Functions

☐ Graph 1 shows the area of a triangle with the base 15 cm and the height h. Table 2 shows the volume V of a cube with the side length of x cm. Table 3 shows the area A of a rectangle with the side lengths a and b, where
a = 6 cm. Which of the functions is non-linear? Be sure to explain your answer.

Graph 1

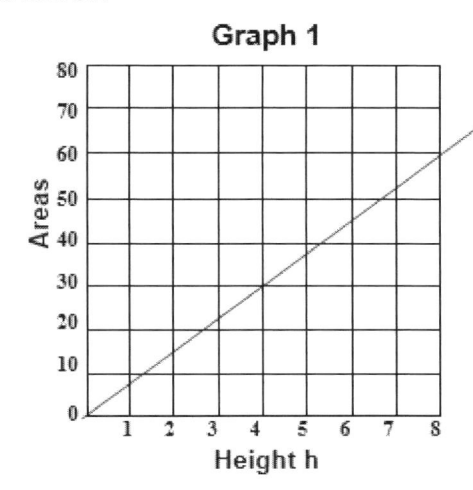

Table 2

x	1	2	5	6
V	1	8	125	216

Table 3

b	2	4	6	8
A	12	24	36	48

A   graph 1   C   table 3

B   table 2   D   none of the above

Use the graph above to answer the questions.

☐ Which of the linear functions has a greater change of rate? Be sure to explain your answer.

A   graph 1   C   table 3

B   table 2   D   all have the same rate

Use the graph above to answer the questions.

☐ Which of the linear functions is decreasing? Be sure to show your work.

A   graph 1   C   table 3

B   table 2   D   none of the above

©Teachers' Treasures Publishing

Name_____

PRACTICE

Common Core Standard 8.F.B.5 – Functions

☐ When Diana got her puppy, it weighed 1 pound. The graph represents the changes in her puppy's weight over the course of a year spent in Diana's ownership. Is this function linear or non-linear? Is this function increasing, decreasing or both? Be sure to explain your answer.

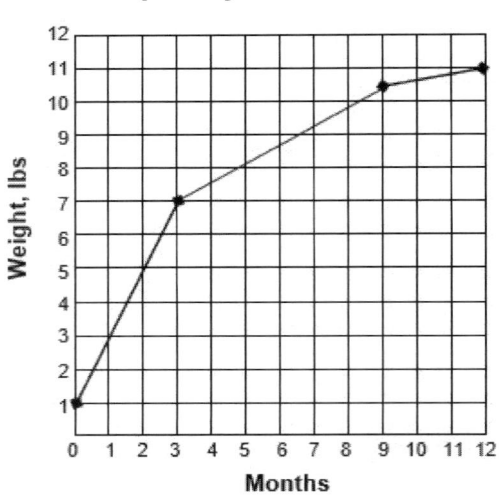

_____

_____

_____

_____

_____

Use the graph above to answer the questions.

☐ In which interval of months puppy's rate of change was the greatest? Be sure to explain your answer.

A   1–3 months   C   9–12 months

B   3–9 months   D   3–12 months

Use the graph above to answer the questions.

☐ In which interval of months puppy's rate of change was the lowest? Be sure to show your work.

A   1–3 months

B   3–9 months

C   9–12 months

D   3–12 months

©Teachers' Treasures Publishing

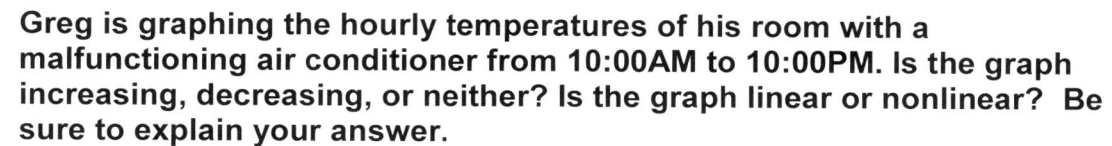

Name_____

ASSESSMENT

Common Core Standard 8.F.B.5 – Functions

☐ Greg is graphing the hourly temperatures of his room with a malfunctioning air conditioner from 10:00AM to 10:00PM. Is the graph increasing, decreasing, or neither? Is the graph linear or nonlinear? Be sure to explain your answer.

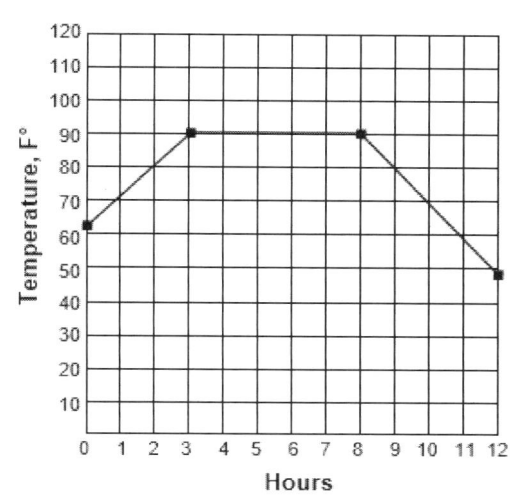

_____
_____
_____
_____
_____

Use the graph above to answer the questions.

☐ At what time does the temperature in the room start dropping? Does the graph represent a decreasing or increasing function from 6:00PM to 10:00PM? Be sure to explain your answer.

A   6:00PM; increasing   C   8:00PM; increasing

B   6:00PM; decreasing   D   8:00PM; decreasing

Use the graph above to answer the questions.

☐ At what time does the temperature in the room reach its highest point? What is the rate of temperature change from 2:00 to 5:00 pm? Be sure to show your work.

A   3:00PM; 1

B   1:00PM; 1

C   3:00PM; 0

D   1:00PM; 0

©Teachers' Treasures Publishing

Name_____

ASSESSMENT

Common Core Standard 8.F.B.5 – Functions

☐ The Meeks family have a small swimming pool. They drained the pool and refilled it after a while. This graph below shows the relationship between the number of gallons of water in the swimming pool and time in hours. Does the graph represent a linear function? Be sure to explain your answer.

_____

_____

_____

_____

_____

_____

Use the graph above to answer the questions.

☐ What is the maximum number of gallons of water in the pool? For how long is the water level increasing? Be sure to explain your answer.

A 600 gallons; 3 hours   C 1100 gallons; 5 hours

B 600 gallons; 9 hours   D 1100 gallons; 9 hours

Use the graph above to answer the questions.

☐ For how long is the water level decreasing? Be sure to show your work.

A 4 hours

B 3 hours

C 1 hour

D 5 hours

©Teachers' Treasures Publishing

Name_____   DIAGNOSTIC

Use the graph below to answer the questions.

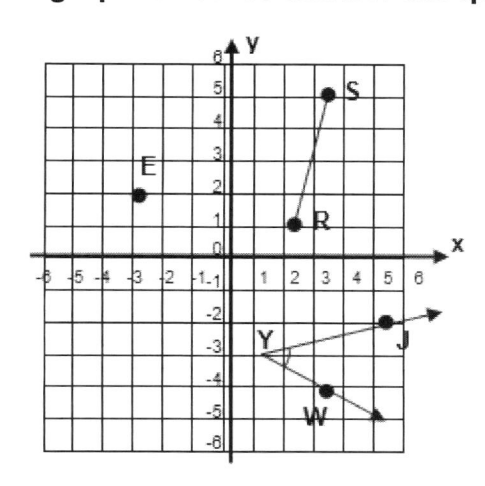

Common Core Standard 8.G.A.1 – Geometry

☐   What will be the coordinates of points R and S if the segment RS is rotated 180° clockwise around the origin? Graph the image of the segment RS after the rotation. Be sure to show your work.

    A   R'(−2; −1); S'(−3; −5)   C   R'(2; 1); S'(3; 5)

    B   R'(2; −1); S'(3; −5)   D   R'(− 2; 1); S'(−3; 5)

Common Core Standard 8.G.A.1 – Geometry

☐   Graph the image of E after a translation 7 units down. What will be the coordinates of the point E after the translation? Be sure to show your work.

    A   E'(−3; 5)   C   E'(−3; −5)

    B   E'(3; 5)   D   E'(3; −5)

Common Core Standard 8.G.A.1 – Geometry

☐   What will be the coordinates of the point Y if the angle JYW is reflected across the y-axis? Graph the image of ∠JYW after the reflection. Be sure to show your work.

    A   Y'(−1; 3)   C   Y'(1; 3)

    B   Y'(−1; −3)   D   Y'(1; −3)

©Teachers' Treasures Publishing

Name_____

DIAGNOSTIC

Use the graph below to answer the questions.

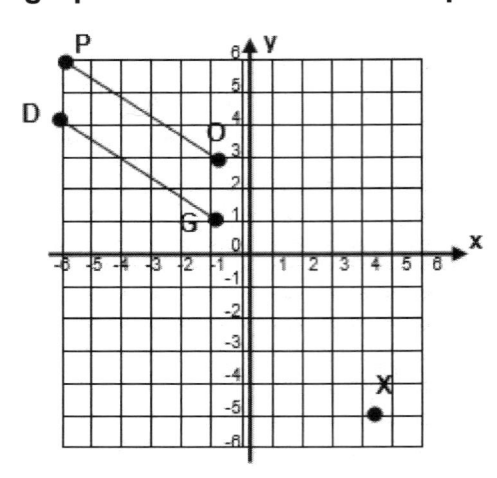

Common Core Standard 8.G.A.1 – Geometry

☐ Graph the line segments DG and PO after they are reflected across the x-axis. What will be the coordinates of points D and O after the translation? Are the segments still parallel? Be sure to show your work.

A   D'(6; 4);   O'(−1;−3);   no

B   D'(−6; 4);   O'(−1;3);   yes

C   D'(−6; −4);   O'(−1;−3);   yes

D   D'(6; 4);   O'(1;3);   no

Common Core Standard 8.G.A.1 – Geometry

☐ Graph the image of X after a translation 6 units left and 2 units up. What will be its new coordinates? Be sure to show your work.

A   X'(−2;3)

B   X'(2;3)

C   X'(2;−3)

D   X'(−2;−3)

Common Core Standard 8.G.A.1 – Geometry

☐ Graph the image of X after a rotation 90° counterclockwise around the origin. What will be the coordinates of the point X after the rotation? Be sure to show your work.

A   X'(5;−4)

B   X'(2;−3)

C   X'(5;4)

D   X'(−4;5)

©Teachers' Treasures Publishing

Name_____

PRACTICE

Common Core Standard 8.G.A.1 – Geometry

☐ What will be the coordinates of the point V(−2,−5) after a translation 4 units up? Be sure to show your work.

    A   V'(−2, 5)   C   V'(−2, −9)

    B   V'(2, −5)   D   V'(−2, −1)

Common Core Standard 8.G.A.1 – Geometry

☐ The image of the point (2, −3) under a reflection across the x-axis is (−2, 3). Is the statement true or false? Be sure to explain your answer.

_____
_____
_____
_____

Common Core Standard 8.G.A.1 – Geometry

☐ The image of the point (3, −5) under a reflection across the y-axis is (−3, 5). Is the statement true or false? Be sure to show your work.

_____
_____
_____
_____

Common Core Standard 8.G.A.1 – Geometry

☐ What will be the coordinates of the point V(−6,−7) after a translation 5 units down? Be sure to show your work.

    A   V'(−6,−7)   C   V'(−6, 7)

    B   V'(−6,−12)   D   V'(−6,−2)

©Teachers' Treasures Publishing

Name_____

PRACTICE

Use the graph below to answer the questions.

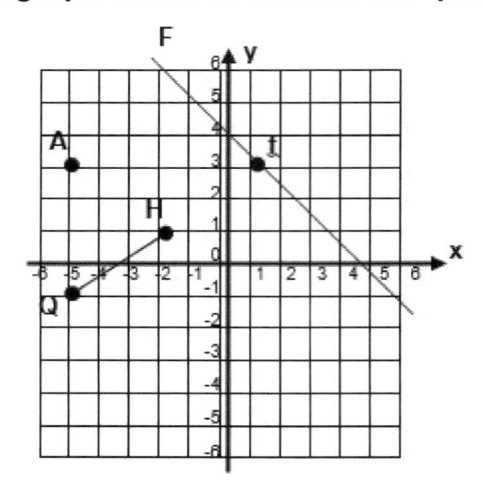

Common Core Standard 8.G.A.1 – Geometry

☐ Graph the image of A after a translation 3 units up. What will be the coordinates of the point A after the rotation? Be sure to show your work.

A A'(−5;6)   C A' (−5; 0)

B A'(5;3)   D A'(−5;3)

Common Core Standard 8.G.A.1 – Geometry

☐ Determine the image of the straight line F under a clockwise rotation of 90° about the origin. What will be the coordinates of the point f, that belongs to the line F, under the rotation? Be sure to show your work.

A f'(−1;3)   C f '(1;−3)

B f'(3;1)   D f '(3;−1)

Common Core Standard 8.G.A.1 – Geometry

☐ Graph the line segment QH after a rotation 270° clockwise around the origin. What will be the coordinates of the point H after the rotation? Be sure to show your work.

A H'(−1;2)   C H '(2;−1)

B H'(2;1)   D H'(−1;−2)

©Teachers' Treasures Publishing

Name_____

PRACTICE

Common Core Standard 8.G.A.1 – Geometry

☐ What will be the coordinates of the point G(2;−1) after a translation 4 units up and 3 units left? Be sure to show your work.

A   G'(−2; 2)   C   G'(−1; 3)

B   G'(−2; 3)   D   G'(5; 3)

Common Core Standard 8.G.A.1 – Geometry

☐ What will be the coordinates of the point K(0;−1) after a translation 5 units down and 2 units right? Be sure to show your work.

A   K'(2;−6)   C   K(−2;−6)

B   K(1;−5)   D   K(2; 4)

Common Core Standard 8.G.A.1 – Geometry

☐ The image of the point (14,−2) under a reflection across the x-axis is (14, 2). Is the statement true or false? Be sure to show your work.

_____

_____

_____

_____

Common Core Standard 8.G.A.1 – Geometry

☐ The image of the point (−9, 12) under a reflection across the y-axis is (−9,−12). Is the statement true or false? Be sure to show your work.

_____

_____

_____

_____

©Teachers' Treasures Publishing

Name_____

PRACTICE

Use the graph below to answer the questions.

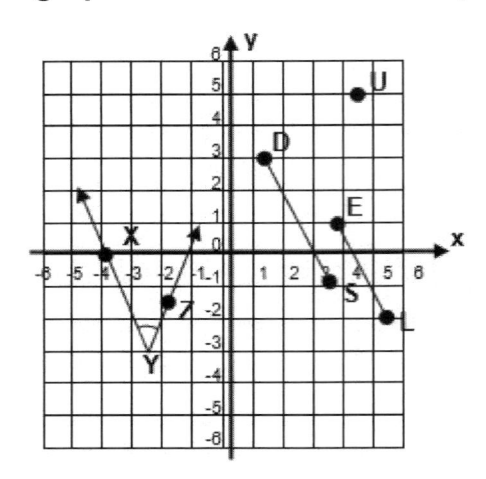

Common Core Standard 8.G.A.1 – Geometry

Graph the line segments DS and EL after they are translated 4 units left and 2 units up. What will be the coordinates of the point L after the translation? Are DS and EL still parallel? Be sure to show your work.

A   L' (9; 0); no

B   L' (1; 0); yes

C   L' (9;−4); no

D   L' (3; 2); yes

Common Core Standard 8.G.A.1 – Geometry

Graph the image of U after a rotation 180° clockwise around the origin. What will be the coordinates of the point U after the rotation? Be sure to show your work.

A   U'(−5;4)

B   U'(5; 4)

C   U'(4; 5)

D   U'(−4;−5)

Common Core Standard 8.G.A.1 – Geometry

What will be the coordinate of X after ∠XYZ is reflected over the y-axis? Would the measure of ∠XYZ change? Be sure to show your work.

A   X'(−4; 0); no

B   X'(4; 0); no

C   X'(4; 0); yes

D   X'(−4; 0); yes

©Teachers' Treasures Publishing

Name _____   **ASSESSMENT**

Use the graph below to answer the questions.

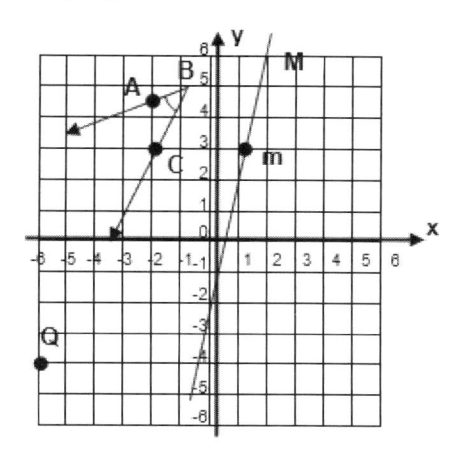

Common Core Standard 8.G.A.1 – Geometry

☐ What will be the coordinates of the point C if ∠ABC is rotated 270° counterclockwise around the origin? Graph the image of ∠ABC after the rotation. Be sure to show your work.

A   C '(−2;3)   C   C'(2;−3)

B   C '(3; 2)   D   C '(−3;−2)

Common Core Standard 8.G.A.1 – Geometry

☐ Graph the image of the line M after a reflection over the y-axis. What will be the coordinates of the point m, that belongs to the line M, after the reflection? Be sure to show your work.

A   m'(−1;3)   C   m'(1;−3)

B   m'(1; 3)   D   m '(−3;1)

Common Core Standard 8.G.A.1 – Geometry

☐ Graph the image of Q after a rotation 180° clockwise around the origin. What will be the coordinates of the point Q after the rotation. Be sure to show your work.

A   G(−6;4)   C   G'(4;−6)

B   G'(6; 4)   D   G '(−6; −4

©Teachers' Treasures Publishing   Page 127

Name_____

ASSESSMENT

Use the graph below to answer the questions.

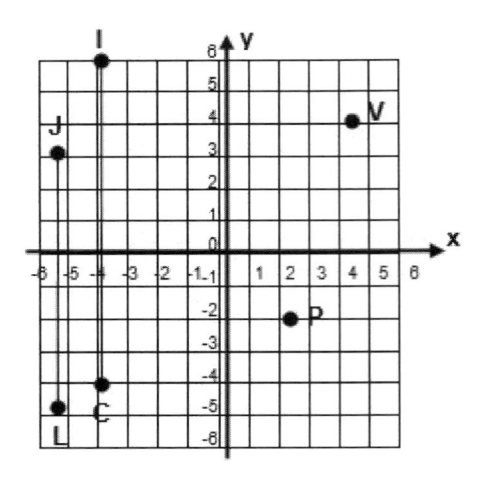

Common Core Standard 8.G.A.1 – Geometry

☐ Graph the line segments JL and IC after they are rotated 90° clockwise around the origin. What will be the coordinates of the point I after the rotation? Are the segments JL and IC still parallel? Be sure to show your work.

A   I '(−4;6)

B   I '(6; 4)

C   I '(6;−4)

D   I '(−6;−4)

Common Core Standard 8.G.A.1 – Geometry

☐ Graph the image of V after a translation 2 units right and 9 units down. What will be its new coordinates? Be sure to show your work.

A   V '(−5;2)

B   V '(6; 9)

C   V '(2;−5)

D   V '(6;−5)

Common Core Standard 8.G.A.1 – Geometry

☐ Graph the image of P after a rotation 90° counterclockwise around the origin. What will be the coordinates of the point P after the rotation? Be sure to show your work.

A   P '(−2;2)

B   P '(3; 2)

C   P '(2; 2)

D   P '(−2;−2)

©Teachers' Treasures Publishing

Page 128

Name_____   DIAGNOSTIC

Use the graph below to answer the questions.

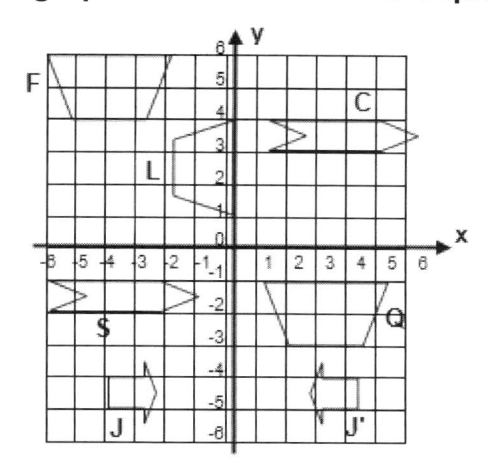

Common Core Standard 8.G.A.2 – Geometry

☐   Which of the Figures above is/are congruent to Figure F? Be sure to show your work.

   A   Figure S   C   Figure Q

   B   Figures L and Q   D   Figure L

Common Core Standard 8.G.A.2 – Geometry

☐   Describe the sequence of transformations that take place to change Figure S into Figure C. Be sure to explain your answer.

   A   translation 7 units right and 5 units up

   B   translation 2 units right and 4 units up

   C   rotation by 90°

   D   reflection across the y-axis

Common Core Standard 8.G.A.2 – Geometry

☐   Is Figure J congruent to Figure J'? Be sure to explain your answer.

   _____

   _____

   _____

Name_____

DIAGNOSTIC

Use the graph below to answer the questions.

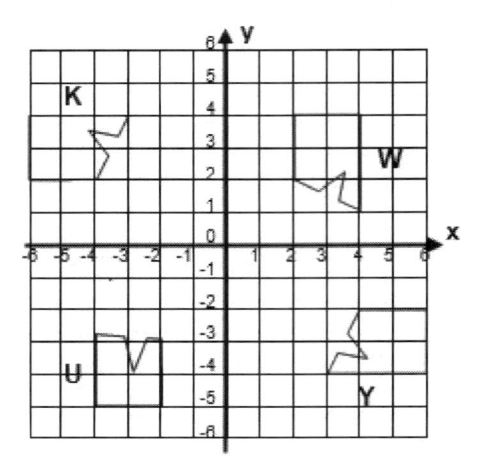

Common Core Standard 8.G.A.1 – Geometry

☐ Figure K is rotated 90° clockwise around the origin, then translated 2 units down. Which of the Figures shows Figure K after these translations? Be sure to show your work.

A   Figure W   C   Figure Y

B   Figure U   D   none of the above

Common Core Standard 8.G.A.1 – Geometry

☐ Describe the sequence of transformations that take place to change Figure W into Figure Y. Be sure to show your work.

A   rotation, then translation   C   reflection, then translation

B   translation   D   none of the above

Common Core Standard 8.G.A.1 – Geometry

☐ Which of the Figures above is not congruent to Figure K? Be sure to show your work.

A   Figure W   C   Figure Y

B   Figure U   D   none of the above

©Teachers' Treasures Publishing

Name_____

PRACTICE

Common Core Standard 8.G.A.1 – Geometry

☐ Is Figure B congruent to Figure B'? Be sure to explain your answer.

_____
_____
_____
_____
_____

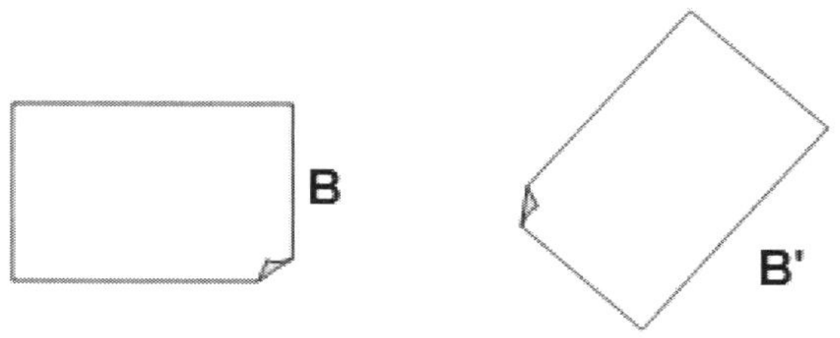

Common Core Standard 8.G.A.1 – Geometry

☐ Which of the Figures below is/are congruent to Figure G?

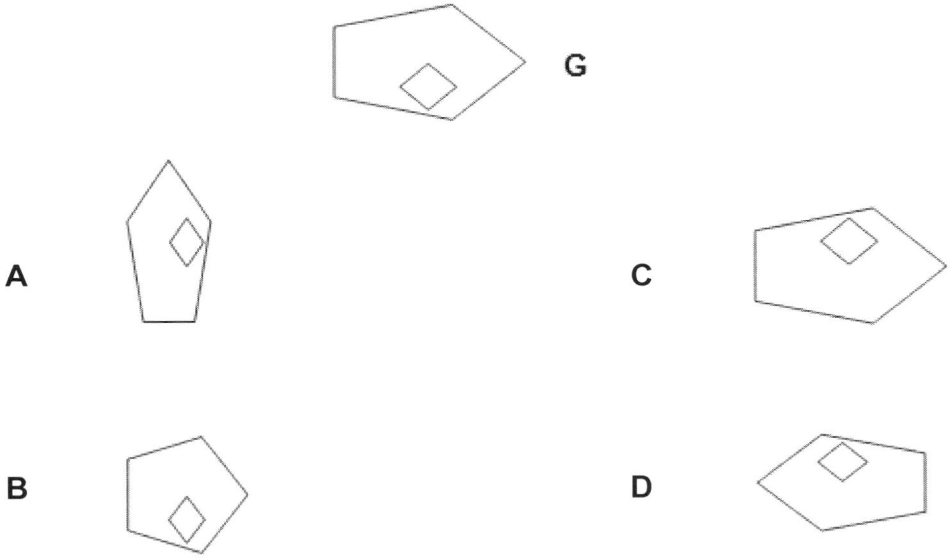

G

A

B

C

D

Common Core Standard 8.G.A.1 – Geometry

☐ Which of the following statements is true? Be sure to show your work.

A   Congruent figures are the same size and color.

B   Congruent figures are the same shape only.

C   Congruent figures are the same color and shape.

D   Congruent figures are the same size and shape.

©Teachers' Treasures Publishing

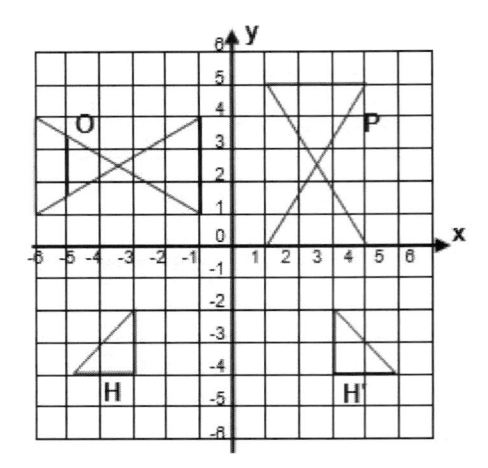

Name_____

PRACTICE

Use the graph below to answer the questions.

Common Core Standard 8.G.A.2 – Geometry

☐ Is Figure H congruent to Figure H'? Be sure to explain your answer.

_____

_____

_____

Common Core Standard 8.G.A.2 – Geometry

☐ Describe the sequence of transformations that take place to change Figure O into Figure P. Be sure to explain your answer.

    A   rotation, then translation   C   reflection

    B   translation   D   none of the above

Common Core Standard 8.G.A.2 – Geometry

☐ Describe the sequence of transformations that take place to change Figure H into Figure H'. Be sure to explain your answer.

    A   rotation, then translation   C   reflection

    B   translation   D   none of the above

©Teachers' Treasures Publishing

Name_____

PRACTICE

Common Core Standard 8.G.A.1 – Geometry

☐ What other words can be used to describe rotation, reflection and translation? Choose the answer in the respective order. Be sure to show your work.

A   flip, turn, slide

C   turn, slide, flip

B   slide, turn, flip

D   turn, flip, slide

Common Core Standard 8.G.A.1 – Geometry

☐ What word can be used to describe a reflection? Be sure to show your work.

A   turn

C   flip

B   slide

D   none of the above

Common Core Standard 8.G.A.1 – Geometry

☐ Which of the Figures below is/are congruent to Figure G?

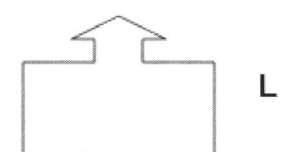

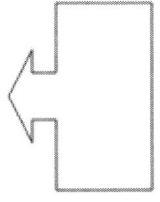

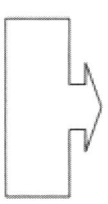

©Teachers' Treasures Publishing

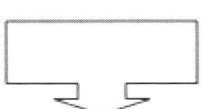

Page 133

Name_____

PRACTICE

Use the graph below to answer the questions.

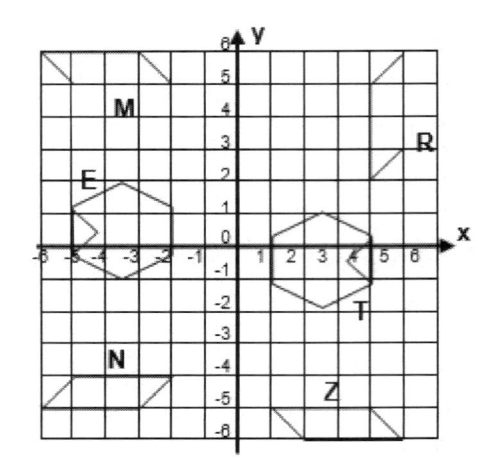

Common Core Standard 8.G.A.2 – Geometry

☐   Figure N is reflected across the x-axis, then translated 1 unit up. Which of the Figures shows Figure N after these translations? Be sure to show your work.

A   Figure M   C   Figure E

B   Figure Z   D   Figure R

Common Core Standard 8.G.A.2 – Geometry

☐   Describe the sequence of transformations that take place to change Figure T into Figure E. Be sure to explain your answer.

A   rotation   C   reflection, then translation

B   translation   D   none of the above

Common Core Standard 8.G.A.2 – Geometry

☐   Describe the sequence of transformations that take place to change Figure R into Figure Z. Be sure to explain your answer.

A   rotation, then translation   C   reflection, then translation

B   translation   D   none of the above

©Teachers' Treasures Publishing

Name_____

ASSESSMENT

Use the graph below to answer the questions.

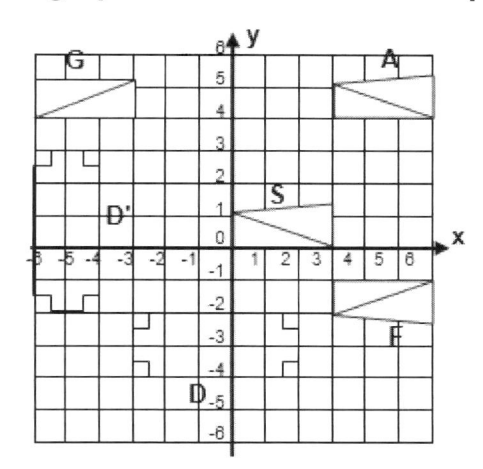

Common Core Standard 8.G.A.2 – Geometry

☐ Which of the Figures above is/are not congruent to Figure A? Be sure to show your work.

A   Figure S   C   Figure G

B   Figures S and F   D   Figure F

Common Core Standard 8.G.A.2 – Geometry

☐ Describe the sequence of transformations that take place to change Figure D into Figure D'. Be sure to explain your answer.

A   translation 7 units right and 5 units up

B   rotation 90° counterclockwise around the origin

C   rotation, then translation

D   reflection across the y-axis

Common Core Standard 8.G.A.2 – Geometry

☐ Is Figure F congruent to Figure S? Be sure to explain your answer.

_____

_____

_____

©Teachers' Treasures Publishing

Name_____

ASSESSMENT

Use the graph below to answer the questions.

Common Core Standard 8.G.A.2 – Geometry

☐ Figure T is rotated 180° counterclockwise around the origin, then translated 3 units down. Which of the Figures shows Figure T after these translations? Be sure to show your work.

A   Figure M   C   Figure V

B   Figure N   D   none of the above

Common Core Standard 8.G.A.2 – Geometry

☐ Describe the sequence of transformations that take place to change Figure V into Figure T. Be sure to explain your answer.

A   translation 5 units left and 4 units down

B   rotation 90° counterclockwise around the origin

C   rotation, then translation

D   reflection across the y-axis

Common Core Standard 8.G.A.2 – Geometry

☐ Is Figure M congruent to Figure M'? Be sure to explain your answer.

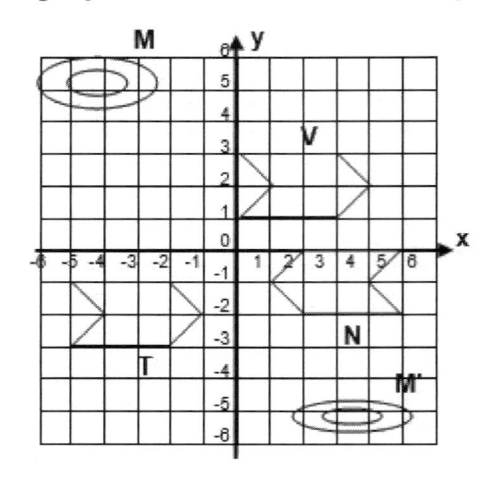

_____

_____

_____

©Teachers' Treasures Publishing

Name_____

DIAGNOSTIC

Common Core Standard 8.G.A.3 – Geometry

☐ **Which pattern could have been created using only translations? Be sure to explain your answer.**

A

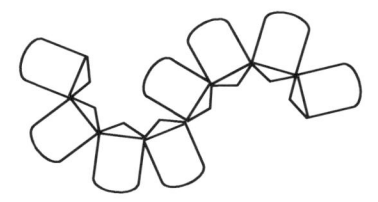

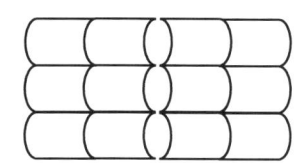

B

C

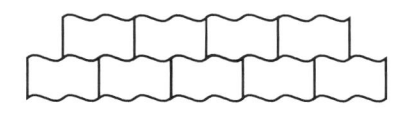

D

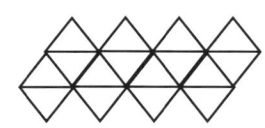

Common Core Standard 8.G.A.3 – Geometry

☐ **Find the vertices of polygon H'J'K'L' after polygon HJKL is dilated using the scale factor $\frac{1}{4}$, if H(8, 2), J(8, 12), K(−2, 4) and L(−4, 16). Be sure to explain your answer.**

    A   H(2, 1), J(2, 3), K(−1, 1) and L(−1, 4)

    B   H(2, 0.5), J(2, 3), K(−0.5, 1) and L(−1, 4)

    C   H(4, 1), J(4, 6), K(−2, 2) and L(−2, 8)

    D   H(2, 0.5), J(2, 3), K(−1, 1) and L(−1, 4)

Common Core Standard 8.G.A.3 – Geometry

☐ **The dashed shape is a dilation of the solid line shape. Is it an enlargement or a reduction? Be sure to explain your answer.**

_____
_____
_____
_____

©Teachers' Treasures Publishing   Page 137

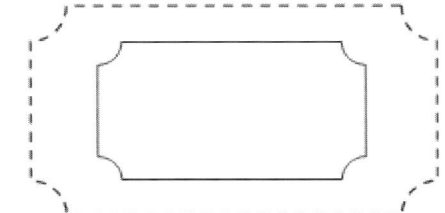

Name_____

DIAGNOSTIC

Use the graph below to answer the questions.

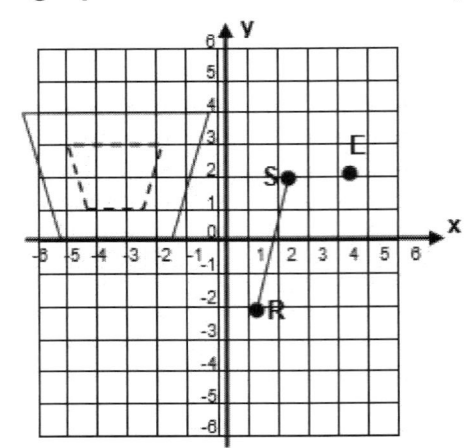

Common Core Standard 8.G.A.3 – Geometry

☐ Find the image of point E(4, 2) for a dilation with center (0, 0) and scale factor $\frac{1}{2}$. What will be the coordinates of the point E after the dilation? Be sure to explain your answer.

A E'(4, 2)   C E'(2, 1)

B E'(−2, 1)   D E(8, 4)

Common Core Standard 8.G.A.3 – Geometry

☐ The line segment RS is translated by the following motion rule: (x,y) → (x+3, y−4). What will be the coordinates of points R and S after the translation? Be sure to explain your answer.

A R'(1,−2) and S'(2, 2)   C R'(−3,−6) and S'(−2,−2)

B R'(4,1) and S'(5, 5)   D R'(4,−6) and S'(5,−2)

Common Core Standard 8.G.A.3 – Geometry

☐ The dashed trapezoid is the image of the solid line trapezoid under a dilation. Is the scale factor greater than 1? Be sure to explain your answer.

_____

_____

_____

©Teachers' Treasures Publishing

Name_____

PRACTICE

Common Core Standard 8.G.A.3 – Geometry

☐ What is the scale factor of the dilation (with center at the origin) if point L (6, 3) becomes L' (24, 12)? Be sure to show your work.

A 3

B 9

C 4

D 2

Common Core Standard 8.G.A.3 – Geometry

☐ The dashed square is the image of the solid square under a dilation. What is the scale factor? Be sure to show your work.

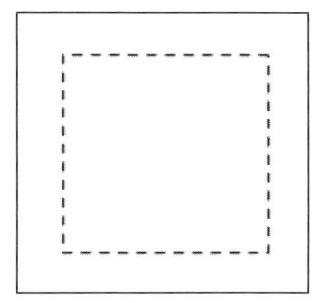

A 2

B $-\frac{1}{3}$

C $\frac{2}{3}$

D $\frac{4}{3}$

Common Core Standard 8.G.A.3 – Geometry

☐ Which of the following statements is not true? Be sure to explain your answer.

A When the scale factor of a dilation > 1, the dilation is an enlargement.

B When the scale factor of a dilation < 1, the dilation is a reduction.

C The image produced by enlarging or reducing a figure is called a dilation.

D The image produced by a dilation is always congruent to the original figure.

©Teachers' Treasures Publishing
Page 139

Name_____

PRACTICE

Use the graph below to answer the questions.

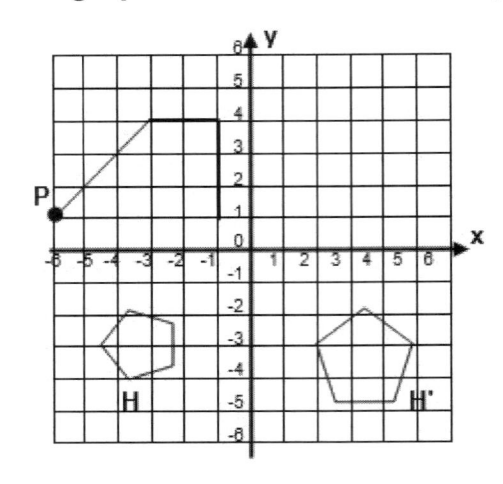

Common Core Standard 8.G.A.3 – Geometry

☐ Is Figure H congruent to Figure H'? Be sure to explain your answer.

_____

_____

_____

Common Core Standard 8.G.A.3 – Geometry

☐ The trapezoid is translated 5 units to the right, and then reflected across the x-axis. Which ordered pair describes the image of point P? Be sure to explain your answer.

A   P'(−6, 1)   C   P'(1, −1)

B   P'(−1, −1)   D   P'(−1, 1)

Common Core Standard 8.G.A.3 – Geometry

☐ Which transformation describes the change from Figure H to Figure H'? Be sure to explain your answer.

A   rotation and dilation   C   reflection

B   translation   D   reflection and translation

©Teachers' Treasures Publishing

Name_____

PRACTICE

Common Core Standard 8.G.A.3 – Geometry

☐ Find the coordinates of the vertices of triangle JKS after the rotation 180° about the origin, if J(2, −2), K(1, 2), and S(5, 4). Be sure to show your work.

A   J'(−2, 2), K'(−1, −2), and S'(5, 4)

B   J'(−2, 2), K'(−1, −2), and S'(−5, −4)

C   J'(−2, −2), K'(2, −1), and S'(4, −5)

D   J'(2, 2), K'(−2, 1), and S'(−4, 5)

Common Core Standard 8.G.A.3 – Geometry

☐ The dashed square is the image of the solid square under a dilation. What is the scale factor? Be sure to show your work.

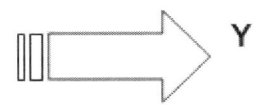

Y

A

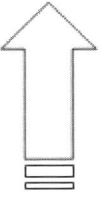

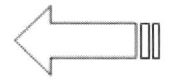

B

C

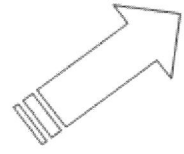

D

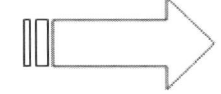

Common Core Standard 8.G.A.3 – Geometry

☐ What word can best describe a dilation? Be sure to explain your answer.

A   resizing

B   reduction

C   shrinking

D   enlargement

©Teachers' Treasures Publishing

Name_____

PRACTICE

Use the graph below to answer the questions.

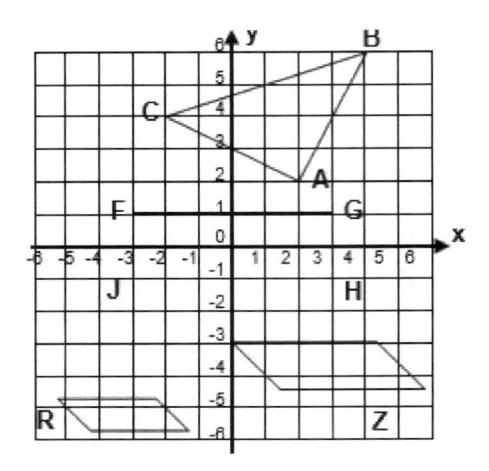

Common Core Standard 8.G.A.3 – Geometry

☐ What is the image of Triangle ABC after a dilation of 0.5? What will be the coordinates of vertices A, B and C after the dilation? Be sure to explain your answer.

    A   A'(4, 4), B'(8, 12) and C'(−4, 8)

    B   A'(0.5, 1), B'(2, 2) and C'(1, 4)

    C   A'(1, 1), B'(2, 3) and C'(−1, 2)

    D   A'(2, 2), B'(4, 6) and C'(−2, 4)

Common Core Standard 8.G.A.3 – Geometry

☐ A dilation of scale factor 3 is applied to rectangle FGHJ, centered at the origin. What are the coordinates of H after the dilation? Be sure to explain your answer.

    A   H'(−3, 1)   C   H'(−3, −1)

    B   H'(9, −3)   D   H'(9, 3)

Common Core Standard 8.G.A.3 – Geometry

☐ Describe the sequence of transformations that took place to change Figure R into Figure Z. Be sure to explain your answer.

    A   rotation   C   reflection and translation

    B   dilation and translation   D   translation

©Teachers' Treasures Publishing

Name_____

ASSESSMENT

Common Core Standard 8.G.A.3 – Geometry

☐ Which pattern could have been created using only translations? Be sure to show your work.

A

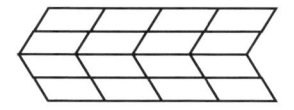

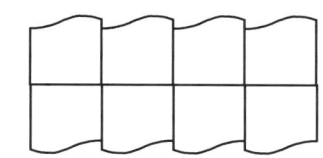

B

C

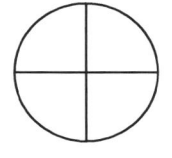

D

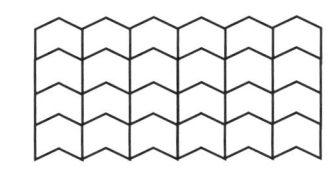

Common Core Standard 8.G.A.3 – Geometry

☐ Find the vertices of Triangle A'B'C' after Triangle ABC is dilated using the scale factor $\frac{2}{3}$, if A(3, 6), B(9, 6) and C(3,−3). Be sure to show your work.

A   A(1, 2), B(3, 2) and C(1,−1)

B   A(2, 3), B(6, 2) and C(6,−1)

C   A(2, 4), B(6, 2) and C(2,−2)

D   A(2, 4), B(6, 4) and C(2,−2)

Common Core Standard 8.G.A.3 – Geometry

☐ The dashed circle is the image of the solid line circle under a dilation. Is the scale factor greater than 1? Be sure to explain your answer.

_____
_____
_____
_____

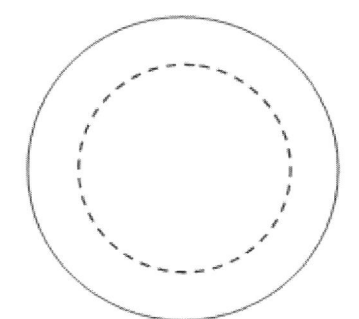

©Teachers' Treasures Publishing   Page 143

Name_____

ASSESSMENT

Use the graph below to answer the questions.

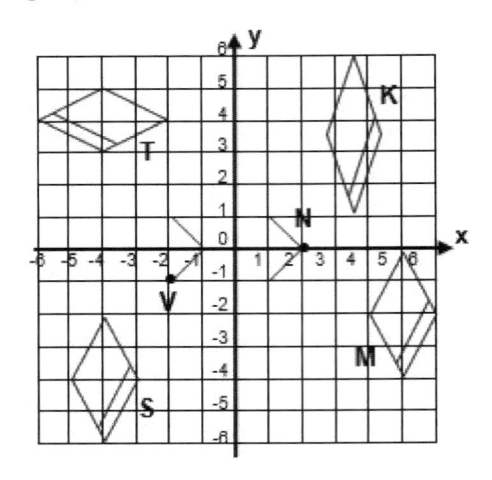

Common Core Standard 8.G.A.3 – Geometry

☐ A dilation of scale factor 4 is applied to the polygon, centered at the origin. What are the coordinates of the points N and V after the dilation? Be sure to explain your answer.

A   N'(−2, −1); V'(−8, 2)

B   N'(−8, −4); V'(8, 0)

C   N'(2, 0); V'(−8,−4)

D   N'(8, 0); V'(−8, 2)

Common Core Standard 8.G.A.3 – Geometry

☐ Describe the sequence of transformations that took place to change Figure S into Figure T. Be sure to explain your answer.

A   translation 8 units left and 1 unit up

B   rotation 90° clockwise around the origin

C   reflection across the y-axis

D   reflection across the x-axis

Common Core Standard 8.G.A.3 – Geometry

☐ Is Figure T congruent to Figure K? Be sure to explain your answer.

_____

_____

_____

©Teachers' Treasures Publishing

Page 144

Name_____

DIAGNOSTIC

Common Core Standard 8.G.A.4 – Geometry

☐ **Rectangle ABCD is similar to A'B'C'D'. What is the scale factor from rectangle ABCD to rectangle A'B'C'D'? Be sure to explain your answer.**

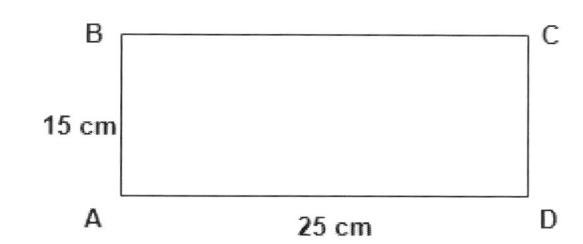

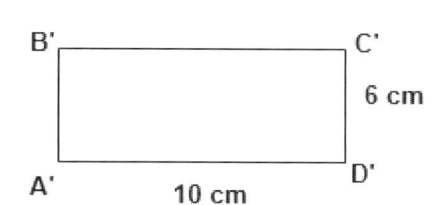

B ───────────── C   B' ───────── C'
│   │   │   │
15 cm   │   │   6 cm
│   │   │   │
A ───────────── D   A' ────────── D'
      25 cm   10 cm

A $\frac{2}{5}$ C $\frac{3}{2}$

B   2.5   D   5

Common Core Standard 8.G.A.4 – Geometry

☐ **Find the value for x using the similarity of the triangles shown below. Be sure to explain your answer.**

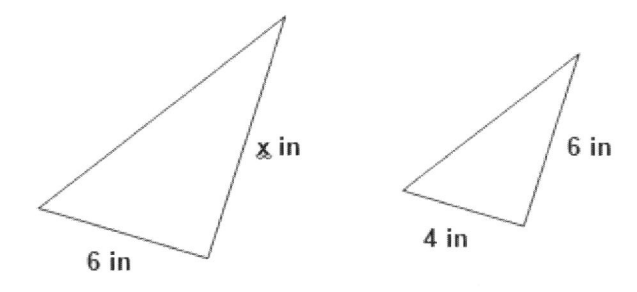

x in ... 6 in
6 in ... 4 in

A   x = 12 in   C   x = 8 in

B   x = 10 in   D   x = 9 in

Common Core Standard 8.G.A.4 – Geometry

☐ **Any two squares are always similar to each other. Is the statement true or false? Be sure to explain your answer.**

_____

_____

_____

©Teachers' Treasures Publishing

Name_____

DIAGNOSTIC

Use the graph below to answer the questions.

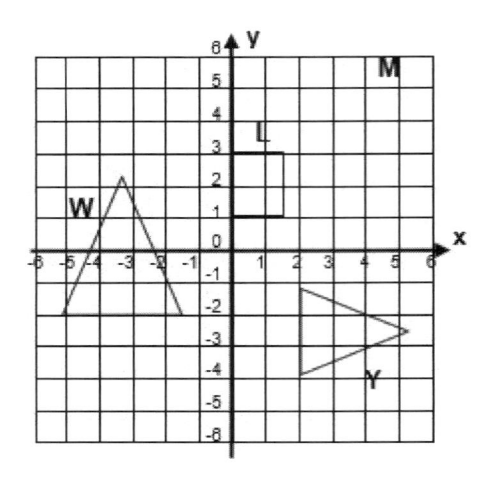

Common Core Standard 8.G.A.4 – Geometry

☐ Figure L is the result of the sequence of transformations of Figure M. Is Figure L similar to Figure M? If yes, find the scale factor.

A   Figure L is similar to Figure M;   scale factor: $\frac{1}{4}$

B   Figure L is similar to Figure M;   scale factor: 2

C   Figure L is similar to Figure M;   scale factor: 3

D   Figure L is not similar to Figure M

Common Core Standard 8.G.A.4 – Geometry

☐ Describe the sequence of transformations that results in the transformation of Figure W to Figure Y. Is Figure W similar to Figure Y? Be sure to explain your answer.

A   rotation and translation;   no

B   dilation, rotation and translation;   yes

C   reflection and dilation;   yes

D   none of the above

©Teachers' Treasures Publishing

Name_____

PRACTICE

Common Core Standard 8.G.A.4 – Geometry

☐ Is Figure B similar to Figure B'? Be sure to explain your answer.

_____
_____
_____
_____

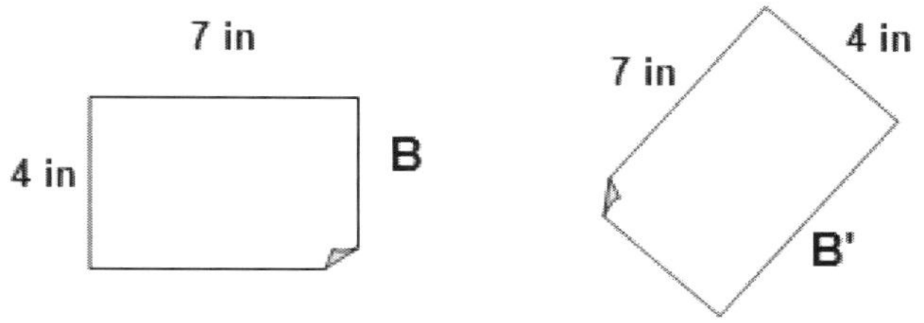

7 in
4 in
B

7 in
4 in
B'

Common Core Standard 8.G.A.4 – Geometry

☐ Which of the figures below is similar to Figure G? Be sure to explain your answer.

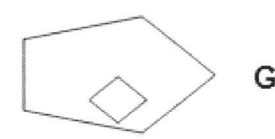

G

A

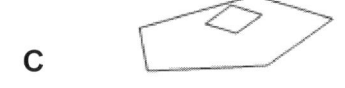

B

C

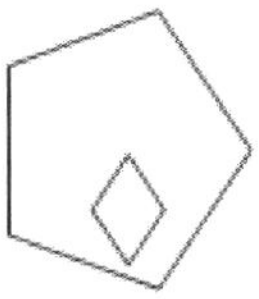

D

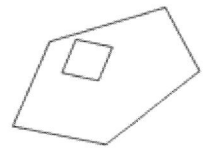

Common Core Standard 8.G.A.4 – Geometry

☐ Which polygons are always similar to each other? Be sure to explain your answer.

A   rectangles

B   right triangles

C   equilateral triangles

D   trapezoids

©Teachers' Treasures Publishing

Name_____

PRACTICE

Use the graph below to answer the questions.

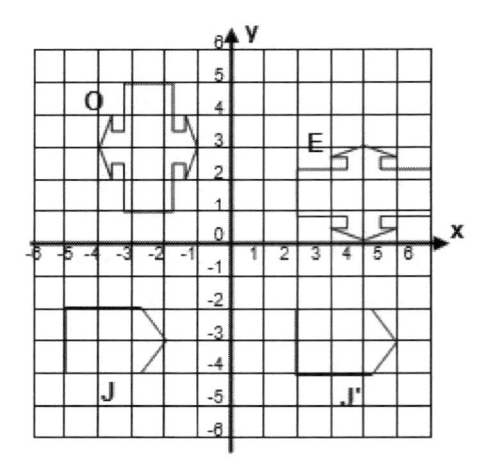

Common Core Standard 8.G.A.4 – Geometry

☐ After which transformation(s) will the two figures stay similar? Be sure to explain your answer.

A   rotation   C   reflection

B   dilation   D   all of the above

Common Core Standard 8.G.A.4 – Geometry

☐ Describe the sequence of transformations that took place to change Figure O into Figure E. Is Figure O similar to Figure E? Be sure to explain your answer.

A   rotation and translation; yes   C   reflection; no

B   translation; yes   D   none of the above

Common Core Standard 8.G.A.4 – Geometry

☐ Describe the sequence of transformations that took place to change Figure J into Figure J'. Be sure to explain your answer.

A   rotation   C   reflection

B   translation   D   dilation

©Teachers' Treasures Publishing

Name_____

PRACTICE

Common Core Standard 8.G.A.4 – Geometry

☐ Find the value for x using the similarity of the triangles shown below. Be sure to show your work.

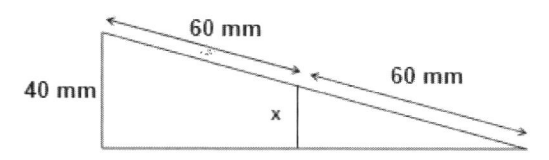

60 mm
60 mm
40 mm
x

A   x = 30 mm

B   x = 40 mm

C   x = 10 mm

D   x = 20 mm

Common Core Standard 8.G.A.4 – Geometry

☐ Two congruent polygons are always similar. Is this statement true or false? Be sure to explain your answer.

_____

_____

_____

Common Core Standard 8.G.A.4 – Geometry

☐ Which of the figures below is similar to Figure G? Be sure to explain your answer.

L

A

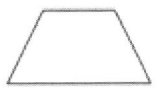

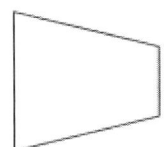

B

C

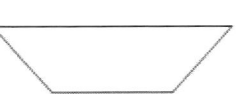

D

©Teachers' Treasures Publishing

Page 149

Name_____

PRACTICE

Use the graph below to answer the questions.

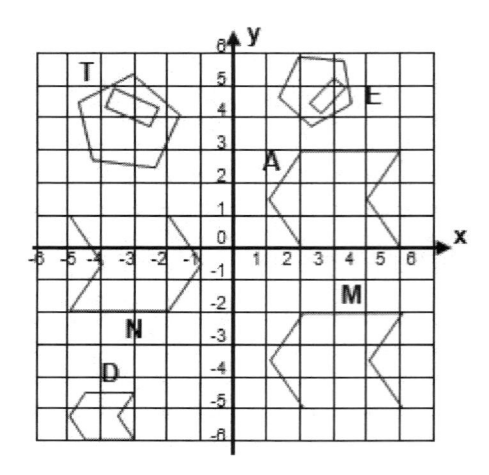

Common Core Standard 8.G.A.4 – Geometry

☐   Figure N is reflected across the y-axis, then translated 3 unit down. Which of the figures shows Figure N after these translations? Is the transformed figure similar to Figure N? Be sure to explain your answer.

A   Figure M; yes   C   Figure A; yes

B   Figure M; no   D   Figure D; no

Common Core Standard 8.G.A.4 – Geometry

☐   Describe the sequence of transformations that took place to change Figure T into Figure E. Is Figure T similar to Figure E? Be sure to explain your answer.

A   rotation, dilation; yes   C   reflection, dilation; no

B   translation, dilation; yes   D   none of the above

Common Core Standard 8.G.A.4 – Geometry

☐   What is the scale factor from Figure D to Figure A, if they are similar? Be sure to explain your answer.

A   2   C   4

B   0.5   D   0.25

©Teachers' Treasures Publishing

Name_____

ASSESSMENT

Use the graph below to answer the questions.

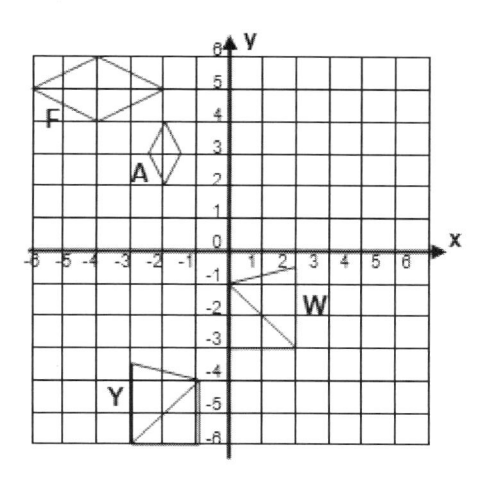

Common Core Standard 8.G.A.4 – Geometry

☐ Figure F is the result of the sequence of transformations of Figure A. Is Figure F similar to Figure A? If yes, find the scale factor.

A   Figure A is similar to Figure F; scale factor: $\frac{1}{3}$

B   Figure A is similar to Figure F; scale factor: 2

C   Figure A is similar to Figure F; scale factor: 3

D   Figure A is not similar to Figure F

Common Core Standard 8.G.A.4 – Geometry

☐ Describe the sequence of transformations that results in the transformation of Figure W to Figure Y. Is Figure W similar to Figure Y? Be sure to explain your answer.

A   reflection and translation; yes

B   dilation and translation; no

C   reflection and dilation; yes

D   none of the above

©Teachers' Treasures Publishing

Name_____

ASSESSMENT

Common Core Standard 8.G.A.4 – Geometry

☐ Trapezoid ABCD is similar to Trapezoid A'B'C'D'. What is the scale factor from A'B'C'D' to ABCD? Find values of A'B and B'C' for A'B'C'D'? Be sure to explain your answer.

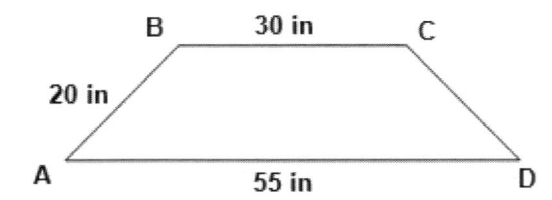

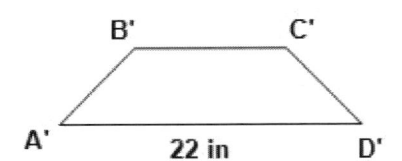

A   Scale factor: 2.5; A'B' = 8 in; B'C' = 12 in

B   Scale factor: 3; A'B' = 12 in; B'C' = 16 in

C   Scale factor: 0.5; A'B' = 10 in; B'C' = 15 in

D   Scale factor: 2; A'B' = 6 in; B'C' = 12 in

Common Core Standard 8.G.A.4 – Geometry

☐ Describe the sequence of transformations that results in the transformation of Figure W to Figure W' shown below. Are they similar? Be sure to explain your answer.

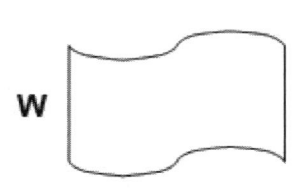

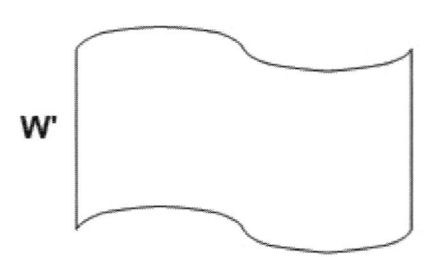

A   reflection; yes

B   reflection; no

C   reflection and dilation; yes

D   reflection and dilation; no

©Teachers' Treasures Publishing

Name_____

DIAGNOSTIC

Common Core Standard 8.G.A.5 – Geometry

☐ Find the measures of ∠1 and ∠2 in the figure below. Be sure to show your work.

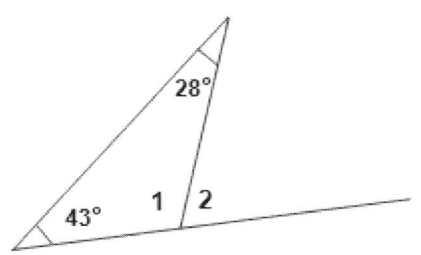

A 109° and 71°	C 99° and 81°
B 118° and 62°	D 75° and 115°

Common Core Standard 8.G.A.5 – Geometry

☐ Find the measures of ∠1 and ∠2 in the figure below. Be sure to show your work.

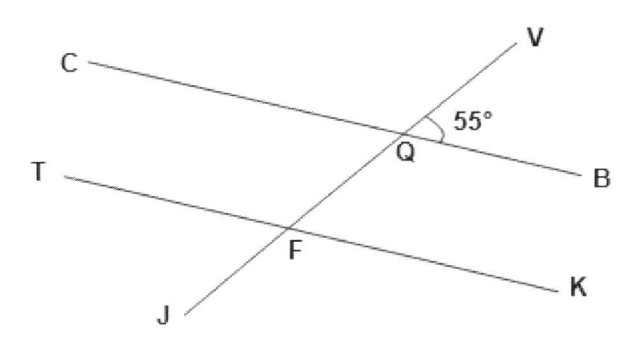

A 115°	C 125°
B 55°	D 110°

Common Core Standard 8.G.A.5 – Geometry

☐ How many degrees are there in the sum of the exterior angles of a regular triangle? Be sure to explain your answer.

A 120°	C 180°
B 360°	D 270°

©Teachers' Treasures Publishing

Name_____

DIAGNOSTIC

Use the graph below to answer the questions.

[Diagram: Two parallel lines MN and GB, with transversals from E through D to O (on line GB near B), and from R through D to Z (on line GB). The angle at O between the transversal and line toward B is marked 120°.]

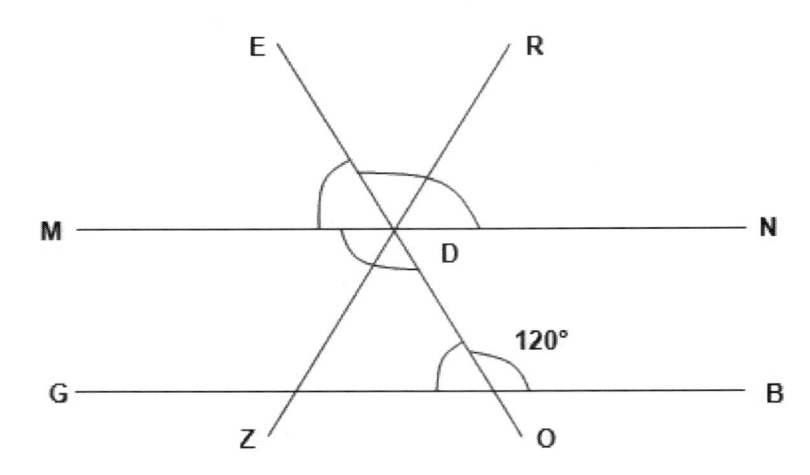

Common Core Standard 8.G.A.5 – Geometry

☐ MN and GB are parallel lines and RZ is a transversal. What is the value of ∠ MDE? Be sure to explain your answer.

A   120°   C   60°

B   80°   D   70°

Common Core Standard 8.G.A.5 – Geometry

☐ MN and GB are parallel lines and EO is a transversal. What are the values of ∠ MDO and ∠ ODN? Be sure to explain your answer.

A   120° and 60°   C   110° and 70°

B   120° and 120°   D   60° and 120°

Common Core Standard 8.G.A.5 – Geometry

☐ Find the measures of ∠EDR and ∠NDE, if the measure of ∠EDN is twice as large as ∠MDE. Be sure to explain your answer.

A   120° and 60°   C   110° and 70°

B   120° and 120°   D   60° and 120°

©Teachers' Treasures Publishing

Name_____

PRACTICE

Common Core Standard 8.G.A.5 – Geometry

☐ What is the total number degrees of all interior angles of a triangle? Be sure to explain your answer.

A   120°

B   360°

C   180°

D   270°

Common Core Standard 8.G.A.5 – Geometry

☐ S and D are two parallel lines and ∠1 = 36° in the figure shown. Find the measures of ∠3 and ∠5. Be sure to show your work.

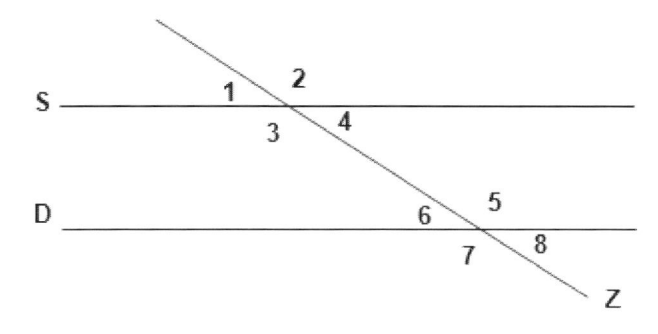

A   144° and 36°

B   154° and 36°

C   154° and 154°

D   144° and 144°

Common Core Standard 8.G.A.5 – Geometry

☐ Triangle SFR is similar to triangle DFE. Find the measure of ∠F. Be sure to explain your answer.

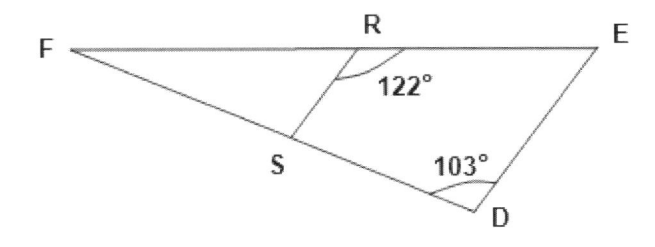

A   19°

B   36°

C   58°

D   27°

Name_____

PRACTICE

Use the graph below to answer the questions.

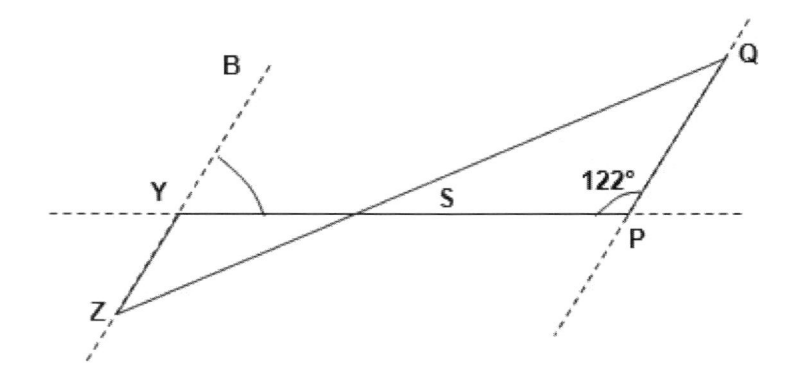

Common Core Standard 8.G.A.5 – Geometry

☐ Triangle SQP is similar to triangle SZY. Which segment is corresponding to segment YS? Be sure to explain your answer.

A   SQ   C   PS

B   ZS   D   PQ

Common Core Standard 8.G.A.5 – Geometry

☐ Triangle SQP is similar to triangle SZY. Find the measure of ∠Z, if the measure of ∠Q is 10° more than the measure of ∠S. Be sure to explain your answer.

A   34°   C   58°

B   24°   D   122°

Common Core Standard 8.G.A.5 – Geometry

☐ Triangle PQX is similar to triangle XYZ. Find the measure of ∠SYP. Be sure to explain your answer.

A   34°   C   58°

B   24°   D   122°

©Teachers' Treasures Publishing

Name_____

PRACTICE

Common Core Standard 8.G.A.5 – Geometry

☐ What is the measure of one interior angle of a regular pentagon? Be sure to explain your answer.

A   120°

C   108°

B   180°

D   540°

Common Core Standard 8.G.A.5 – Geometry

☐ How many degrees are there in the sum of the exterior angles of a regular hexagon? Be sure to explain your answer.

A   120°

C   270°

B   180°

D   360°

Common Core Standard 8.G.A.5 – Geometry

☐ Triangle SFR is similar to triangle DFE. Find the measure of ∠F. Be sure to explain your answer.

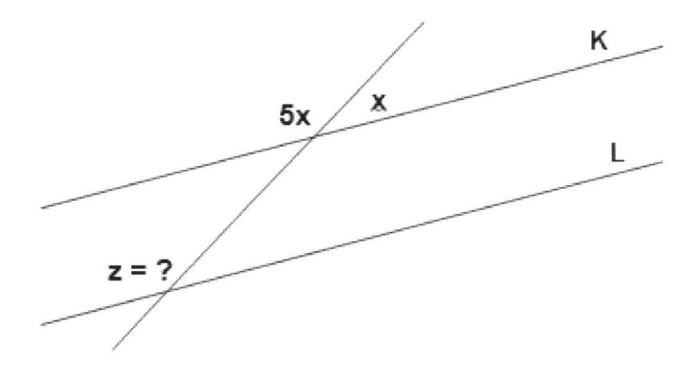

[Figure: two lines labeled K and L crossed by a transversal; angles marked 5x and x at the upper intersection, z = ? at the lower intersection]

A   36°

C   150°

B   144°

D   60°

©Teachers' Treasures Publishing

Name_____

PRACTICE

Use the graph below to answer the questions.

[Figure: triangle with angle A at bottom left, angle B at top, angle C at bottom right with exterior angle 136°, and angle D above B formed by extended lines]

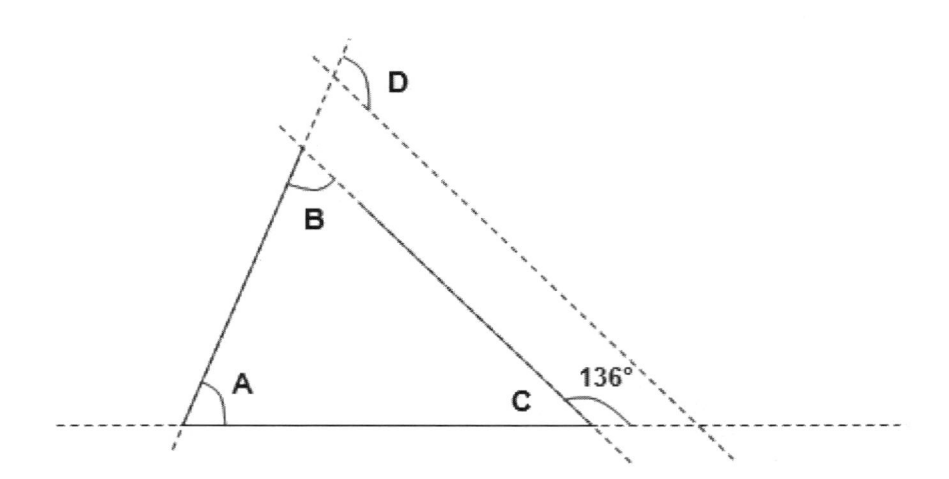

Common Core Standard 8.G.A.5 – Geometry

☐ ∠A and ∠B are equal. ∠C's exterior angle = 136°. Find the measure of ∠A in the figure. Be sure to explain your answer.

    A   34°   C   44°

    B   68°   D   136°

Common Core Standard 8.G.A.5 – Geometry

☐ ∠A and ∠B are equal. ∠C's exterior angle = 136°. Find the measure of ∠D in the figure. Be sure to explain your answer.

    A   102°   C   112°

    B   68°   D   136°

Common Core Standard 8.G.A.5 – Geometry

☐ Find the sum of the measures of ∠B and ∠C in the figure. Be sure to explain your answer.

    A   102°   C   112°

    B   68°   D   136°

©Teachers' Treasures Publishing

Name_____

ASSESSMENT

Common Core Standard 8.G.A.5 – Geometry

☐ The line SD is drawn parallel to the base BC in the triangle ABC. If the ∠A = 51°, find ∠S. Be sure to explain your answer.

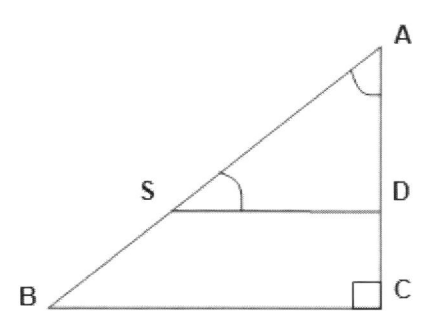

A	51°	C	109°
B	49°	D	39°

Common Core Standard 8.G.A.5 – Geometry

☐ E and O are two parallel lines and the line G is a transversal shown in the figure below. Find all angles that are congruent to ∠4. Be sure to explain your answer.

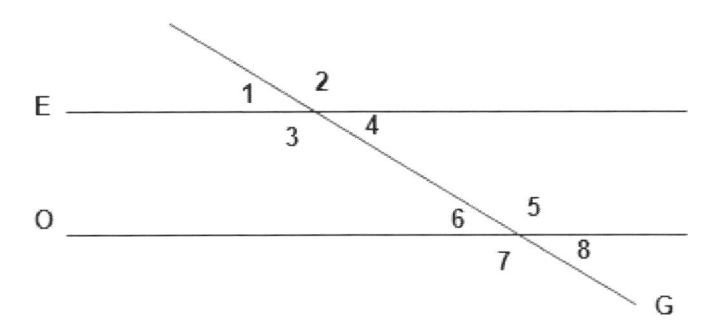

A	∠1, ∠4, ∠8	C	∠1, ∠4, ∠6
B	∠3, ∠2, ∠5	D	∠6, ∠8, ∠1

©Teachers' Treasures Publishing   Page 159

Name_____

ASSESSMENT

Use the graph below to answer the questions.

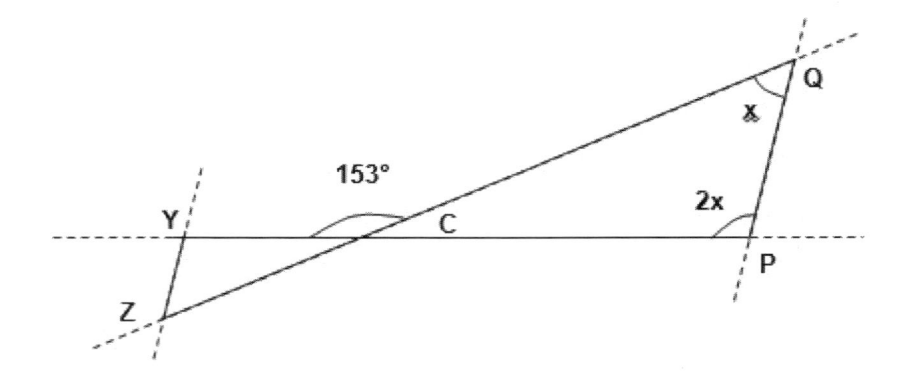

Common Core Standard 8.G.A.5 – Geometry

☐ **Triangle CQP is similar to triangle CZY. Find the measure of ∠C in the figure, if ∠C's exterior angle = 153°. Be sure to explain your answer.**

A   27°   C   53°

B   37°   D   80°

Common Core Standard 8.G.A.5 – Geometry

☐ **Triangle CQP is similar to triangle CZY. Find the measure of ∠Y, if the measure of ∠P is twice as large as the measure of ∠Q. Be sure to explain your answer.**

A   27°   C   51°

B   54°   D   102°

Common Core Standard 8.G.A.5 – Geometry

☐ **Triangle CQP is similar to triangle CZY. Find the measure of ∠Z, if the measure of ∠P is twice as large as the measure of ∠Q. Be sure to explain your answer.**

A   27°   C   51°

B   54°   D   102°

©Teachers' Treasures Publishing

Name_____

DIAGNOSTIC

Common Core Standard 8.G.B.6 – Geometry

☐ What is the length of the hypotenuse? Be sure to explain your answer.

A   9 yd

B   10 yd

C   14 yd

D   12 yd

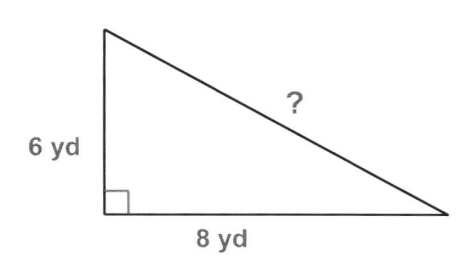

6 yd
8 yd
?

Common Core Standard 8.G.B.6 – Geometry

☐ Does this triangle have a right angle? Be sure to explain your answer.

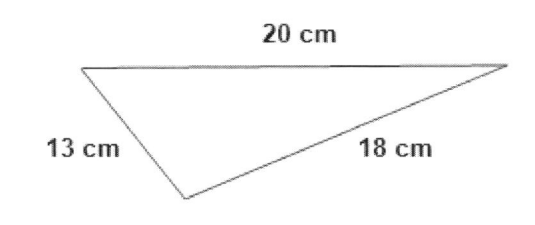

_____
_____
_____
_____

20 cm
13 cm
18 cm

Common Core Standard 8.G.B.6 – Geometry

☐ A triangle has sides with lengths of 12 centimeters, 19 centimeters, and 20 centimeters. Is it a right triangle? Be sure to explain your answer.

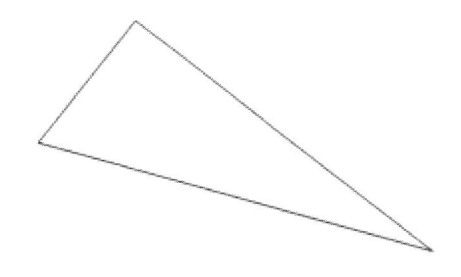

_____
_____
_____
_____

©Teachers' Treasures Publishing

Name_____

DIAGNOSTIC

Common Core Standard 8.G.B.6 – Geometry

☐ A triangle has sides with lengths of 7 centimeters, 10 centimeters, and 11 centimeters. Is it a right triangle? Be sure to explain your answer.

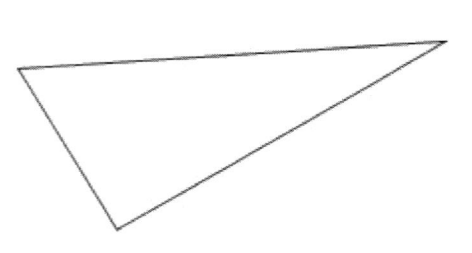

_____

_____

_____

_____

Common Core Standard 8.G.B.6 – Geometry

☐ What is the length of the missing leg? Be sure to explain your answer.

A   4.3 km

B   4 km

C   3 km

D   3.7 km

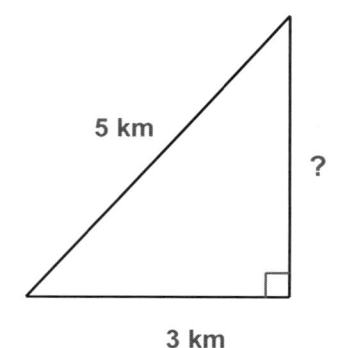

(Right triangle with hypotenuse 5 km, base 3 km, missing leg ?)

Common Core Standard 8.G.B.6 – Geometry

☐ A car drives 10 miles east and then 24 miles due north. How far is it from where it started? Be sure to explain your answer.

A   32

B   20.6

C   26

D   34

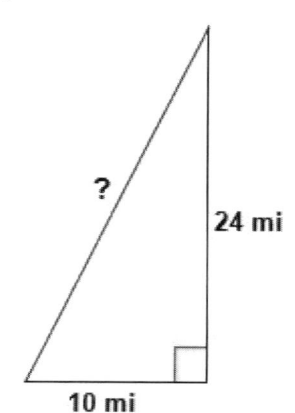

(Right triangle with legs 10 mi and 24 mi, hypotenuse ?)

©Teachers' Treasures Publishing

Name_____

PRACTICE

Common Core Standard 8.G.B.6 – Geometry

☐ Does the triangle with side lengths of 26, 13, and 34 have a right angle? Be sure to explain your answer.

_____
_____
_____
_____
_____

Common Core Standard 8.G.B.6 – Geometry

☐ Which of the following statements describes the Pythagorean Theorem? Be sure to explain your answer.

A   A right angle is an angle that has a measure of 90° which is indicated by a square drawn at the corner formed by the angle.

B   If a and b are the lengths of the legs of a right triangle and c is the length of the hypotenuse, then $a^2 + b^2 = c^2$.

C   A triangle with a right angle is called a right triangle.

D   The longest side of the right triangle is called a "hypotenuse".

Common Core Standard 8.G.B.6 – Geometry

☐ A triangle has side lengths of 21 miles, 28 miles, and 35 miles. Is it a right triangle? Be sure to explain your answer.

_____
_____
_____
_____
_____

©Teachers' Treasures Publishing

Name_____

PRACTICE

Common Core Standard 8.G.B.6 – Geometry

☐ What is the diagonal distance across a square of size 1? Round to the nearest hundredth. Be sure to explain your answer.

A   2.33

B   1.41

C   1.11

D   1.31

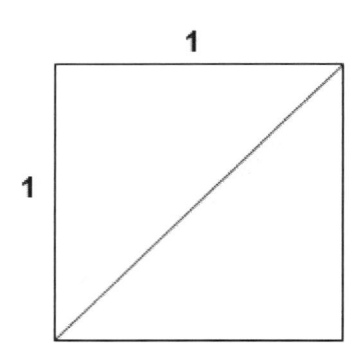

Common Core Standard 8.G.B.6 – Geometry

☐ Find x, if AB = 5, BC = 6 and CA = x. Be sure to explain your answer.

A   61

B $\sqrt{61}$

C   7.9

D   7

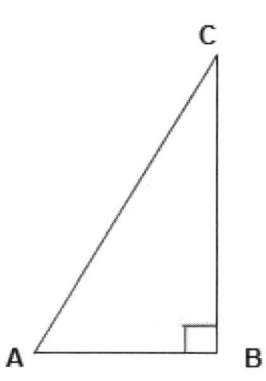

Common Core Standard 8.G.B.6 – Geometry

☐ The side lengths of right triangles are 15, 30, 37. Determine which length represents the hypotenuse. Be sure to explain your answer.

A   15

B   30

C   37

D   none of the above

©Teachers' Treasures Publishing

Name_____

PRACTICE

Common Core Standard 8.G.B.6 – Geometry

☐ Calculate the height of a triangle with sides at lengths of 15 feet, 39 feet. Be sure to explain your answer.

A   38

B   36

C   41.78

D   16

Common Core Standard 8.G.B.6 – Geometry

☐ Does an 8, 15, 16 triangle have a right angle? Be sure to explain your answer.

Common Core Standard 8.G.B.6 – Geometry

☐ A triangular section on the map has sides with lengths of 5 kilometers, 5 kilometers, and 9 kilometers. Is it a right triangle? Be sure to explain your answer.

©Teachers' Treasures Publishing   Page 165

Name_____

PRACTICE

Common Core Standard 8.G.B.6 – Geometry

☐ The area of a college campus is a triangle and has sides with lengths of 9 kilometers, 12 kilometers, and 15 kilometers. Find out if it is a right triangle. Be sure to explain your answer.

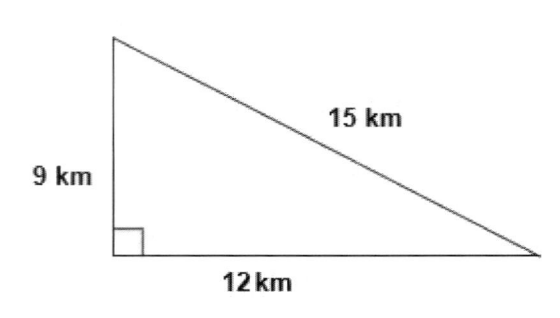

_____

_____

_____

_____

Common Core Standard 8.G.B.6 – Geometry

☐ If WY and YX are doubled, what will be the change in the hypotenuse XW? Be sure to explain your answer.

A   XW will stay the same

B   XW will decrease by 2

C   XW will increase by 10

D   XW will be doubled

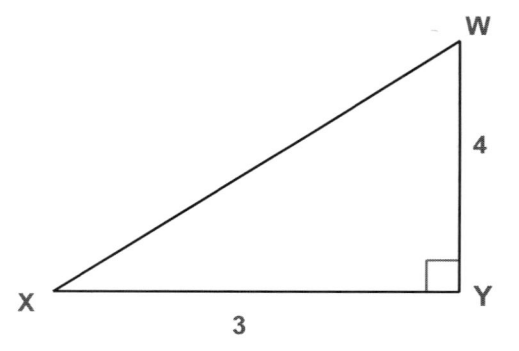

Common Core Standard 8.G.B.6 – Geometry

☐ A box is in the shape of a square with the side length 32 cm. What is its diagonal? Round to the nearest hundredth. Be sure to explain your answer.

A   45.30

B   45.25

C   45.20

D   44.52

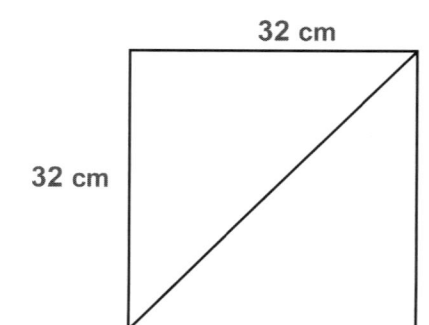

©Teachers' Treasures Publishing

Name_____

ASSESSMENT

Common Core Standard 8.G.B.6 – Geometry

☐ A triangle has sides with lengths of 3 centimeters, 4 centimeters, and 6 centimeters. Is it a right triangle? Be sure to explain your answer.

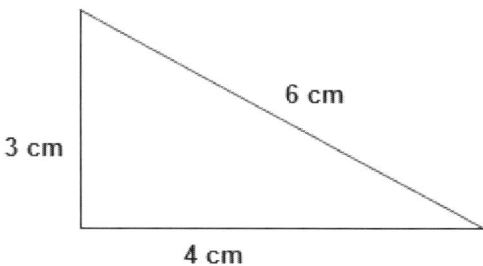

_____
_____
_____
_____
_____

3 cm, 6 cm, 4 cm

Common Core Standard 8.G.B.6 – Geometry

☐ Does this triangle have a right angle? Be sure to explain your answer.

_____
_____
_____
_____
_____

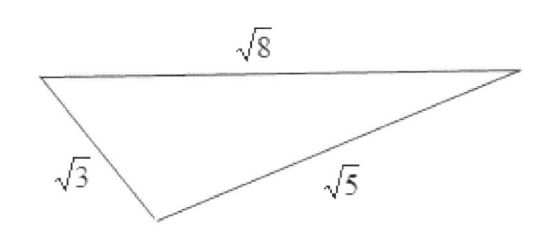

$\sqrt{8}$, $\sqrt{3}$, $\sqrt{5}$

Common Core Standard 8.G.B.6 – Geometry

☐ A triangle has sides with lengths of 5 centimeters, 12 centimeters, and 13 centimeters. Is it a right triangle? Be sure to explain your answer.

_____
_____
_____
_____
_____

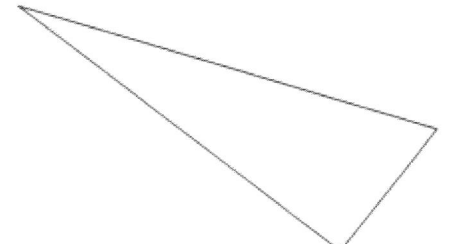

©Teachers' Treasures Publishing

Name_____

ASSESSMENT

Common Core Standard 8.G.B.6 – Geometry

☐ Fran bicycles 4 miles west to get from her house to school. After school, she bicycles 3 miles north to her friend Nina's house. How far is Fran's house from Nina's house, measured in a straight line? Be sure to explain your answer.

A 6 miles

B 5 miles

C 7 miles

D 8 miles

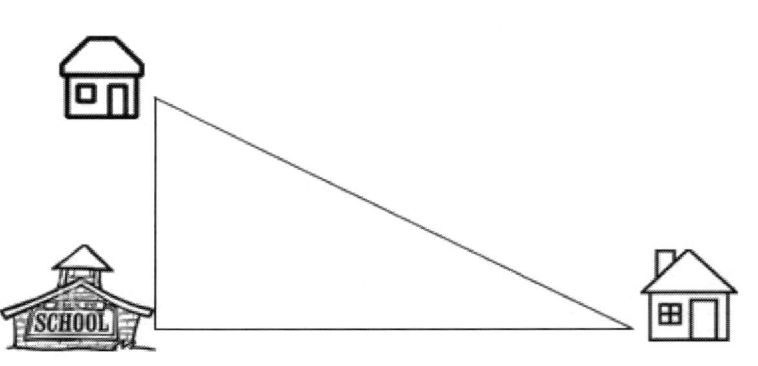

Common Core Standard 8.G.B.6 – Geometry

☐ What is the length of the missing leg? Be sure to explain your answer.

A 4 feet

B 5 feet

C 6 feet

D 7 feet

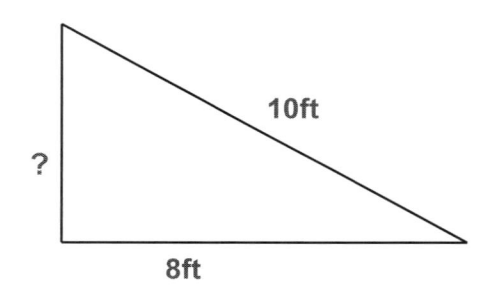

Common Core Standard 8.G.B.6 – Geometry

☐ Mr. Bullock calculated the distance across his garden from point W to point Y using the measurements shown on the picture. What is the distance from point X to point Y? Be sure to explain your answer.

A 8 feet

B 13 feet

C 18 feet

D 24 feet

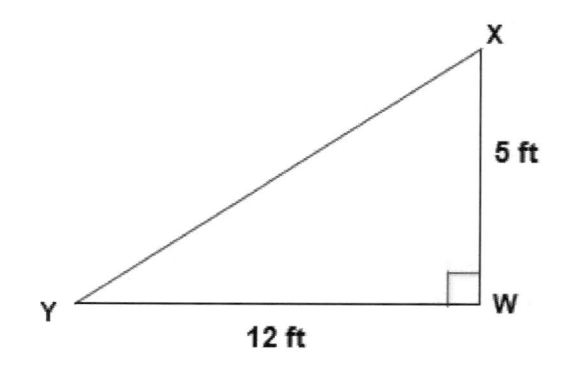

©Teachers' Treasures Publishing

Name_____

DIAGNOSTIC

Common Core Standard 8.G.B.7 – Geometry

☐ A school bus goes by Allen High School, when it transports students from Murphy Middle School to Carpenter High School. When the new highway is built, the bus will go directly from Murphy Middle School to Carpenter High School. What is the shortest distance this new highway could be? Round to the nearest tenth if necessary. Be sure to explain your answer.

    A   34.9 km

    B   38 km

    C   40 km

    D   36.5 km

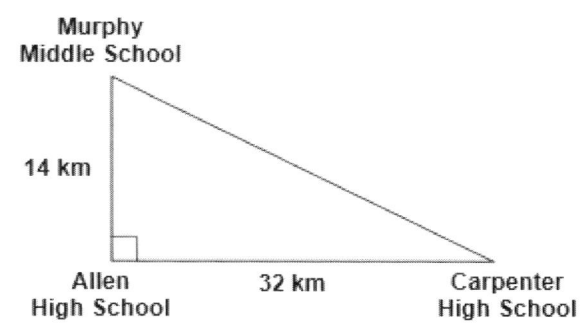

Common Core Standard 8.G.B.7 – Geometry

☐ A tree in Andrew's yard is 16 meters tall. In the afternoon, it casts a shadow that measures 20 meters from the top of the tree to the end of the shadow. What is the length of the shadow? Be sure to explain your answer.

    A   36 m

    B   12 m

    C   16 m

    D   21 m

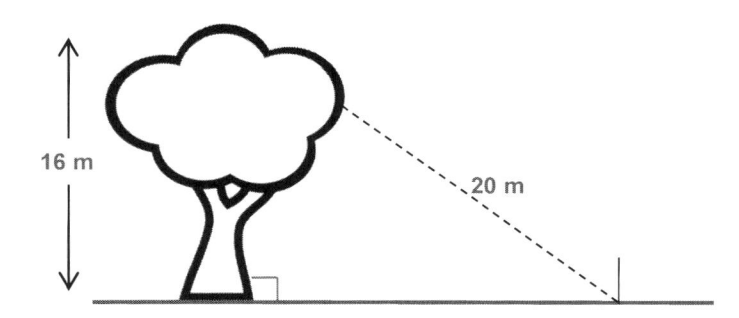

Common Core Standard 8.G.B.7 – Geometry

☐ Neil rides his car 12 km north and then 7 km west. How far is he from his starting point? Be sure to explain your answer.

    A   17 km

    B   15 km

    C $\sqrt{193}$ km

    D $\sqrt{139}$ km

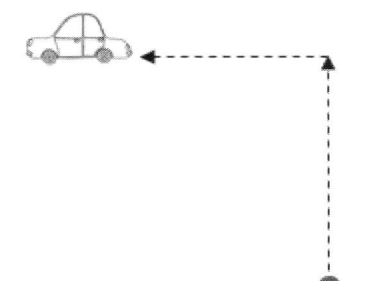

©Teachers' Treasures Publishing

Name_____

DIAGNOSTIC

Common Core Standard 8.G.B.7 – Geometry

☐ Sam walks 2 km in an east to west direction. He stops and then walks in a west to south direction for 1 km. How much distance does he have to walk to reach from initial point to end point? Round to the nearest tenth if necessary. Be sure to explain your answer.

A   2.2 km

B   3.2 km

C $\sqrt{6}$ km

D   4.2 km

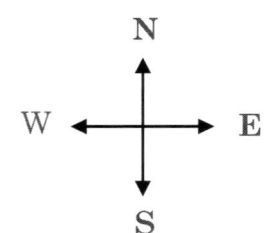

Common Core Standard 8.G.B.7 – Geometry

☐ Calculate the length of the missing side of the given triangle. Be sure to explain your answer.

A $\sqrt{115}$ in

B $5\sqrt{17}$ in

C   15 in

D   12 in

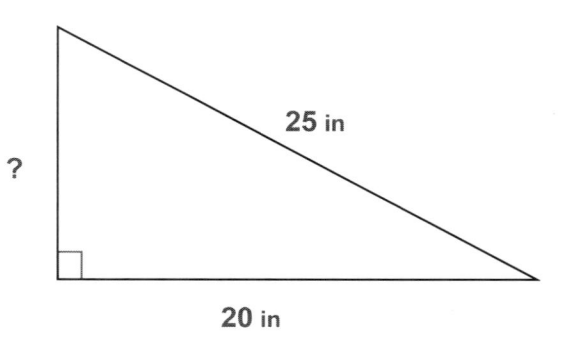

(Triangle with hypotenuse 25 in, base 20 in, missing side ?)

Common Core Standard 8.G.B.7 – Geometry

☐ A store built a loading ramp at the back of the warehouse. The ramp is 10 feet long. It meets the ground 8 feet from the side of the warehouse. How tall is the ramp? Be sure to explain your answer.

A   5 ft

B   6 ft

C   8 ft

D   7 ft

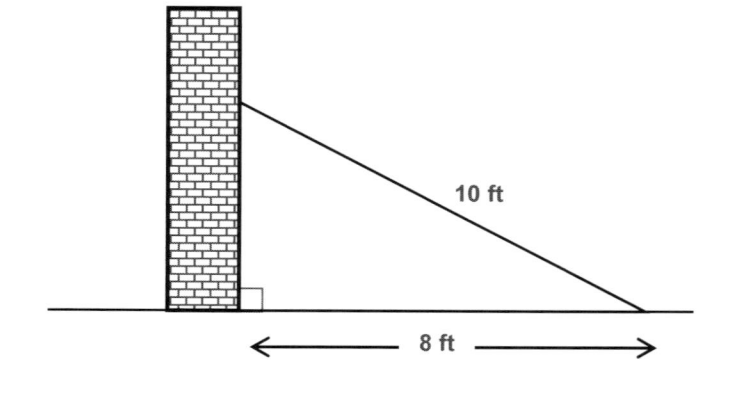

©Teachers' Treasures Publishing

Name_____

PRACTICE

Common Core Standard 8.G.B.7 – Geometry

☐ It is 15 kilometers from Amy's house to Melinda's house, and 12 kilometers from Melinda's house to Kathy's house. What is the shortest distance from Amy's house to Kathy's house? Be sure to explain your answer.

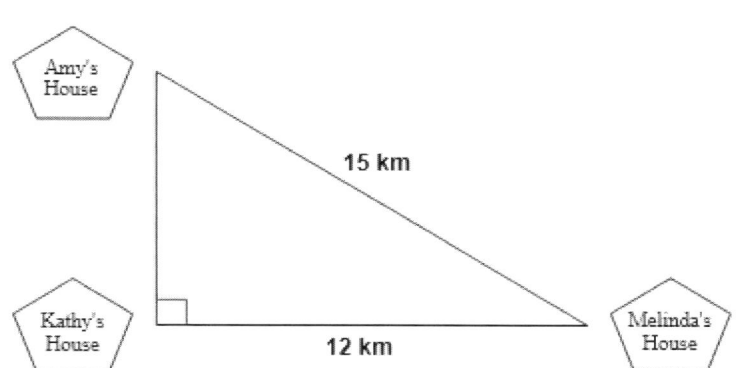

A   3.4 km

B   9 km

C   6 km

D   24 km

Common Core Standard 8.G.B.7 – Geometry

☐ Patrick and his brother Bob are mowing a rectangular shaped lot that measures 20 feet long and 25 feet diagonally. What is the width of the lot? Be sure to explain your answer.

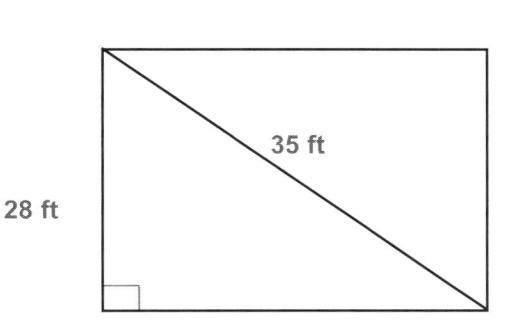

A   15 ft

B   32 ft

C   25 ft

D   21 ft

Common Core Standard 8.G.B.7 – Geometry

☐ Calculate the length of the missing side of the given triangle. Be sure to explain your answer.

A $\sqrt{338}$ in

B $\sqrt{167}$ in

C $\sqrt{274}$ in

D $4\sqrt{21}$ in

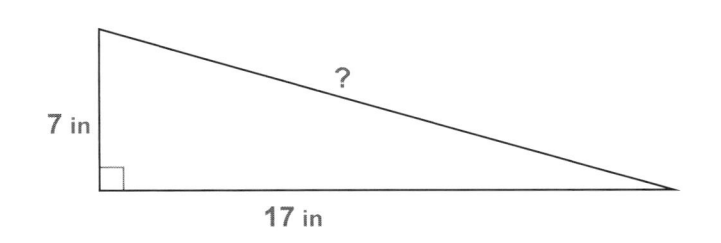

©Teachers' Treasures Publishing

Name_____

PRACTICE

Common Core Standard 8.G.B.7 – Geometry

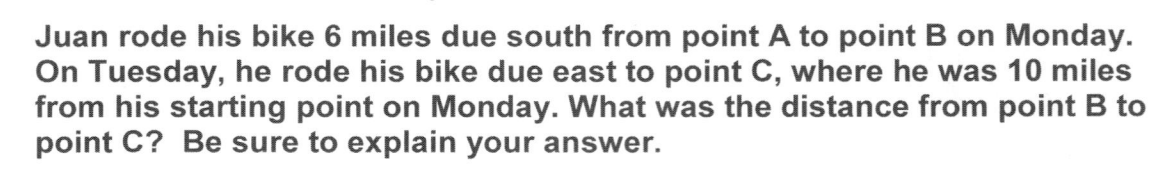

☐ Juan rode his bike 6 miles due south from point A to point B on Monday. On Tuesday, he rode his bike due east to point C, where he was 10 miles from his starting point on Monday. What was the distance from point B to point C? Be sure to explain your answer.

- A   18 mi
- B   32 mi
- C   27 mi
- D   38 mi

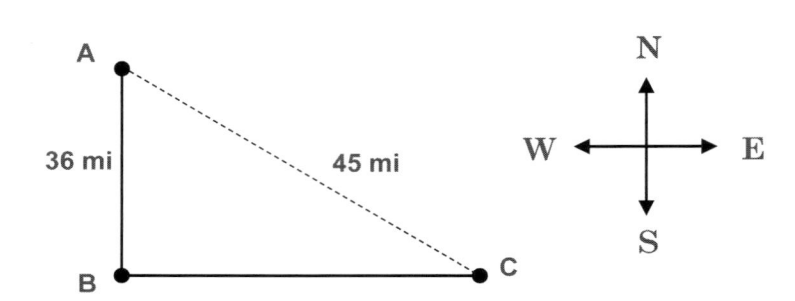

(Triangle diagram: A at top, B below A with 36 mi between them, C to the right of B with 45 mi hypotenuse from A to C. Compass rose showing N, S, E, W.)

Common Core Standard 8.G.B.7 – Geometry

☐ On Sunday Maxwell walks to his grandparents' house from his home. He moves 4 miles south and then he moves 5 miles east. How much distance is between home and his grandparents' house? Round to the nearest tenth if necessary. Be sure to explain your answer.

- A   7 miles
- B   6.4 miles
- C   7.2 miles
- D   7.9 miles

Common Core Standard 8.G.B.7 – Geometry

☐ Calculate the length of the missing side of the given triangle. Be sure to explain your answer.

- A $\sqrt{391}$ in
- B $5\sqrt{15}$ in
- C   28 in
- D   32 in

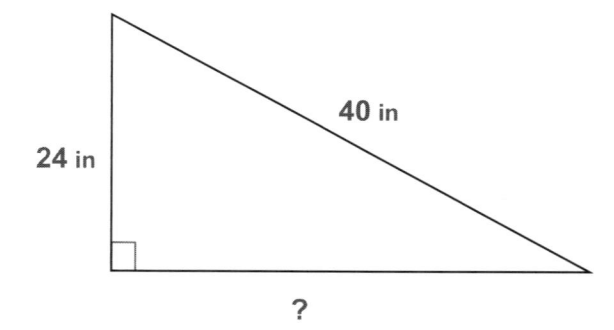

(Right triangle with legs 24 in and ?, hypotenuse 40 in.)

©Teachers' Treasures Publishing

Name_____

PRACTICE

Common Core Standard 8.G.B.7 – Geometry

☐ Erik rides his bike 11 km south and then 11 km east. How far is he from his starting point? Be sure to explain your answer.

    A   23

    B $11\sqrt{2}$

    C $7\sqrt{7}$

    D   14

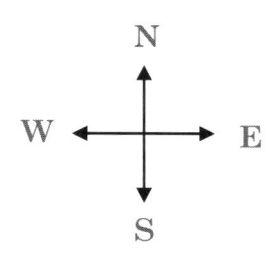

Common Core Standard 8.G.B.7 – Geometry

☐ Heather is flying a kite that is 20 m from her along the ground and 10 m above her. How long is the string between Heather and the kite? Be sure to explain your answer.

    A   32.16 m

    B   23.13 m

    C   33.21 m

    D   22.36 m

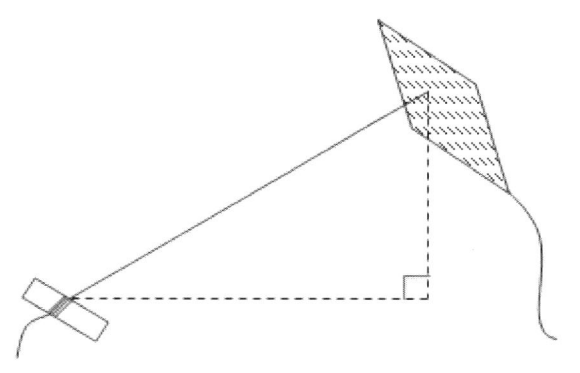

Common Core Standard 8.G.B.7 – Geometry

☐ A frame maker checks his work by making a diagonal measurement between the two pieces of molding. What should he read on the ruler if the sides of the frame form a right angle? Be sure to explain your answer.

    A $15\sqrt{2}$

    B $\sqrt{218}$

    C $13\sqrt{5}$

    D   32

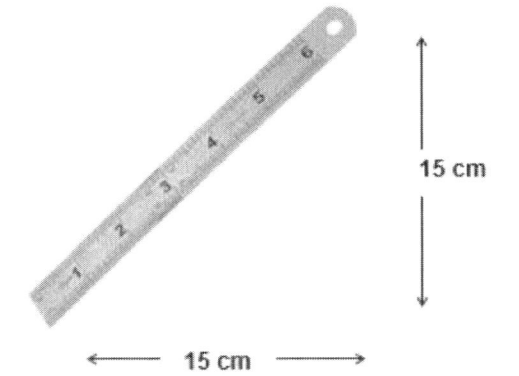

15 cm

15 cm

©Teachers' Treasures Publishing

Name_____

PRACTICE

Common Core Standard 8.G.B.7 – Geometry

☐ A trucking company attached a wire cable to a flagpole 30 feet from the base of the pole. The wire cable meets the ground 40 feet from the base of the flagpole. How long is the wire cable? Be sure to explain your answer.

A   35 ft

B   50 ft

C   125 ft

D   12 ft

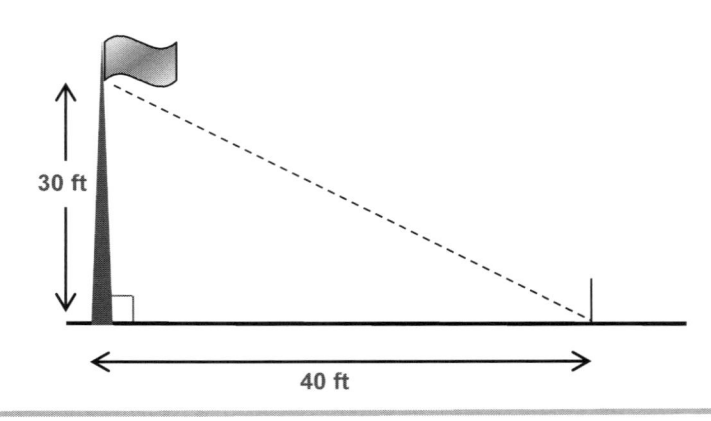

30 ft

40 ft

Common Core Standard 8.G.B.7 – Geometry

☐ Find the width of a triangle that has a 9 cm height and a hypotenuse of 19 cm. Round to the nearest tenth if necessary. Be sure to explain your answer.

A   17.6   C   18.6

B   16.7   D   16.9

Common Core Standard 8.G.B.7 – Geometry

☐ What is the shortest distance from Camp A to Camp C? Be sure to explain your answer.

A   17 km

B   18 km

C   21 km

D   23 km

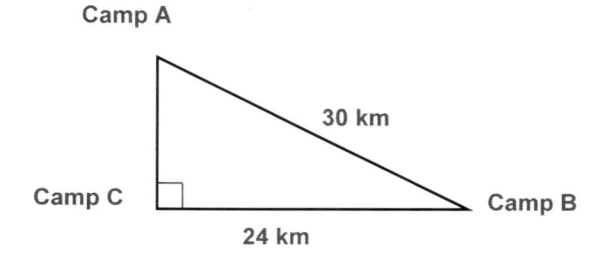

Camp A

30 km

Camp C   Camp B

24 km

©Teachers' Treasures Publishing

Name_____

ASSESSMENT

Common Core Standard 8.G.B.7 – Geometry

☐ The map shows the location of movie theatres in a city in Texas. Discount Cinema is due north of Super Cinema and due west of Double Screen Theater. What is the shortest distance from Discount Cinema to Super Cinema? Be sure to explain your answer.

A $4\sqrt{33}$ mi

B 14 mi

C 15 mi

D $3\sqrt{41}$ mi

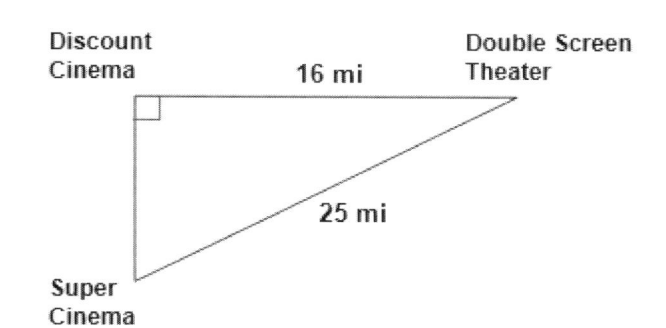

Discount Cinema — 16 mi — Double Screen Theater
25 mi
Super Cinema

Common Core Standard 8.G.B.7 – Geometry

☐ A school athletic club wants to build a new swimming pool. The plans call for the pool to be 20 meters wide and 99 meters long. How long will a large banner hung diagonally across the pool need to be? Be sure to explain your answer.

A 79 m

B 10 m

C 101 m

D 119 m

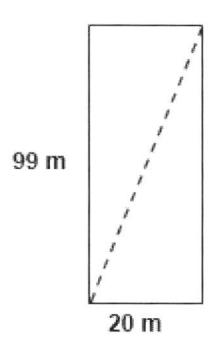

99 m
20 m

Common Core Standard 8.G.B.7 – Geometry

☐ Calculate the length of the missing side of the given triangle. Be sure to explain your answer.

A $\sqrt{513}$ in

B $7\sqrt{87}$ in

C 35 in

D 32 in

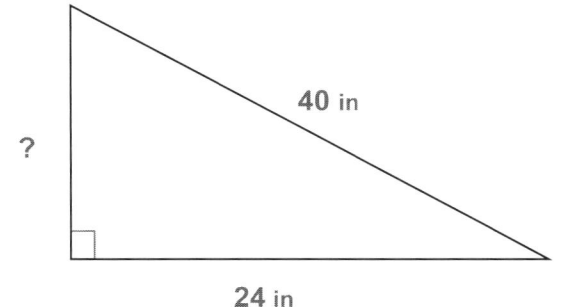

40 in
?
24 in

©Teachers' Treasures Publishing   Page 175

Name_____

ASSESSMENT

Common Core Standard 8.G.B.7 – Geometry

☐ Matt uses a guy wire to support a young tree. He attaches it to a point 6 ft up the tree trunk and stretches the wire to stake 8 ft from the tree trunk. How long must the wire be? Be sure to explain your answer.

A   12 ft

B   10 ft

C   14 ft

D   12.5 ft

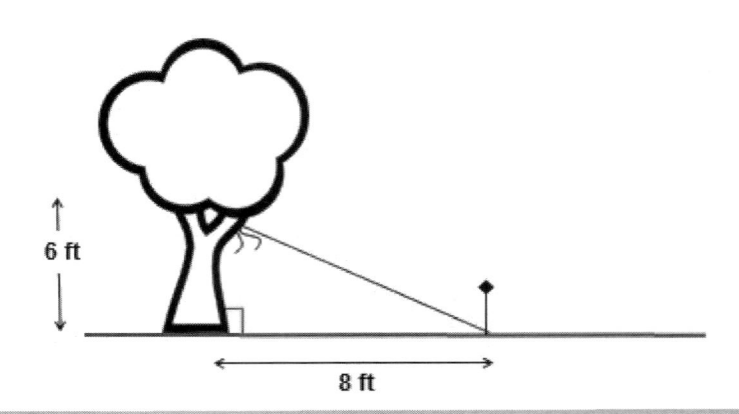

Common Core Standard 8.G.B.7 – Geometry

☐ Lily walks 46 meters in an east to west direction. Then she walks in a west to south direction for 37 meters. How much distance does she have to walk to reach from initial point to end point? Round to the nearest tenth if necessary. Be sure to explain your answer.

A   58.7 m

B   49.8 m

C   52 m

D   59 m

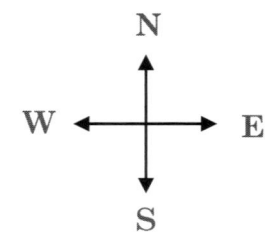

Common Core Standard 8.G.B.7 – Geometry

☐ Mr. Cane wants to hang banners across the front of the parking lot at his store. If he hangs the banners from point R to point S using the measurements on the diagram, how many yards of banners should be in order? Be sure to explain your answer.

A   35 yd

B   49 yd

C   7 yd

D   12 yd

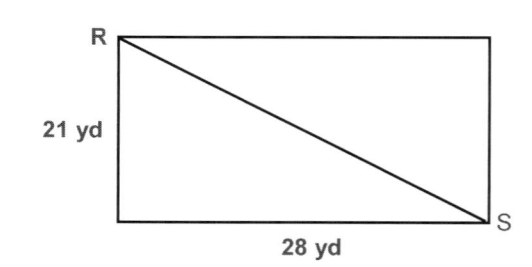

©Teachers' Treasures Publishing

Name_____

DIAGNOSTIC

Common Core Standard 8.G.B.8 – Geometry

☐ Apply the Pythagorean Theorem to find the distance between the two points in a coordinate system. Be sure to show your work.

A $\sqrt{7}$

B $4\sqrt{2}$

C   5

D   6

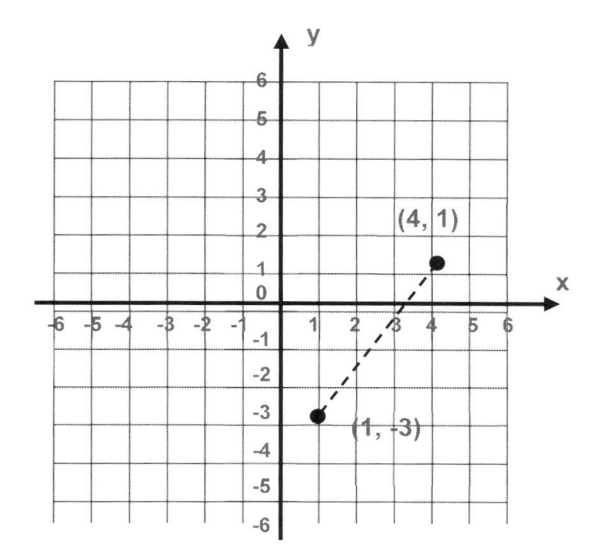

Points shown: (4, 1) and (1, -3)

Common Core Standard 8.G.B.8 – Geometry

☐ Suzy rides her bike 6 km north and then 8 km west. Determine how far she is from her starting point S, by graphing and connecting the points, and applying the Pythagorean Theorem. Be sure to show your work.

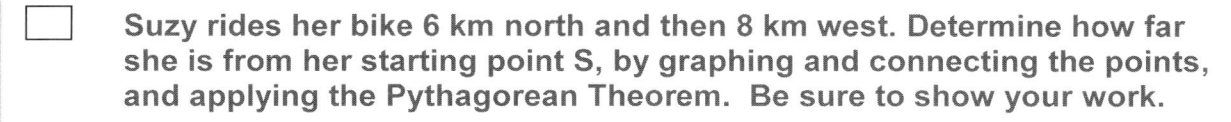

A $\sqrt{163}$

B   10

C   14

D $\sqrt{112}$

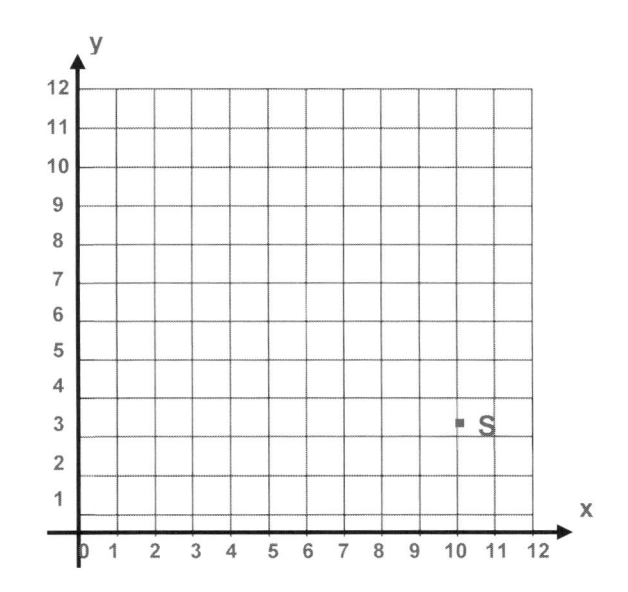

©Teachers' Treasures Publishing

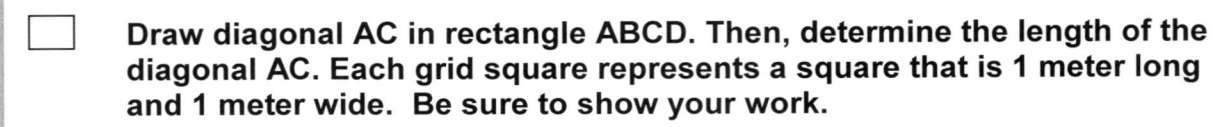

Name_____

DIAGNOSTIC

Common Core Standard 8.G.B.8 – Geometry

☐ Draw diagonal AC in rectangle ABCD. Then, determine the length of the diagonal AC. Each grid square represents a square that is 1 meter long and 1 meter wide. Be sure to show your work.

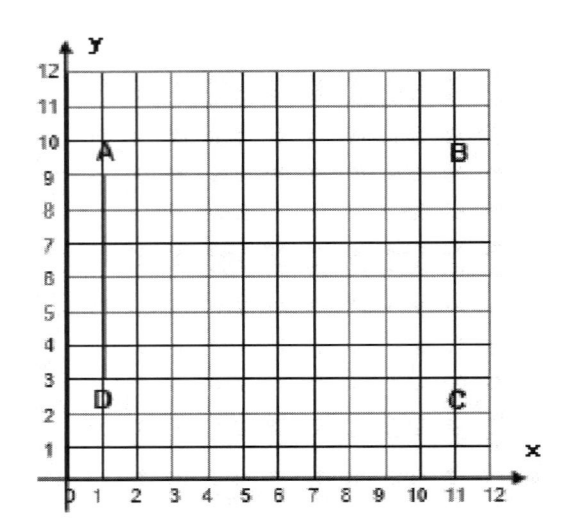

A   12.4 meters

B   11.2 meters

C $8\sqrt{17}$ meters

D $2\sqrt{34}$ meters

Common Core Standard 8.G.B.8 – Geometry

☐ The school team is having a soccer practice. Zack and Ben are the closest to the ball. How far is Zack from the ball? How far is Ben from the ball? Each grid square represents a square that is 3 feet long and 3 feet wide. Be sure to show your work.

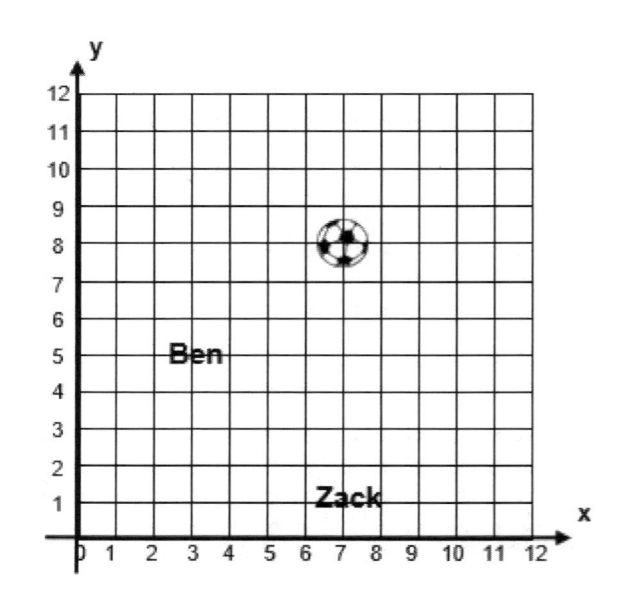

A   21 feet; 17 feet

B   21 feet; 15 feet

C   17 feet; 21 feet

D   23 feet; 15 feet

©Teachers' Treasures Publishing

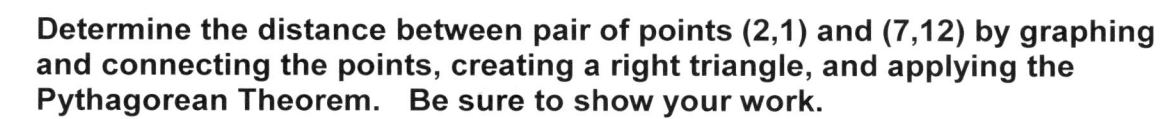

Name_____

PRACTICE

Common Core Standard 8.G.B.8 – Geometry

☐ **Determine the distance between pair of points (2,1) and (7,12) by graphing and connecting the points, creating a right triangle, and applying the Pythagorean Theorem. Be sure to show your work.**

A   12

B $\sqrt{146}$

C   13

D $12\sqrt{2}$

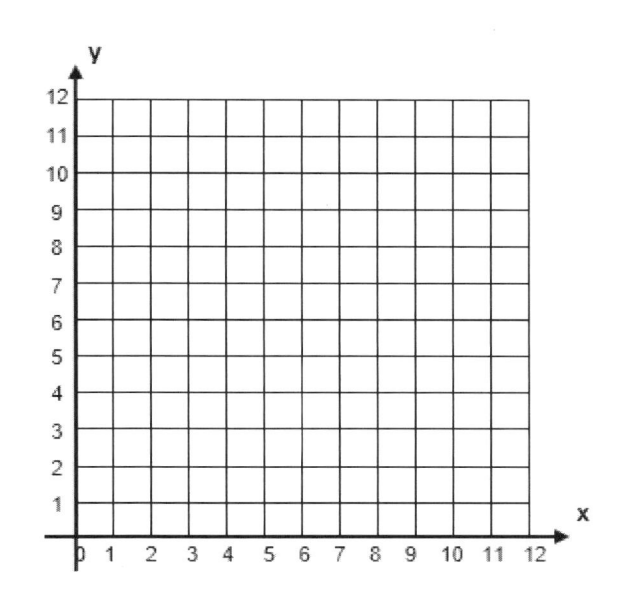

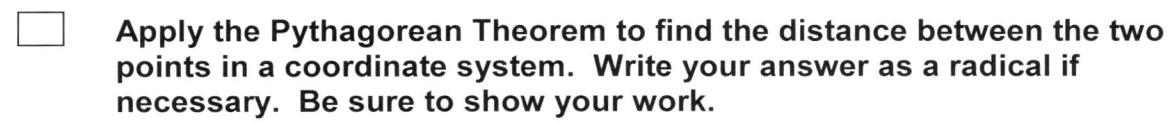

Common Core Standard 8.G.B.8 – Geometry

☐ **Apply the Pythagorean Theorem to find the distance between the two points in a coordinate system. Write your answer as a radical if necessary. Be sure to show your work.**

A   14

B $\sqrt{93}$

C $7\sqrt{2}$

D   3.5

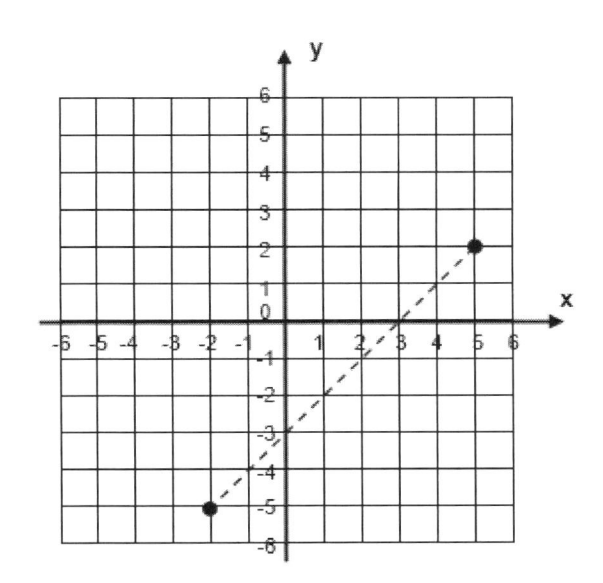

©Teachers' Treasures Publishing

Name_____

PRACTICE

Common Core Standard 8.G.B.8 – Geometry

☐ Find the distance between (−5,3) and (1,−4). Write your answer as a radical if necessary. Be sure to show your work.

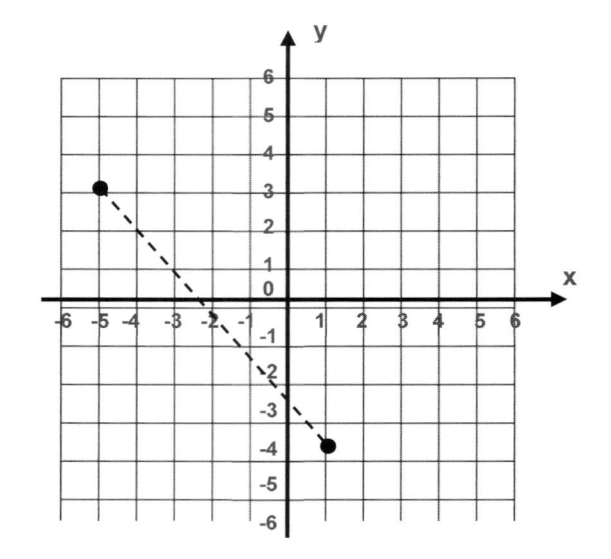

A $\sqrt{97}$

B $\sqrt{85}$

C   9.5

D   9

Common Core Standard 8.G.B.8 – Geometry

☐ Find the distance between (−2,1) and (−4,4). Write your answer as a radical if necessary. Be sure to show your work.

A $\sqrt{13}$

B $\sqrt{14}$

C $\sqrt{15}$

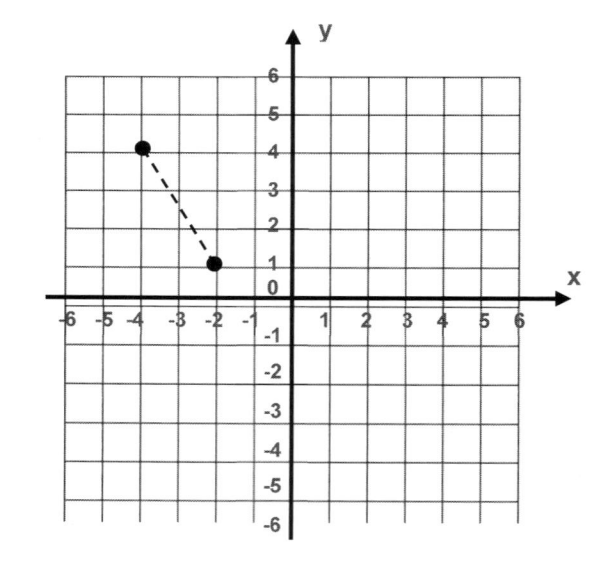

D   4

©Teachers' Treasures Publishing

Name_____

PRACTICE

Common Core Standard 8.G.B.8 – Geometry

☐ Find the length of the line segment whose endpoints are (−3,6) and (5,0). Write your answer as a radical if necessary. Be sure to show your work.

A   12

B $5\sqrt{6}$

C $6\sqrt{5}$

D   10

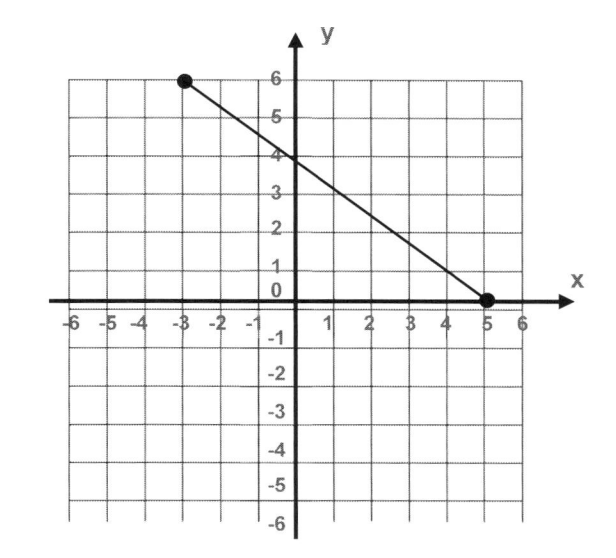

Common Core Standard 8.G.B.8 – Geometry

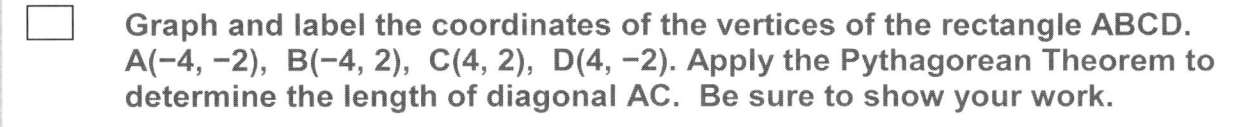

☐ Graph and label the coordinates of the vertices of the rectangle ABCD. A(−4, −2), B(−4, 2), C(4, 2), D(4, −2). Apply the Pythagorean Theorem to determine the length of diagonal AC. Be sure to show your work.

A $4\sqrt{5}$

B   8

C   10

D $4\sqrt{15}$

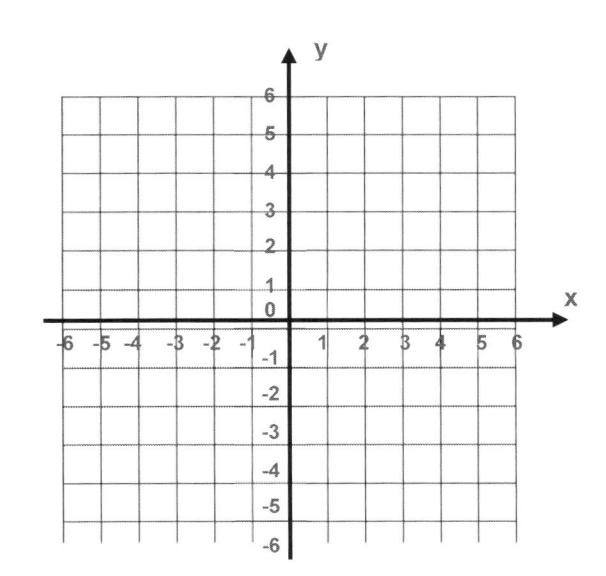

©Teachers' Treasures Publishing

Page 181

Name_____

PRACTICE

Common Core Standard 8.G.B.8 – Geometry

☐ **Justin rides his toy truck 32 inches north and then 8 inches west to get to his toy garage. Determine how far he is from his starting point by graphing and connecting the points, and applying the Pythagorean Theorem. Each grid square represents a square 4 x 4 inches. Be sure to show your work.**

A   33 inches

B   32 inches

C $8\sqrt{17}$ inches

D $7\sqrt{18}$ inches

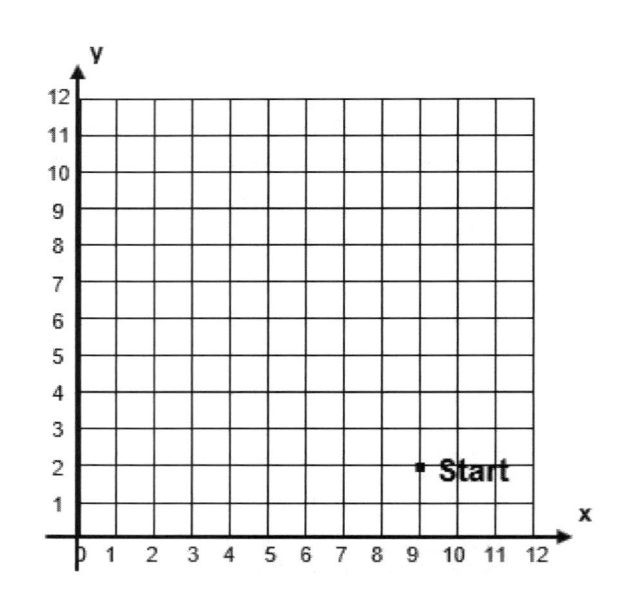

Common Core Standard 8.G.B.8 – Geometry

☐ **Apply the Pythagorean Theorem to find the hypotenuse of the right triangle ABC. Write your answer as a radical if necessary. Each grid square represents a square 1 x 1 inches. Be sure to show your work.**

A $\sqrt{70}$ inches

B $\sqrt{130}$ inches

C   11 inches

D   12 inches

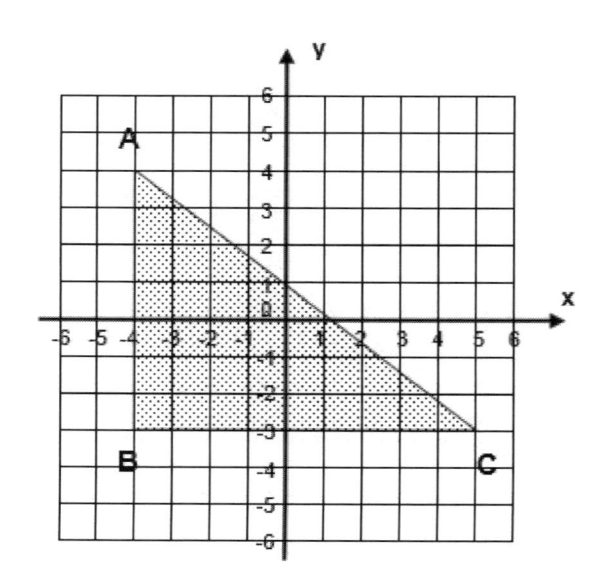

©Teachers' Treasures Publishing

Name_____

ASSESSMENT

Common Core Standard 8.G.B.8 – Geometry

☐ Find the length of the line segment whose endpoints are (0, 0) and (-6, 6). Write your answer as a radical if necessary. Be sure to show your work.

A $6\sqrt{2}$

B $6\sqrt{23}$

C   9

D   8

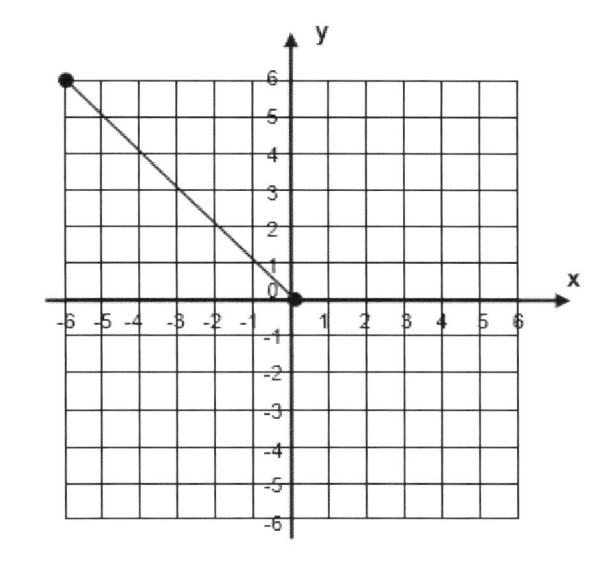

Common Core Standard 8.G.B.8 – Geometry

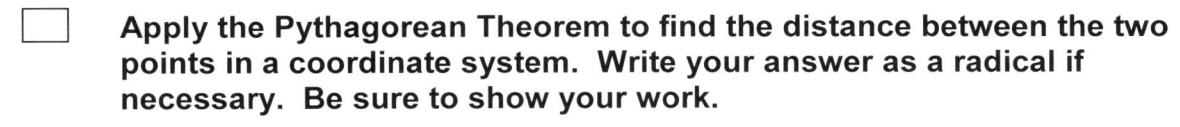

☐ Apply the Pythagorean Theorem to find the distance between the two points in a coordinate system. Write your answer as a radical if necessary. Be sure to show your work.

A   13

B $3\sqrt{10}$

C $\sqrt{90}$

D   10.7

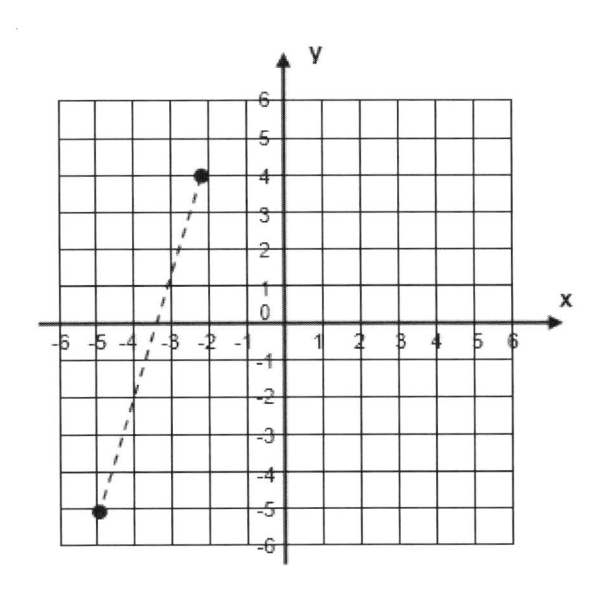

©Teachers' Treasures Publishing

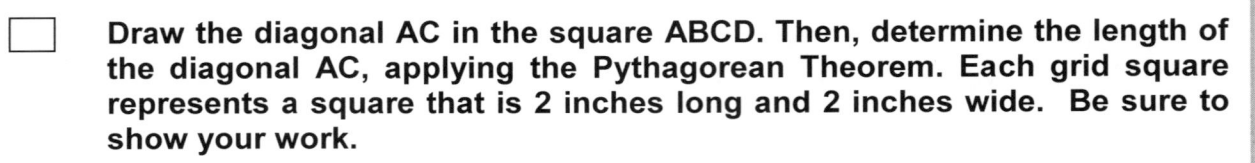

Name_____

ASSESSMENT

Common Core Standard 8.G.B.8 – Geometry

Draw the diagonal AC in the square ABCD. Then, determine the length of the diagonal AC, applying the Pythagorean Theorem. Each grid square represents a square that is 2 inches long and 2 inches wide. Be sure to show your work.

A $12\sqrt{3}$ inches

B $12\sqrt{2}$ inches

C   12 inches

D   15 inches

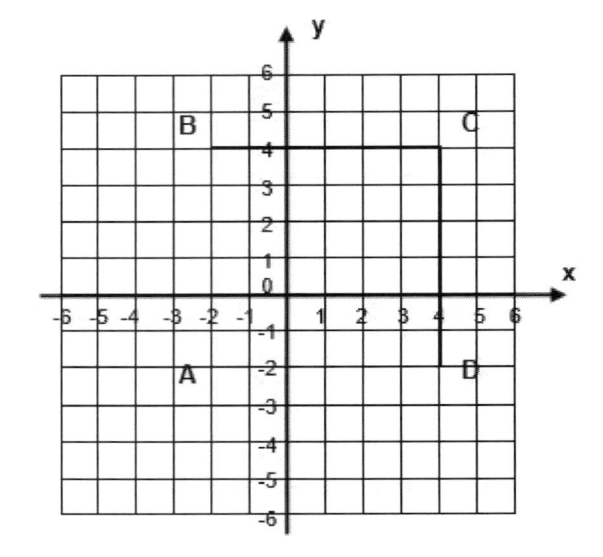

Common Core Standard 8.G.B.8 – Geometry

Cameron walks 12 meters south, then 16 meters east. Determine how far he is from his starting point C by graphing and connecting the points, and applying the Pythagorean Theorem. Each grid square represents a square of 1 x 1 meters. Be sure to show your work.

A   26 meters

B   24 meters

C   22 meters

D   20 meters

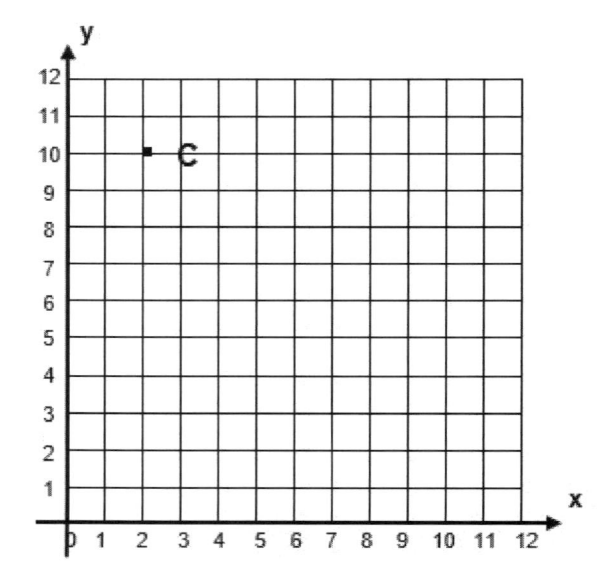

©Teachers' Treasures Publishing

Name_____

DIAGNOSTIC

Common Core Standard 8.G.C.9 – Geometry

☐ A cylindrical container with a radius of 100 cm and a height of 50 cm is filled with oil. What is the volume of oil that container could hold? Use π = 3.14. Be sure to explain your answer.

   A   175000 cm³

   B   1570000 cm³

   C   157000 cm³

   D   1750000 cm³

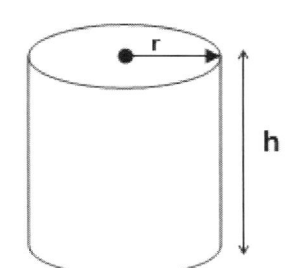

Common Core Standard 8.G.C.9 – Geometry

☐ At the store, Mr. Katz was looking for a new cylindrical water tank for his farm. He could not decide between two white tanks with radium of 3 feet and a height of 2 feet and a blue tank with a radius of 2 feet and a height of 4 feet. Which choice will hold more water? Use π = 3.14. Be sure to show your work.

   A   two white tanks

   B   a blue tank

   C   they have the same volume

   D   two blue tanks

Common Core Standard 8.G.C.9 – Geometry

☐ In math class Irine is asked to find the volume of a cone with a radius of 20 millimeters and a height of 80 millimeters. Karine was asked to find the diameter of a sphere with the same volume as Irine's cone. What is the diameter of Karine's sphere? Use π = 3. Be sure to explain your answer.

   A   200 millimeters

   B   20 millimeters

   C   40 millimeters

   D   100 millimeters

©Teachers' Treasures Publishing

Name_____

DIAGNOSTIC

Common Core Standard 8.G.C.9 – Geometry

☐ Alina and her older sister, Daria, were making conical witch hats for their Halloween party. Alina's hat had a radius of 6 cm and a height of 25 cm, while Daria's hat had a radius of 8 cm and a height of 30 cm. By how much does the volume of Daria's hat differ from the volume of Alina's hat? Use π = 3. Be sure to explain your answer.

A   1120 cm³

B   1200 cm³

C   120 cm³

D   1020 cm³

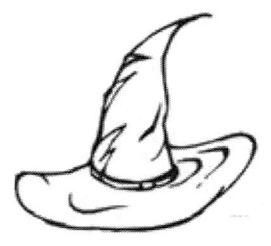

Common Core Standard 8.G.C.9 – Geometry

☐ The Yummy Bakery decided to change the signature cookies, Crispy Cones, to Crunchy Cylinders. How will the volume of the new cookies change if the radius and the height remain the same? Use π = 3.14. Be sure to show your work.

A   increase by 2

B   increase by 3

C   decrease by 2

D   decrease by 3

Common Core Standard 8.G.C.9 – Geometry

☐ Find the volume of air in a beach ball that has a 15 inch diameter. Round the answer to the nearest whole number. Use π = 3.14. Be sure to explain your answer.

A   235 cubic inches

B   1766 cubic inches

C   1324 cubic inches

D   324 cubic inches

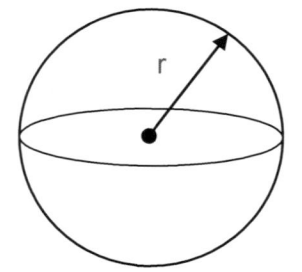

©Teachers' Treasures Publishing

Name_____

PRACTICE

Common Core Standard 8.G.C.9 – Geometry

☐ What is the volume of a regular cylinder that has a radius of 7 cm and a height of 2 cm? Round your answer to the nearest tenth. Use π = 3.14. Be sure to explain your answer.

A   370 cm³

B   370.7 cm³

C   307 cm³

D   307.7 cm³

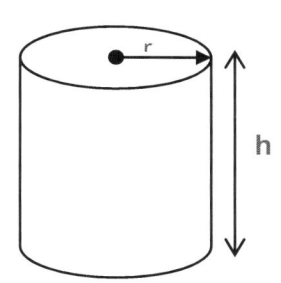

Common Core Standard 8.G.C.9 – Geometry

☐ How many cubic inches of oil can fill 10 cylindrical tanks with a radius of 12 inches and a height of 20 inches? Use π = 3.14. Be sure to show your work.

A   90422 cubic inches

B   90442 cubic inches

C   90432 cubic inches

D   90423 cubic inches

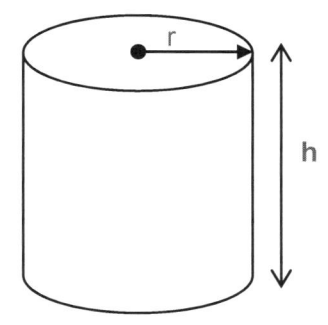

Common Core Standard 8.G.C.9 – Geometry

☐ A cone with a volume of 314 cubic feet has a height of 3 feet. What is its radius? Use π = 3.14. Be sure to explain your answer.

A   12 ft

B   10 ft

C   20 ft

D   16 ft

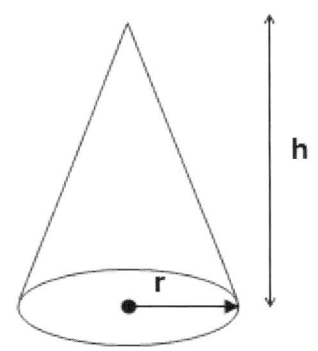

©Teachers' Treasures Publishing

Name_____

PRACTICE

Common Core Standard 8.G.C.9 – Geometry

☐ Ian went to the grocery store to buy canned beans. All the cans had the same height of 9 centimeters, but varied in diameter. By how much will a volume of a can with the diameter of 6 centimeters be greater than a can with the diameter of 4 centimeters? Use π = 3.14. Be sure to explain your answer.

A   565.2 cubic centimeters

B   150 cubic centimeters

C   140.5 cubic centimeters

D   240.2 cubic centimeters

Common Core Standard 8.G.C.9 – Geometry

☐ Find the sum of the volume of a cone with the radius of 1 cm, a height of 5 cm and the volume of a sphere with the radius of 1 cm. Round your answer to the nearest tenth. Use π = 3.14. Be sure to show your work.

A   9.4 cm^3

B   7.4 cm^3

C   9 cm^3

D   7 cm^3

Common Core Standard 8.G.C.9 – Geometry

☐ What is the volume of a sphere with a diameter of 24.8? Round your answer to the nearest whole number. Use π = 3. Be sure to explain your answer.

A   3625.7

B   7626

C   3486

D   6286

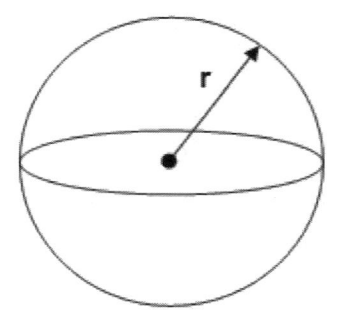

©Teachers' Treasures Publishing

Page 188

Name_____

PRACTICE

Common Core Standard 8.G.C.9 – Geometry

☐ Gloria's favorite type of ice cream is a cone. It has a radius of 6 cm and a height of 12 cm. Find the volume of the ice cream cone in cubic centimeters. Round the answer to the nearest whole number. Use π = 3.14. Be sure to explain your answer.

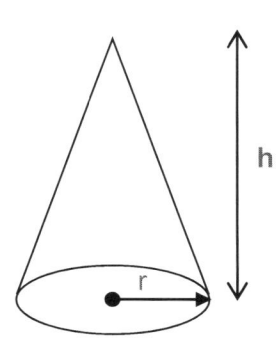

A   430 cm³

B   226 cm³

C   150 cm³

D   452 cm³

Common Core Standard 8.G.C.9 – Geometry

☐ Find the sum of the volume of a cylinder with the radius of 1 in, a height of 5 in and the volume of a sphere of radius 3 in. Use π = 3.14. Be sure to show your work.

A   128.74 cubic inches

B   13.345 cubic inches

C   53.38 cubic inches

D   106.76 cubic inches

Common Core Standard 8.G.C.9 – Geometry

☐ How many times greater will the volume of a sphere with a radius of 15 be if the radius is doubled? Use π = 3.14. Be sure to explain your answer.

A   2

B   4

C   6

D   8

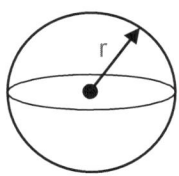

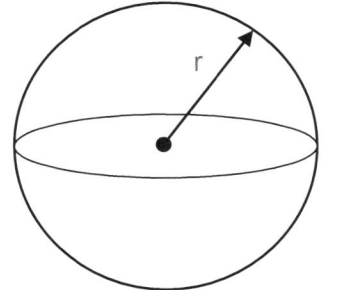

©Teachers' Treasures Publishing

Name_____

PRACTICE

Common Core Standard 8.G.C.9 – Geometry

☐ A cone has a height of 6 units. The diameter of the base is 20 units. What is the volume of the cone? Use π = 3.14. Be sure to explain your answer.

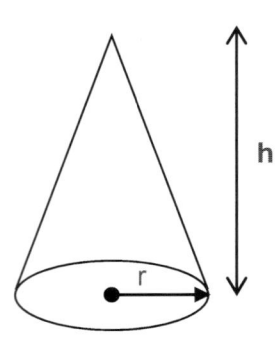

A   753.6 cubic units

B   1256 cubic units

C   2512 cubic units

D   628 cubic units

Common Core Standard 8.G.C.9 – Geometry

☐ Find the difference between the volume of a cylinder with a radius of 10 cm, a height of 50 cm and the volume of a sphere with a radius of 10 cm. Use π = 3. Be sure to show your work.

A   5000 cm^3

B   1000 cm^3

C   11000 cm^3

D   14000 cm^3

Common Core Standard 8.G.C.9 – Geometry

☐ How many milliliters of liquid are needed to fill a cylindrical can with a radius of 4 centimeters and a height of 4.5 centimeters? Note: One milliliter is equivalent to one cubic centimeter of liquid. Use π = 3.14. Be sure to explain your answer.

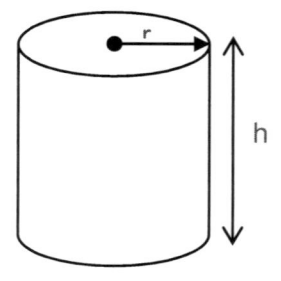

A   42.39 cubic centimeter

B   190.755 cubic centimeter

C   226.08 cubic centimeter

D   278.74 cubic centimeter

©Teachers' Treasures Publishing

Name_____

ASSESSMENT

Common Core Standard 8.G.C.9 – Geometry

☐ Find the sum of the volume of a cone with the radius of 5 inches, the height of 5 inches and the volume of a sphere with the radius of 5 inches. Use π = 3. Be sure to explain your answer.

A   625 cubic inches

B   1000 cubic inches

C   1250 cubic inches

D   925 cubic inches

Common Core Standard 8.G.C.9 – Geometry

☐ A carpenter drilled a hole in a wooden block. Find the volume of the hole if it has a diameter of 16 mm and a depth of 10 mm. Use π = 3.14. Be sure to show your work.

A   251.2 mm³

B   2512 mm³

C   2009.6 mm³

D   1920 mm³

Common Core Standard 8.G.C.9 – Geometry

☐ Find the volume of air in a balloon that has an 18 inch diameter. Assume that the air balloon is a sphere. Round the answer to the nearest whole number. Use π = 3.14. Be sure to explain your answer.

A   2826 cubic inches

B   3052 cubic inches

C   1296 cubic inches

D   12.96 cubic inches

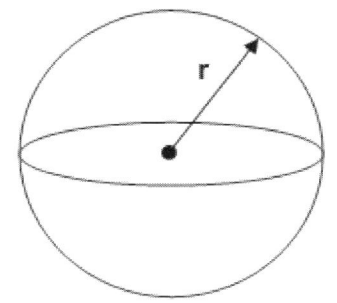

©Teachers' Treasures Publishing

Name_____

ASSESSMENT

Common Core Standard 8.G.C.9 – Geometry

☐ How many times greater will the volume of a sphere with a radius of 15 be if the radius is tripled? Use π = 3.14. Be sure to explain your answer.

    A   3

    B   6

    C   9

    D   27

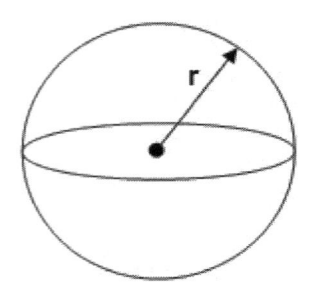

Common Core Standard 8.G.C.9 – Geometry

☐ Workers have to fill a big cylindrical container with a mixture from small cylindrical bottles. The small cylindrical bottles have a radius of 5 inches and a height of 10 inches. How many small bottles are needed to fill the big container, which has a radius of 20 inches and a height of 55 inches? Use π = 3.14. Be sure to show your work.

    A   66

    B   77

    C   88

    D   99

Common Core Standard 8.G.C.9 – Geometry

☐ In math class Naseem is asked to find the volume of a cylinder with a diameter of 12 millimeters and a height of 33 millimeters. Tim was asked to draw a cone with the same volume and radius. What is the height of Tim's cone? Use π = 3. Be sure to explain your answer.

    A   37.5 millimeters

    B $\sqrt{75}$ millimeters

    C   108 millimeters

    D   99 millimeters

©Teachers' Treasures Publishing

Name_____

DIAGNOSTIC

Common Core Standard 8.SP.A.1 – Statistics & Probability

☐ The scatter plot shown gives the relationship between the demand and the price of consumer goods. What correlation does the graph follow? Be sure to explain your answer.

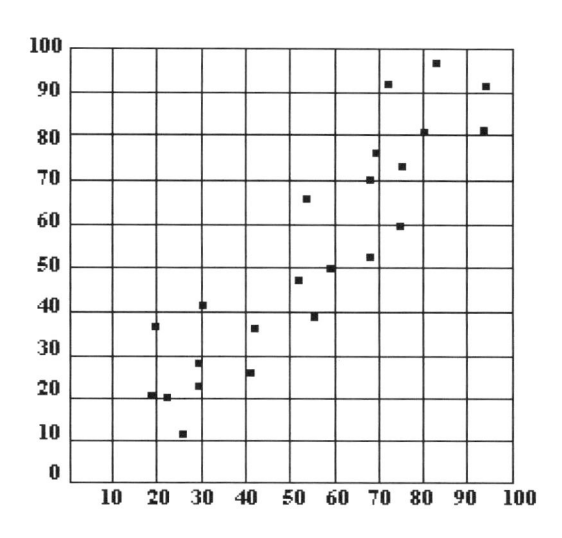

Common Core Standard 8.SP.A.1 – Statistics & Probability

☐ Does the scatter plot below have an outlier? If yes, identify its approximate coordinates? Be sure to explain your answer.

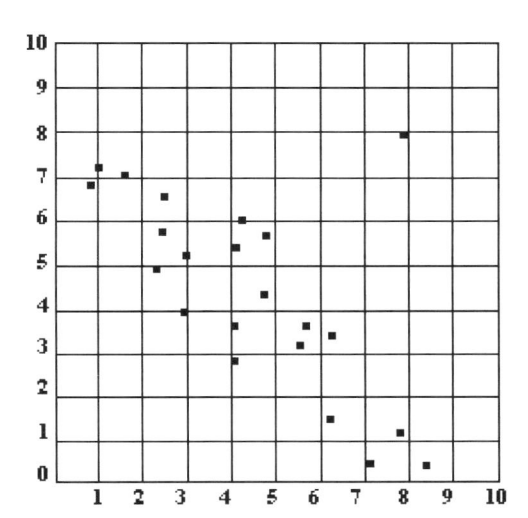

©Teachers' Treasures Publishing

Name_____

DIAGNOSTIC

Use the graph below to answer the questions.

[Scatter plot with Hours on x-axis (1-10) and Dollars on y-axis (0-100)]

Common Core Standard 8.SP.A.1 – Statistics & Probability

☐   The scatter plot shows a relationship between hours worked as a nanny and money earned. Which best describes the relationship between the variables? Be sure to explain your answer.

   A   non-linear, positive correlation

   B   linear, no correlation

   C   linear, positive correlation

   D   linear, negative correlation

Common Core Standard 8.SP.A.1 – Statistics & Probability

☐   Does the scatter plot have an outlier? If yes, identify its approximate coordinates? Be sure to explain your answer.

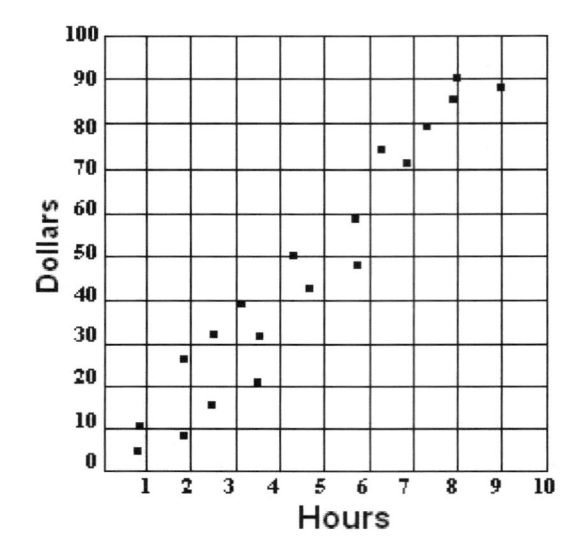

_____

_____

_____

_____

©Teachers' Treasures Publishing

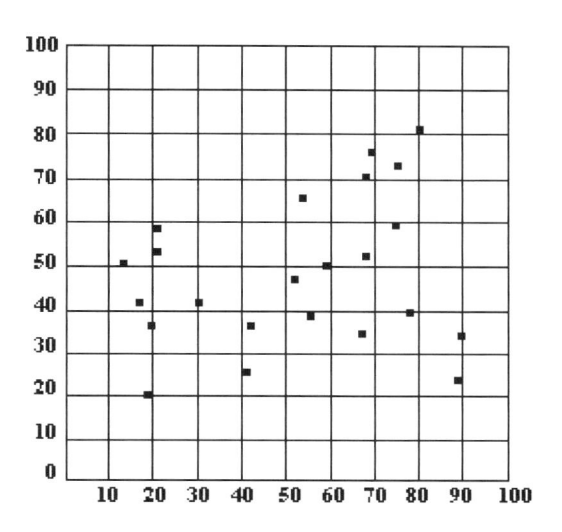

Name_____

PRACTICE

Common Core Standard 8.SP.A.1 – Statistics & Probability

☐ Does this scatter plot show a positive correlation, a negative correlation, or no correlation? Be sure to explain your answer.

_____

_____

_____

_____

_____

Common Core Standard 8.SP.A.1 – Statistics & Probability

☐ The table below shows 10 years of data on the sales of discount boots and sweaters at Bon Boutique. Describe the correlation between the number of sales of boots and sweaters. Be sure to explain your answer.

Years	1	2	3	4	5	6	7	8
Boots	40	43	21	88	100	67	70	71
Sweaters	57	53	68	35	33	50	49	49

A   positive correlation

B   negative correlation

C   no correlation

D   none of the above

©Teachers' Treasures Publishing

Name_____

PRACTICE

Use the graph below to answer the questions.

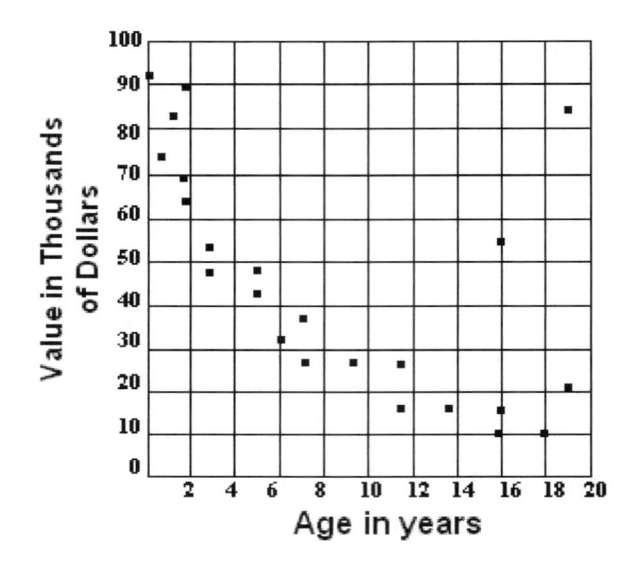

[Scatter plot: Value in Thousands of Dollars vs. Age in years]

Common Core Standard 8.SP.A.1 – Statistics & Probability

☐ This scatter plot shows the relationship between the age of a car and its value. Which best describes the relationship between the variables? Be sure to explain your answer.

   A   non-linear, positive correlation

   B   linear, no correlation

   C   linear, positive correlation

   D   non-linear, negative correlation

Common Core Standard 8.SP.A.1 – Statistics & Probability

☐ Identity any points that appear to be outliers. If found, write their coordinates. Be sure to show your work.

   A   no outliers

   B   (16, 55); (19, 95)

   C   (16, 55); (19, 85)

   D   (18, 55); (19, 95)

©Teachers' Treasures Publishing

Name_____

PRACTICE

Common Core Standard 8.SP.A.1 – Statistics & Probability

☐ Does this scatter plot show a positive correlation, a negative correlation, or no correlation? Be sure to explain your answer.

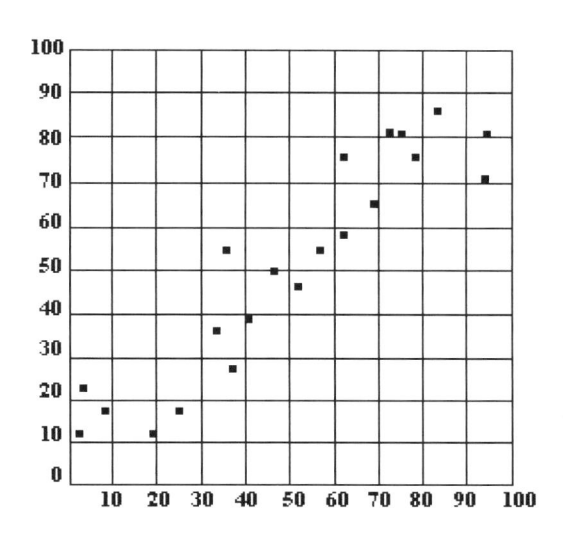

_____

_____

_____

_____

_____

Common Core Standard 8.SP.A.1 – Statistics & Probability

☐ The table below shows the relationship between the number of beverages and sandwiches sold at the cafeteria. Which of the scatter plots best describe the table? Be sure to explain your answer.

Months	1	2	3	4	5	6	7	8
Beverages	32	43	25	18	52	67	70	71
Sandwiches	37	48	31	25	63	70	77	75

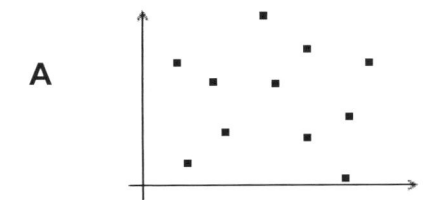

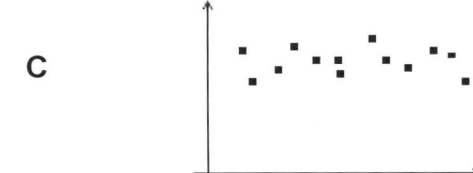

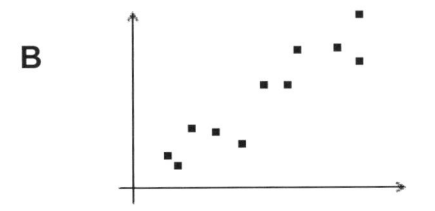

A

B

C

D

©Teachers' Treasures Publishing

Page 197

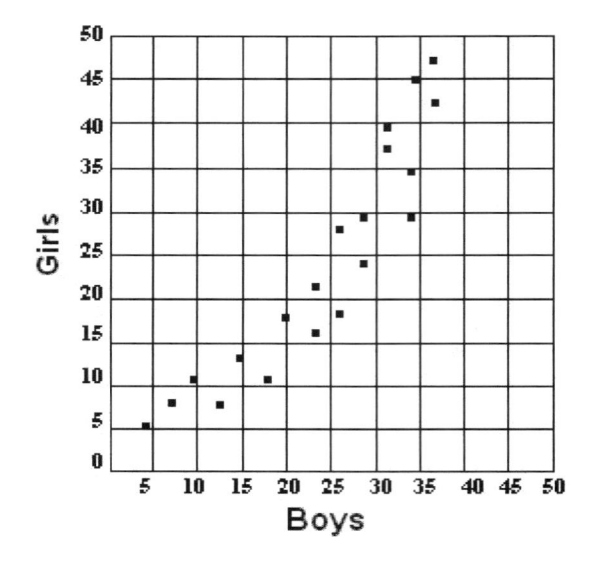

Name_____

PRACTICE

Use the graph below to answer the questions.

[Scatter plot with Boys on x-axis (0-50) and Girls on y-axis (0-50)]

Common Core Standard 8.SP.A.1 – Statistics & Probability

☐ The scatter plot shows a relationship between the number of boys and girls in different grades of a school. Which best describes the relationship between the variables? Be sure to explain your answer.

A   non-linear, positive correlation

B   linear, no correlation

C   linear, positive correlation

D   linear, negative correlation

Common Core Standard 8.SP.A.1 – Statistics & Probability

☐ Does the scatter plot have an outlier? If yes, identify its approximate coordinates? Be sure to explain your answer.

_____
_____
_____
_____

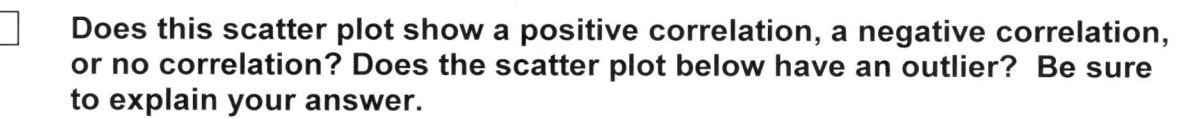

Name_____

ASSESSMENT

Common Core Standard 8.SP.A.1 – Statistics & Probability

☐ Does this scatter plot show a positive correlation, a negative correlation, or no correlation? Does the scatter plot below have an outlier? Be sure to explain your answer.

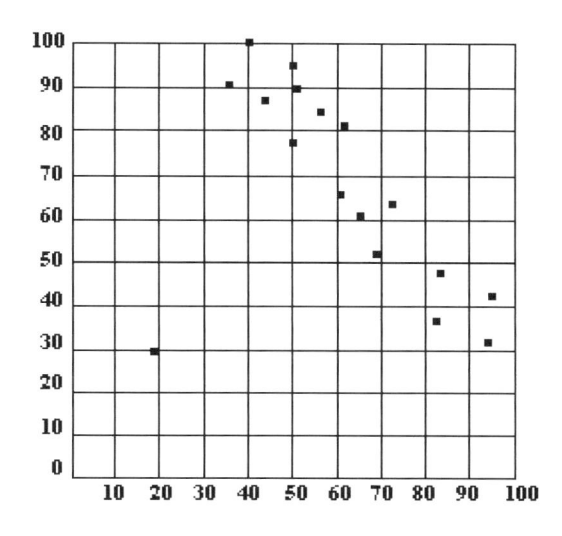

_____

_____

_____

_____

_____

_____

Common Core Standard 8.SP.A.1 – Statistics & Probability

☐ Hester and Martin recorded their weight on the first day of each new year for the last 8 years. Describe the correlation between the weight of Martin and Hester. Be sure to explain your answer.

Years	1	2	3	4	5	6	7	8
Hester	118	120	126	134	128	122	114	110
Martin	130	134	128	145	150	143	147	155

A   positive correlation

B   negative correlation

C   no correlation

D   none of the above

©Teachers' Treasures Publishing

Name_____

ASSESSMENT

Use the graph below to answer the questions.

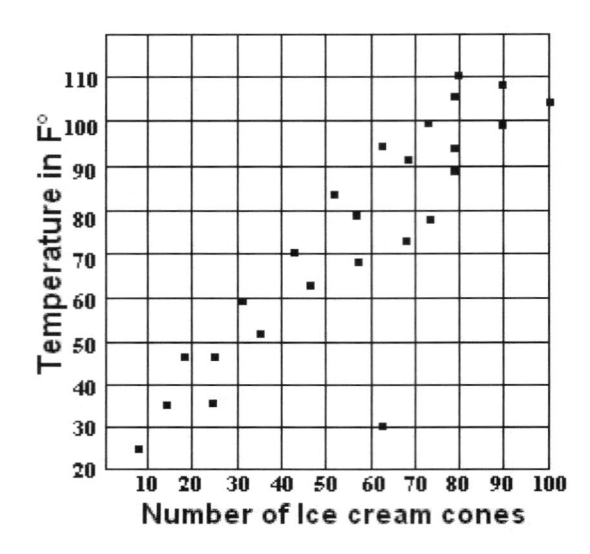

[Scatter plot: Temperature in F° (y-axis, 20–110) vs. Number of Ice cream cones (x-axis, 10–100)]

Common Core Standard 8.SP.A.1 – Statistics & Probability

☐ This scatter plot shows a relationship between the outdoor temperature and the number of ice cream cones sold in different stores. Which best describes the relationship between the variables? Be sure to explain your answer.

A   non-linear, positive correlation

B   linear, no correlation

C   linear, positive correlation

D   linear, negative correlation

Common Core Standard 8.SP.A.1 – Statistics & Probability

☐ Identify any points that appear to be outliers. If found, write their coordinates. Be sure to explain your answer.

A   no outliers

B   (40, 100)

C   (10, 25)

D   (63, 30)

©Teachers' Treasures Publishing

Name_____

DIAGNOSTIC

Common Core Standard 8.SP.A.2 – Statistics & Probability

☐ Usually receptionists spend about 2 minutes routing each incoming phone call. Is there a positive, negative or no relationship between the phone calls routed and the minutes on the phone? Be sure to explain your answer.

Receptionist	Number of calls	Minutes
Louis	2	7
Scott	7	14
Helena	12	46
William	4	6
Olivia	9	49
Julian	16	50
Viola	6	24

_____

_____

Common Core Standard 8.SP.A.2 – Statistics & Probability

☐ Is there a positive, negative or no relationship between the women's shoe size and their heights? Be sure to explain your answer.

Women	Shoe size	Height, cm
Anita	8½	166
Barbara	7	160
Susan	5½	154
Kelly	9	172
Olga	6½	165
Janet	8	169
Patricia	10	181

_____

_____

©Teachers' Treasures Publishing

Name_____

DIAGNOSTIC

Use the graph below to answer the questions.

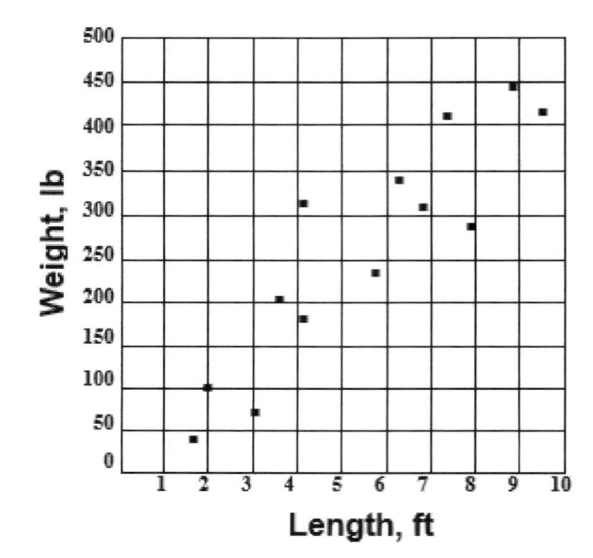

Common Core Standard 8.SP.A.2 – Statistics & Probability

☐ The scatter plot shows the weights and lengths of 10 alligators. Draw a line of best fit. Use your line to predict the length of an alligator that is 300 pounds. Be sure to explain your answer.

    A   3 feet

    B   8 feet

    C   7 feet

    D   6 feet

Common Core Standard 8.SP.A.2 – Statistics & Probability

☐ Describe the relation between weight and length. Is there a positive, negative or no relationship shown on the scatter plot? Be sure to explain your answer.

_____

_____

_____

_____

©Teachers' Treasures Publishing

Name_____

PRACTICE

Common Core Standard 8.SP.A.2 – Statistics & Probability

☐ The scatter plot shows the relationship between the time spent on video games and math grades. Draw a line of best fit. Use the line to determine if there is a positive, negative or no relationship between the variables. Be sure to explain your answer.

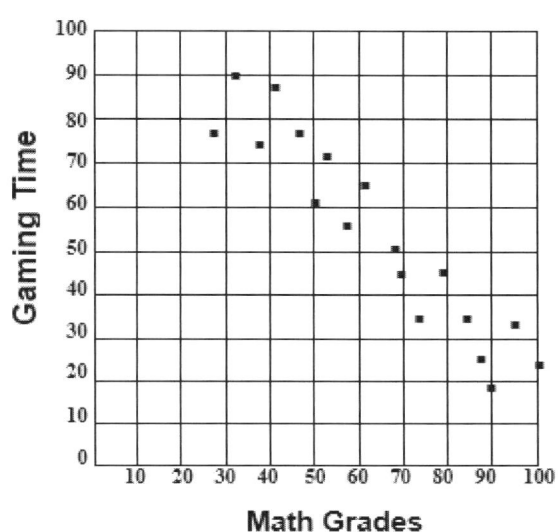

_____
_____
_____
_____

Common Core Standard 8.SP.A.2 – Statistics & Probability

☐ Is there a positive, negative or no relationship between the sale of water bottles in a local store and the outdoor temperature over the course of seven months? Be sure to explain your answer.

Month	Number of bottles	Temperature, °F
February	451	51
March	493	63
April	487	68
May	531	79
June	739	88
July	882	91
August	948	99

_____
_____
_____

©Teachers' Treasures Publishing

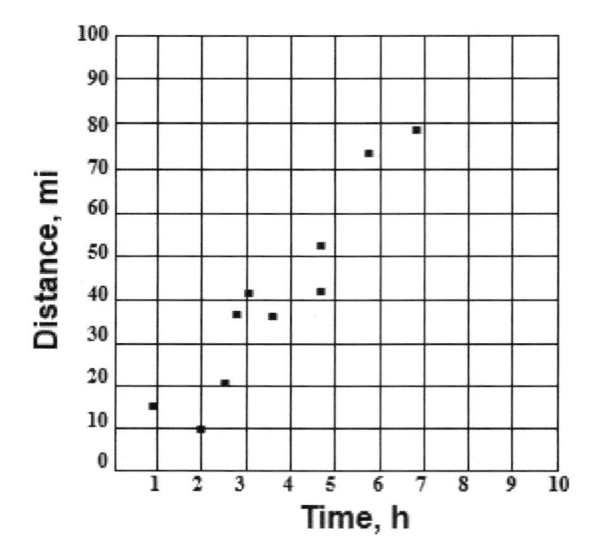

Name_____

PRACTICE

Use the graph below to answer the questions.

[Scatter plot with x-axis "Time, h" from 1 to 10 and y-axis "Distance, mi" from 0 to 100]

Common Core Standard 8.SP.A.2 – Statistics & Probability

☐ The scatter plot shows the distances ridden by different bicyclists over time. Draw a line of best fit. Use the line to estimate the distance covered in 8 hours. Be sure to explain your answer.

A   80 miles

B   76 miles

C   93 miles

D   67 miles

Common Core Standard 8.SP.A.2 – Statistics & Probability

☐ Is there a positive, negative or no relationship shown on the scatter plot? Be sure to explain your answer.

_____

_____

_____

_____

©Teachers' Treasures Publishing

Name_____

PRACTICE

Common Core Standard 8.SP.A.2 – Statistics & Probability

☐ Which of the following graphs best represents the line of best fit? Be sure to explain your answer.

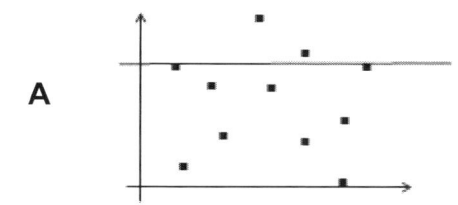

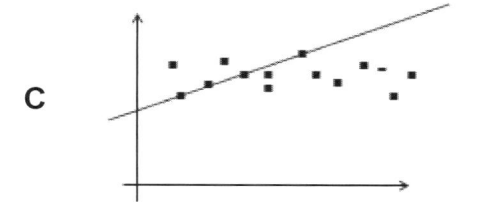

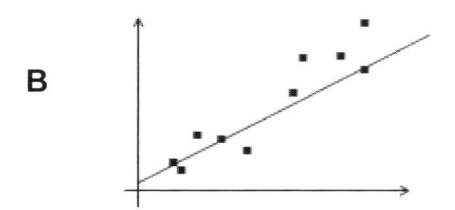

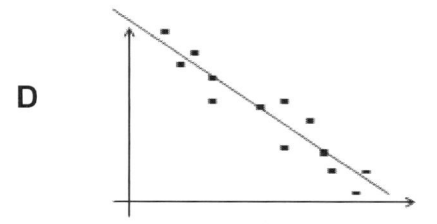

A

B

C

D

Common Core Standard 8.SP.A.2 – Statistics & Probability

☐ Make a scatter plot of the data in the table. Draw a line of best fit. Is there a positive, negative or no relationship between the variables? Be sure to explain your answer.

Day	1	2	3	4	5	6	7	8
Cups sold	11	18	24	35	5	42	39	50
Money earned	27	44	60	84	10	98	90	100

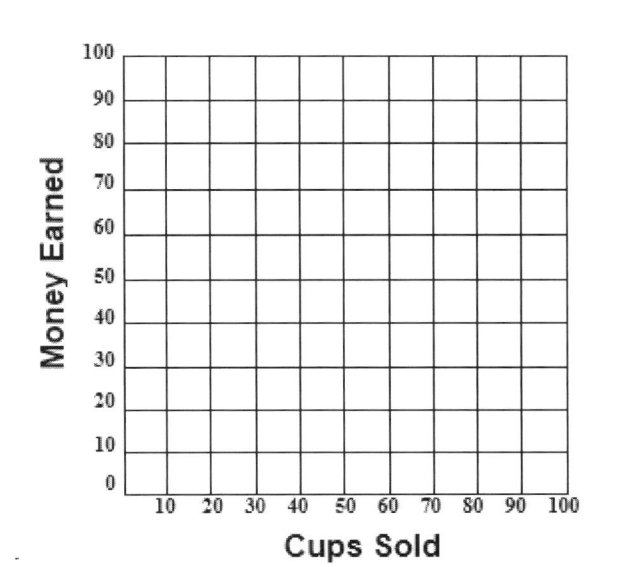

_____

_____

_____

_____

_____

©Teachers' Treasures Publishing

Page 205

Name_____

PRACTICE

Use the graph below to answer the questions.

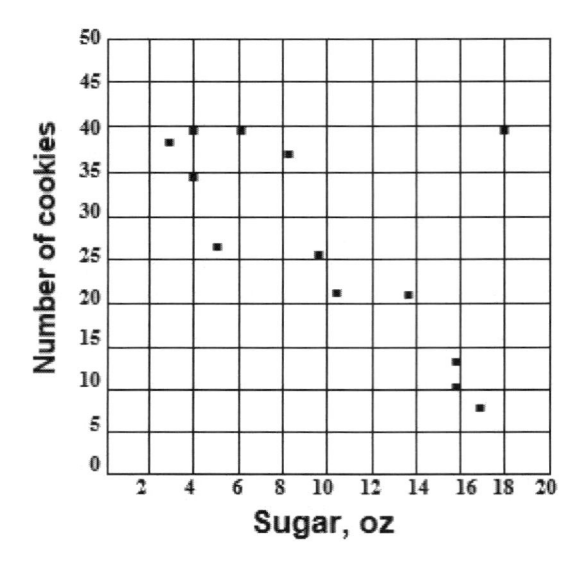

[Scatter plot: Number of cookies vs Sugar, oz]

Common Core Standard 8.SP.A.2 – Statistics & Probability

☐   Bakers in Good Bakes use a 20 oz pack of sugar for each kind of cookie a day. The scatter plot shows the relationship between the amount of sugar left in the pack and the number of different kinds of cookies made. Draw a line of best fit. Use the line to predict the amount of sugar left when 30 cookies baked. Be sure to explain your answer.

A   8 oz

B   2 oz

C   16 oz

D   4 oz

Common Core Standard 8.SP.A.2 – Statistics & Probability

☐   Is there a positive, negative or no relationship between the number of different kinds of cookies baked and sugar left in the pack? Be sure to explain your answer.

_____

_____

_____

©Teachers' Treasures Publishing

Name_____

ASSESSMENT

Common Core Standard 8.SP.A.2 – Statistics & Probability

☐   Is there a positive, negative or no relationship between the speed and travel time? Be sure to explain your answer.

Speed, mph	Travel time, hr
20	10
45	4.5
60	3.5
15	14
35	6

_____

_____

Common Core Standard 8.SP.A.2 – Statistics & Probability

☐   Make a scatter plot of the data in the table. Draw a line of best fit. Is there a positive, negative or no relationship between the variables? Be sure to explain your answer.

Car	1	2	3	4	5	6	7	8
Distance Travelled	102	198	154	16	72	47	128	110
Gas Left	18	9	8	10	12	5	3	10

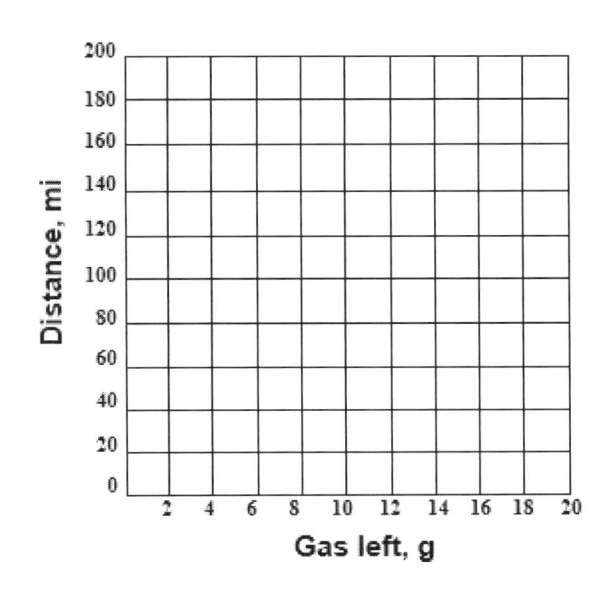

_____

_____

_____

_____

_____

©Teachers' Treasures Publishing

Name_____

ASSESSMENT

Use the graph below to answer the questions.

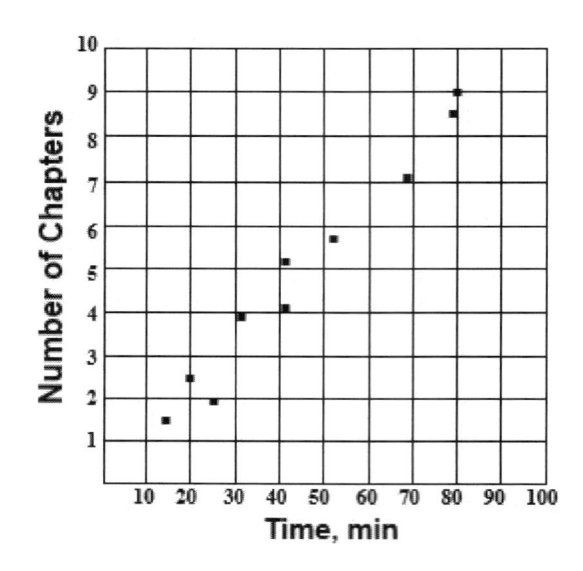

[Scatter plot: Number of Chapters vs Time, min]

Common Core Standard 8.SP.A.2 – Statistics & Probability

☐ The scatter plot shows the relationship between the number of chapters of a book read and the time spent on it by 10 students. Draw a line of best fit. Use the line to predict the time spent on reading 4 chapters. Be sure to explain your answer.

    A   35 min

    B   45 min

    C   23 min

    D   50 min

Common Core Standard 8.SP.A.2 – Statistics & Probability

☐ Is there a positive, negative or no relationship shown on the scatter plot? Be sure to explain your answer.

_____

_____

_____

©Teachers' Treasures Publishing

Name_____

DIAGNOSTIC

Common Core Standard 8.SP.A.3 – Statistics & Probability

☐ The table below represents the relationship between the people invited to an outdoor picnic and the money needed. Make a scatter plot of the data. Draw a line of best fit. Write an equation of the line of best fit. If the trend continued, about how much money is needed for 55 guests? Be sure to explain your answer.

Host	Number of guests	Dollars
Frank	7	89
Alexander	17	152
George	10	102
Peter	19	239
Dmitri	25	183
Mark	41	380
Chris	37	302
Walter	28	242

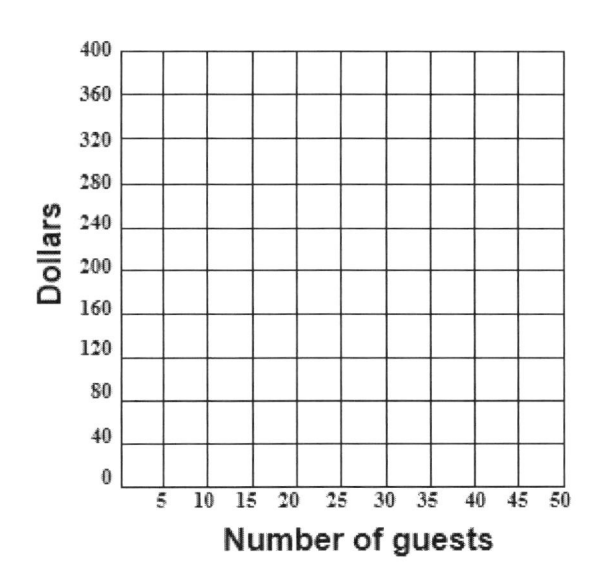

A   y = 40 + 4x; 260

B   y = 20 + 8x; 460

C   y = 280 − 2x; 170

D   y = 5x + 80; 355

©Teachers' Treasures Publishing

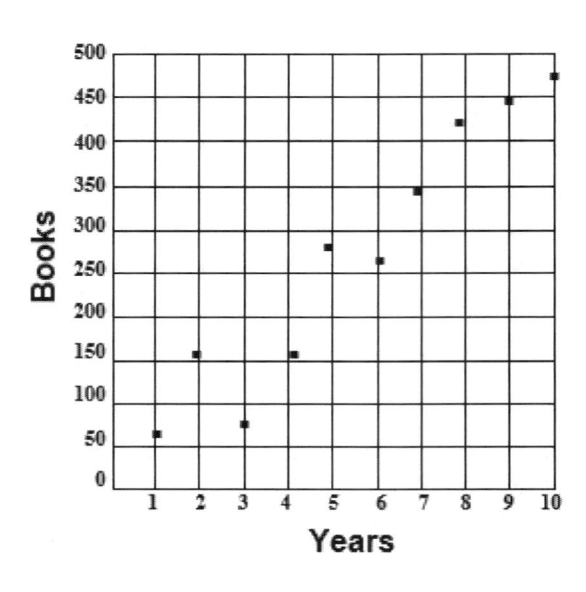

Name_____

DIAGNOSTIC

Use the graph below to answer the questions.

[Scatter plot showing Books (y-axis, 0-500) vs Years (x-axis, 1-10)]

Common Core Standard 8.SP.A.3 – Statistics & Probability

☐ The scatter plot shows the number of cooking books sold at a local store from 2001 to 2010. Draw a line of best fit. What is the equation of the line of best fit? Be sure to explain your answer.

A y = 65 + 25x

B y = 25x

C y = 100 + 50x

D y = 50x

Common Core Standard 8.SP.A.3 – Statistics & Probability

☐ What does the slope of the line mean in the context of this situation? Be sure to explain your answer.

A each book costs $25

B sales decreased over time

C sales increased by 50 books yearly

D sales increased 50 times yearly

©Teachers' Treasures Publishing

Page 210

Name_____

PRACTICE

Common Core Standard 8.SP.A.3 – Statistics & Probability

☐ Use the table below to write an equation that represents the data. Be sure to show your work.

Days	1	2	3	4	5	6	7
Number of cakes	12	37	19	31	17	23	29
Number of slices	84	259	133	217	119	161	203

A $y = 9x$

B $y = 5 + 7x$

C $y = 7x$

D $y = 50 - 9x$

Common Core Standard 8.SP.A.3 – Statistics & Probability

☐ Based on the previous response, choose the statement that best interprets the slope of the equation. Be sure to explain your answer.

A   cakes are cut into 9 slices

B   each cake is cut evenly

C   the number of slices is always greater than the number of cakes

D   each cake is cut into 7 equal slices

Common Core Standard 8.SP.A.3 – Statistics & Probability

☐ Choose an equation showing that each table (y) will serve 2 cakes (x). Be sure to explain your answer.

A $y = 2x$

B $y = x$

C $x = 2y$

D $y = \dfrac{1}{2} x$

©Teachers' Treasures Publishing   Page 211

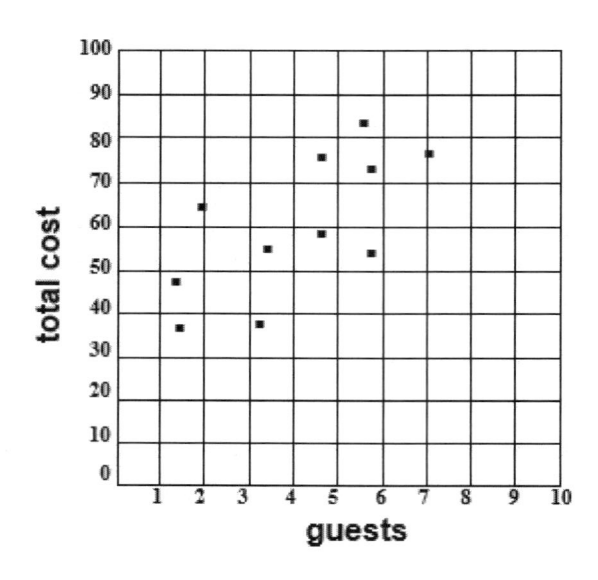

Name _____

PRACTICE

Use the graph below to answer the questions.

[Scatter plot showing total cost vs guests, with points roughly between 1-7 guests and costs from about 35 to 85]

Common Core Standard 8.SP.A.3 – Statistics & Probability

☐ The scatter plot shows the relationship between the guests invited to the birthday party and the total cost with an additional purchase of the birthday cake. Draw a line of best fit. What is the equation of the line of best fit? Be sure to explain your answer.

A   y = 10 + 25x

B   y = 25x − 20

C   y = 25 + 9x

D   y = 15x

Common Core Standard 8.SP.A.3 – Statistics & Probability

☐ Choose the answer that best interprets the y-intercept of the function in context to this situation. Be sure to explain your answer.

A   the person will pay only for birthday cake

B   the person won't pay any payment

C   the person will pay for himself

D   probably the person will pay cancellation fee

©Teachers' Treasures Publishing

Name_____

PRACTICE

Common Core Standard 8.SP.A.3 – Statistics & Probability

☐ Graphs below show different plans of salesmen's salaries, where the x axis represents sales and the y axis represents the salaries. Which of the graphs represents a plan in which the salesmen can receive no income? Be sure to explain your answer.

A

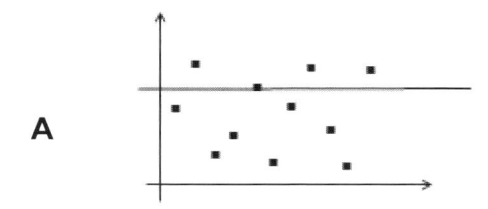

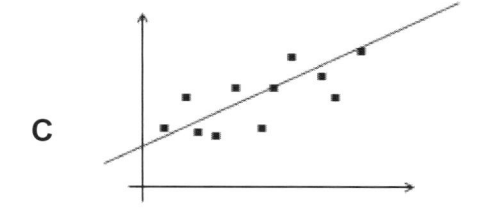

B

C

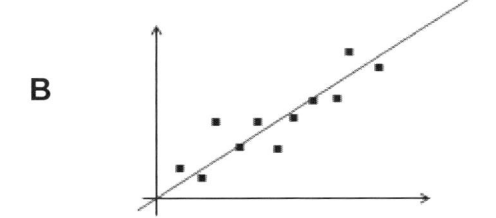

D

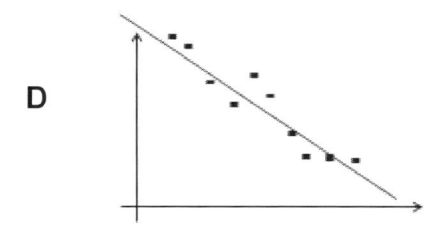

Common Core Standard 8.SP.A.3 – Statistics & Probability

☐ The table below shows the relationship between the number of seed packs planted and the total number of flowers grown. Find the equation that represents the data. What does the y-intercept of the function mean in context to this situation? Be sure to explain your answer.

Season	1	2	3	4	5	6
Seed packs	12	19	22	13	20	17
Flowers grown	24	38	44	26	40	34

A   3 plants can grow with every seed packs

B   more seed packs planted, more flowers grown

C   no seeds planted, no flowers grown

D   number of flowers grown can vary

©Teachers' Treasures Publishing

Name_______________________________

PRACTICE

Use the graph below to answer the questions.

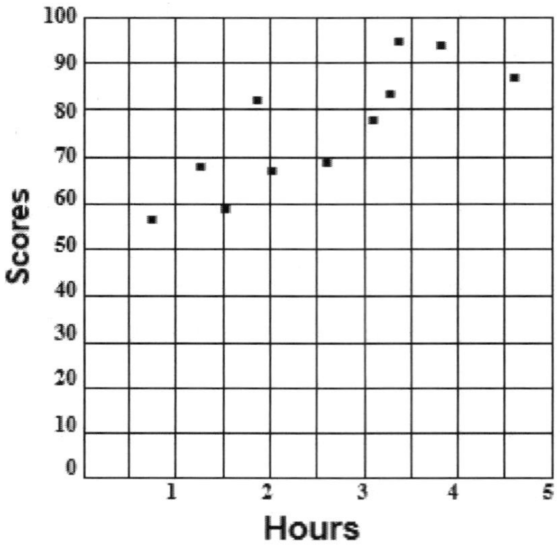

Common Core Standard 8.SP.A.3 – Statistics & Probability

☐ **The scatter plot shows the number of hours spent studying for a French exam and the final test score. Draw in the line of best fit. What is the equation for the line of best fit? Be sure to explain your answer.**

A y = 50 + 10x

B y = 40x − 100

C y = 50 + 30x

D y = 4x + 60

Common Core Standard 8.SP.A.3 – Statistics & Probability

☐ **Predict the grade for a student who studied for more than 5 hours. Be sure to explain your answer.**

A 120

B 115

C 100

D 95

©Teachers' Treasures Publishing

Name_____

ASSESSMENT

Common Core Standard 8.SP.A.3 – Statistics & Probability

☐ The table below represents the relationship between the Christmas gifts and the money left in a wallet. Make a scatter plot of the data. Draw a line of best fit. Write an equation of the line of best fit. Be sure to explain your answer.

Person	Number of gifts	Dollars left
Sally	9	57
Charlie	2	45
Nelson	5	149
Martin	8	109
Bradley	3	210
Judith	7	153
Eli	5	199
Alyx	6	117
Gordon	2	286

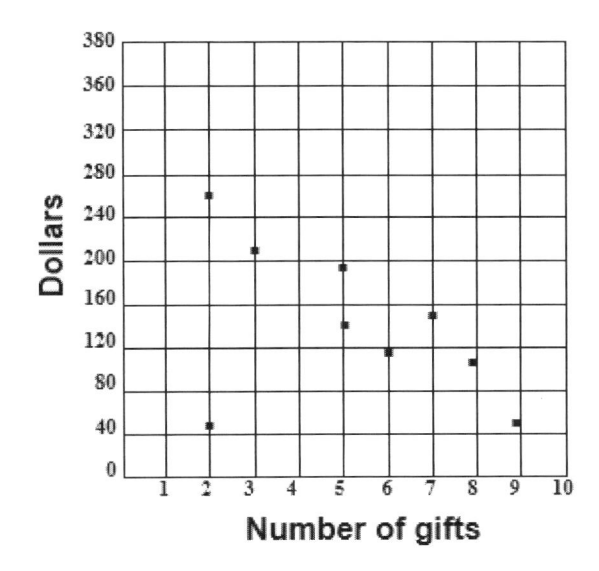

A $y = 250 + 15x$

B $y = 320 - 25x$

C $y = 400 - 20x$

D $y = 30x$

©Teachers' Treasures Publishing

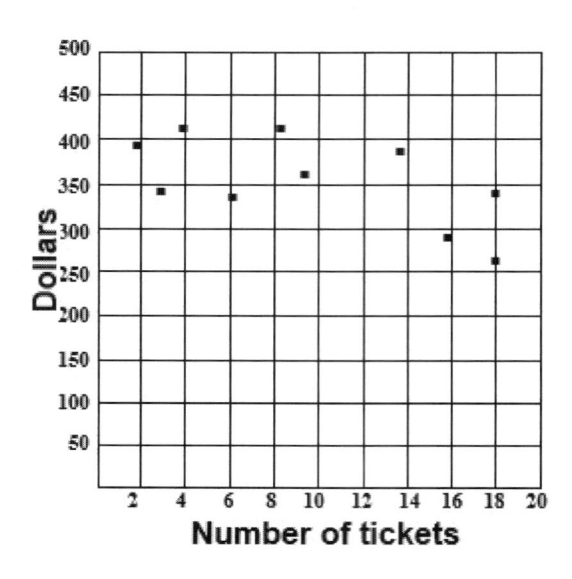

Name _____

ASSESSMENT

Use the graph below to answer the questions.

[Scatter plot: y-axis labeled "Dollars" from 0 to 500, x-axis labeled "Number of tickets" from 2 to 20]

Common Core Standard 8.SP.A.3 – Statistics & Probability

☐ Once a week Larry buys lottery tickets using his weekly income. The scatter plot shows the relationship between the number of lottery tickets and Larry's budget. Draw a line of best fit. What is the equation of the line of best fit? Be sure to explain your answer.

A $y = 2x + 350$

B $y = 500 + 1.5x$

C $y = 600 - 3x$

D $y = 400 - 4x$

Common Core Standard 8.SP.A.3 – Statistics & Probability

☐ What does the y-intercept of the line mean in context to this situation? Be sure to explain your answer.

A   the more tickets he buys, the less money he has left

B   he didn't spend any money on lottery tickets

C   number of lottery tickets can vary

D   he pays $4 for each ticket

©Teachers' Treasures Publishing

Name_____

DIAGNOSTIC

Common Core Standard 8.SP.A.4 – Statistics & Probability

☐ The table below shows the Hispanic populations in North Carolina cities (2015). Calculate the percentage of the Hispanic population in Monroe. Round to the nearest whole number. Be sure to show your work.

City	Hispanic	Non Hispanic
Sanford	7,190	20,904
Monroe	9,651	23,146

(A) 33%

B   29%

C   36%

D   26%

Common Core Standard 8.SP.A.4 – Statistics & Probability

☐ Based on the previous problem, find the percentage of the Hispanic population in Sanford. Round to the nearest whole number. Be sure to show your work.

A   33%

B   29%

(C) 36%

D   26%

Common Core Standard 8.SP.A.4 – Statistics & Probability

☐ Based on the previous problems, is there evidence that the Hispanic populations in North Carolina cities are smaller than the non-Hispanic populations? Be sure to explain your answer.

_____

_____

_____

©Teachers' Treasures Publishing

Name_____

DIAGNOSTIC

Use the graph below to answer the questions.

	Home recycling	No home recycling	Total
School recycling	430	42	472
No school recycling	25	14	39
Total	455	56	511

Common Core Standard 8.SP.A.4 – Statistics & Probability

☐ The table shows the results of a survey of students who separate recycle and trash in the school cafeteria and at home. Is there evidence that those who separate recycle and trash in the school cafeteria also tend to recycle at home? How many students recycle at home but not at school? Be sure to explain your answer.

A   yes;   42

B   yes;   25

C   no;   14

D   no;   29

Common Core Standard 8.SP.A.4 – Statistics & Probability

☐ Find the percentage of the total number of students who recycle in school. Round to the nearest whole number. Be sure to explain your answer.

A   88%

B   75%

C   92%

D   98%

©Teachers' Treasures Publishing

Name _____

PRACTICE

Common Core Standard 8.SP.A.4 – Statistics & Probability

☐ A surveyor collected data about 2 groups of people that attended the carnival booth to get a prize. The table below shows the number of people who won a prize at a carnival booth. Calculate the percentage of people from the second group, who didn't win a prize. Be sure to show your work.

Number of groups	Prize	No Prize
1	7	13
2	10	15

A   70%

B   40%

C   60%

D   55%

Common Core Standard 8.SP.A.4 – Statistics & Probability

☐ Based on the previous problem, find the percentage of people from the first group, who didn't win a prize. Be sure to show your work.

A   65%

B   40%

C   70%

D   55%

Common Core Standard 8.SP.A.4 – Statistics & Probability

☐ Based on the previous problems, is there evidence that the number of winners will be less than the number of people, who didn't win a prize. Be sure to explain your answer.

_____

_____

_____

©Teachers' Treasures Publishing

Name_____

PRACTICE

Use the graph below to answer the questions.

	Soccer	No Soccer	Total
Boys	37	15	52
Girls	45	12	57
Total	82	27	109

Are boys or girls more likely play soccer? Be sure to explain your answer.

_____

_____

_____

Common Core Standard 8.SP.A.4 – Statistics & Probability

☐ **Find the percentage of children who play soccer. Round to the nearest whole number. Be sure to show your work.**

A   62%

B   25%

C   75%

D   38%

Common Core Standard 8.SP.A.4 – Statistics & Probability

☐ **What percent of girls do not play soccer? Round to the nearest whole number. Be sure to explain your answer.**

A   25%

B   32%

C   12%

D   21%

©Teachers' Treasures Publishing

Name_____

PRACTICE

Common Core Standard 8.SP.A.4 – Statistics & Probability

☐ A survey of 11th graders found that 87 students passed their Math test and 74 of those students also passed their Physics test. What is the total number of students who didn't pass their Physics test? Be sure to show your work.

	Passed physics	Didn't pass physics	Total
Passed math	74	13	87
Didn't pass math	10	8	18
Total	84	21	105

A   12

B   13

C   10

D   21

Common Core Standard 8.SP.A.4 – Statistics & Probability

☐ Based on the table above, what is the number of students who didn't pass their Physics test but passed their Math test? Be sure to show your work.

A   12

B   13

C   10

D   21

Common Core Standard 8.SP.A.4 – Statistics & Probability

☐ Based on the table above, is there evidence that students who pass their Math test also tend to pass their Physics test? Be sure to explain your answer.

_____

_____

_____

©Teachers' Treasures Publishing

Name_____

PRACTICE

Common Core Standard 8.SP.A.4 – Statistics & Probability

☐ The table below shows the results of a survey conducted with chefs of Greek and French restaurants in the region. The survey asked if they use red onions or not. Calculate the percentage of Greek chefs who prefer red onions. Round to the nearest whole number. Be sure to show your work.

Restaurant	Red	Not Red
Greek	17	5
French	19	10

A   25%

B   69%

C   82%

D   77%

Common Core Standard 8.SP.A.4 – Statistics & Probability

☐ Based on the table from the previous problem, find the percentage of French chefs who prefer red onions. Round to the nearest whole number. Be sure to show your work.

A   45%

B   66%

C   52%

D   71%

Common Core Standard 8.SP.A.4 – Statistics & Probability

☐ Based on the previous problem, is there evidence that both Greek and French chefs prefer red onions? Be sure to explain your answer.

_____

_____

_____

©Teachers' Treasures Publishing

Name_____

ASSESSMENT

Use the graph below to answer the questions.

	Sew	Don't Sew	Total
Knit	76	48	124
Don't Knit	112	64	176
Total	188	112	300

Common Core Standard 8.SP.A.4 – Statistics & Probability

☐ Women's Crafting Association was conducting a survey in which 300 women were asked whether they could knit or sew. The table shows the results of that survey. Fill out the blank cells in the table. What is the total number of women who can't sew? Be sure to explain your answer.

A   176

B   153

C   188

D   112

Common Core Standard 8.SP.A.4 – Statistics & Probability

☐ Is there evidence that those women who can knit also tend to sew? Find the percentage of those who can knit and sew. Round the answer to the nearest whole number. Be sure to explain your answer.

A   yes; 31%

B   yes; 43%

C   no; 25%

D   no; 19%

©Teachers' Treasures Publishing

Name_____

ASSESSMENT

Use the graph below to answer the questions.

	Sport	No Sport	Total
Music	460	155	615
No Music	120	90	210
Total	580	245	825

Common Core Standard 8.SP.A.4 – Statistics & Probability

☐ The table shows the results of a survey conducted on students from a local school whether they play an instrument or do sports. Fill out the blank cells in the table. How many students do sports but do not play an instrument? Be sure to explain your answer.

A   120

B   155

C   130

D   580

Common Core Standard 8.SP.A.4 – Statistics & Probability

☐ Find the percentage of those students who play an instrument. Round the answer to the nearest whole number. Is there evidence that those who play an instrument also tend to do sports? Be sure to explain your answer.

A   45%; no

B   63%; yes

C   52%; no

D   75%; yes

©Teachers' Treasures Publishing

ANSWER KEY

8.NS.A.1

Page 1 .... C, 0.06, $\frac{87}{100}$

Page 2 .... C, 2, B

Page 3 .... A, D, 1.125

Page 4 .... 11, $3\frac{1}{2}$, A

Page 5 .... C, D, B

Page 6 .... A, C, $0.\overline{629}$

Page 7 .... D, D, 5

Page 8 .... B, $0.1\overline{6}$, $880\frac{1}{25}$

8.NS.A.2

Page 9 .... A, C, 8.8

Page 10 .... 7.7, $20\sqrt{5} + 10\sqrt{15}$, 1.14

Page 11 .... B, A, B

Page 12 .... C, 10.5, B

Page 13 .... D, $17\sqrt{6}$, $6 + 14\sqrt{17}$

Page 14 .... 2.8, $1\frac{2}{3} - \frac{5\sqrt{2}}{7}$, 6.28

Page 15 .... C, B, $10\sqrt{11}$

Page 16 .... C, $12\sqrt{21} + 5\sqrt{5}$, 3.2

8.EE.A.1

Page 17 .... B, C, $3\frac{1}{2}$

Page 18 .... $\frac{2}{7}$, -0.016, B

Page 19 .... C, D, D

Page 20 .... A, B, B

Page 21 .... D, B, D

Page 22 .... 36, 125, 8.41

Page 23 .... A, D, C

Page 24 .... -0.135, 64.04, 225

8.EE.A.2

Page 25 .... B, B, D

Page 26 .... A, C, A

Page 27 .... A, B, A

Page 28 .... C, A, A

Page 29 .... C, B, B

Page 30 .... B, C, A

Page 31 .... B, B, B

Page 32 .... A, C, A

8.EE.A.3

Page 33 .... B, 3.3×10^{-1}, A

Page 34 .... 3.51×10^{-4}, D, B

Page 35 .... B, C, A

Page 36 .... A, 4.4×10^{7}, 1.6×10^{6}

Page 37 .... B, B, A

Page 38 .... B, D, B

Page 39 .... A, D, 1.252×10^{-4}

Page 40 .... B, D, B

8.EE.A.4

Page 41 .... A, B, D

Page 42 .... B, D, A

Page 43 .... B, B, D

Page 44 .... C, A, C

Page 45 .... C, A, C

Page 46 .... D, B, D

Page 47 .... B, A, D

Page 48 .... D, C, B

© Teachers' Treasures Publishing

ANSWER KEY

8.EE.B.5

Page 49 .... Jack, A, B
Page 50 .... Denny, C, A
Page 51 .... C, B, D
Page 52 .... A, C
Page 53 .... Girls, B, A
Page 54 .... Leon, D, C
Page 55 .... YumCake, D, D
Page 56 .... Basketball Team, D, A

8.EE.B.6

Page 57 .... D, D
Page 58 .... A, B
Page 59 .... A, B, D
Page 60 .... B, C
Page 61 .... D, A, C
Page 62 .... B, D
Page 63 .... C, B, C
Page 64 .... D, A

8.EE.C.7

Page 65 .... B, B, A
Page 66 .... B, D, A
Page 67 .... B, A, C
Page 68 .... A, B, D
Page 69 .... C, A, A
Page 70 .... B, C, D
Page 71 .... B, A, C
Page 72 .... B, D, B

8.EE.C.8

Page 73 .... B, B
Page 74 .... A, D, B
Page 75 .... D, No, Yes
Page 76 .... B, B, B
Page 77 .... C, A
Page 78 .... D, B, C
Page 79 .... B, C
Page 80 .... D, D, B

8.F.A.1

Page 81 .... B, A, B
Page 82 .... B, C, A
Page 83 .... Yes, B, D
Page 84 .... A, C, No
Page 85 .... B, B
Page 86 .... D, C, B
Page 87 .... D, A, B
Page 88 .... Yes, A, B

8.F.A.2

Page 89 .... B, B, B
Page 90 .... A, A
Page 91 .... A, B, C
Page 92 .... C, D, D
Page 93 .... A, B
Page 94 .... B, A, B
Page 95 .... A, A
Page 96 .... C, A, B

© Teachers' Treasures Publishing

ANSWER KEY

8.F.A.3

Page 97	Non-Linear, C
Page 98	Linear, No, D
Page 99	B, Non-Linear
Page 100	C, Linear, A
Page 101	B, No
Page 102	Non-Linear, Linear, Yes
Page 103	B, Non-Linear, A
Page 104	Linear, Linear, Linear

8 F.A.4

Page 105	B, A, B
Page 106	D, D, C
Page 107	D, B, D
Page 108	B, D, C
Page 109	A, B, B
Page 110	True, Yes, C
Page 111	D, C, A
Page 112	C, No, B

8 F.B.5

Page 113	No, B, A
Page 114	C, A, D
Page 115	A, B, C
Page 116	D, B
Page 117	B, A, D
Page 118	Non-Linear; Increasing, A, C
Page 119	Neither; Non-Linear, B, D
Page 120	No, C, B

8.G.A.1

Page 121	A, C, B
Page 122	C, D, C
Page 123	D, False, False, B
Page 124	A, D, D
Page 125	C, A, True, False
Page 126	B, D, B
Page 127	B, A, B
Page 128	B, D, C

8.G.A.2

Page 129	C, A, Yes
Page 130	A, A, B
Page 131	Yes, C, D
Page 132	Yes, A, C
Page 133	D, C, A
Page 134	A, C, A
Page 135	C, C, Yes
Page 136	B, A, No

8.G.A.3

Page 137	B, B, Enlargement
Page 138	C, D, No
Page 139	C, C, D
Page 140	No, B, A
Page 141	B, C, A
Page 142	C, B, B
Page 143	D, D, No
Page 144	B, B, No

ANSWER KEY

8.G.A.4
Page 145 .... A, D, True
Page 146 .... B, B
Page 147 .... Yes, C, C
Page 148 .... D, A, B
Page 149 .... D, True, A
Page 150 .... A, A, A
Page 151 .... B, A
Page 152 .... A, C

8.G.A.5
Page 153 .... A, C, B
Page 154 .... C, A, D
Page 155 .... C, D, A
Page 156 .... C, A, A
Page 157 .... C, D, C
Page 158 .... B, C, C
Page 159 .... D, D
Page 160 .... A, D, C

8.G.B.6
Page 161 .... B, No, No
Page 162 .... No, B, C
Page 163 .... No, B, Yes
Page 164 .... B, B, C
Page 165 .... B, No, No
Page 166 .... Yes, D, B
Page 167 .... No, Yes, Yes
Page 168 .... B, C, B

8.G.B.7
Page 169 .... A, B, C
Page 170 .... A, C, B
Page 171 .... B, D, A
Page 172 .... C, B, D
Page 173 .... B, D, A
Page 174 .... B, B, B
Page 175 .... D, C, D
Page 176 .... B, D, A

8.G.B.8
Page 177 .... C, B
Page 178 .... D, B
Page 179 .... B, C
Page 180 .... B, A
Page 181 .... D, A
Page 182 .... C, B
Page 183 .... A, C
Page 184 .... B, D

8.G.B.9
Page 185 .... B, A, B
Page 186 .... D, B, B
Page 187 .... D, C, B
Page 188 .... A, A, B
Page 189 .... D, A, D
Page 190 .... D, C, C
Page 191 .... A, C, B
Page 192 .... D, C, D

© Teachers' Treasures Publishing

ANSWER KEY

8.SP.A.1

Page 193 .... Positive Correlation, Yes (8:8)
Page 194 .... C, No
Page 195 .... No Correlation, B
Page 196 .... D, C
Page 197 .... Positive Correlation, B
Page 198 .... A, No
Page 199 .... Negative Correlation; Yes, C
Page 200 .... C, D

8.SP.A.2

Page 201 .... Positive Relationship, Positive Relationship
Page 202 .... D, Positive Relationship
Page 203 .... Negative Relationship, Positive Relationship
Page 204 .... C, Positive Relationship
Page 205 .... D, Positive Relationship
Page 206 .... A, Negative Relationship
Page 207 .... Negative Relationship, No Relationship
Page 208 .... A, Positive Relationship

8.SP.A.3

Page 209 .... B
Page 210 .... D, C
Page 211 .... C, D, A
Page 212 .... C, A
Page 213 .... B, C
Page 214 .... A, C
Page 215 .... B
Page 216 .... D, B

8.SP.A.4

Page 217 .... B, D, Yes
Page 218 .... B, C
Page 219 .... C, A, Yes
Page 220 .... Girls, C, D
Page 221 .... D, B, Yes
Page 222 .... D, B, Yes
Page 223 .... D, C
Page 224 .... A, D

© Teachers' Treasures Publishing

Made in the USA
Middletown, DE
22 October 2015